Urban Nightlife

almost all black & white

- own exper
→ limits

South

Space
Black

Appreciate anecdotes

not familiar w/ region or local culture BUT some things were universal

Athlete, frat boy → racialized terms

many friends
almost exclusively friends

152
surprising to some
↳ extent
race is an issue

↓

Disarming Black men → voice talk after pressure from authority

boundies
pre-game, clubs, friends
econ
culturally entrenched
"integrated segregation"
wall guards to entry

to that extent does some even if the individuals are recognized as such

less banter than... Black women

128
-few meaningful conv.
happen outside racial boundaries

Talking stories on the streets
→ negative reps - get built

Race Talk
-rarely serious
jokes, small quips
→ no deeply analysis

Urban Nightlife

Entertaining Race, Class, and Culture in Public Space

REUBEN A. BUFORD MAY

Rutgers University Press

New Brunswick, New Jersey and London

Library of Congress Cataloging-in-Publication Data
May, Reuben A. Buford, 1965–
    Urban nightlife : entertaining race, class, and culture in public space / Reuben A. Buford May.
       pages   cm
    Includes bibliographical references and index.
    ISBN 978-0-8135-6939-0 (hardcover : alk. paper) — ISBN 978-0-8135-6938-3 (pbk. : alk.
paper) — ISBN 978-0-8135-6940-6 (e-book)
    1. African Americans—Social life and customs. 2. Middle class—United States—Social life
and customs. 3. City and town life—United States. 4. Social interaction—United States. 5. United
States—Race relations. I. Title.
    E185.6.M467 2014
    305.896'073—dc23
    2013046602

A British Cataloging-in-Publication record for this book is available from the British Library.

Visit our website: http://rutgerspress.rutgers.edu

Manufactured in the United States of America

To my wife Lyndel
Thank you for your continued love and support

I got the burdened to disprove
You watch my every move
Trying to get a clue of what to do
I'm scaring you
What did I do
Let's see
Walk, talk, look, like a human

—Reginald S. Stuckey,
"Burden to Disprove"

Contents

Preface

What happens when groups of nightlife participants from different racial, class, and cultural backgrounds come together in urban public space to have fun? Sociological studies provide a glimpse into the use of urban public space, and even urban nightlife, yet none of them explicitly answer this question. This is curious given the existence of nightlife areas in most cities, the diversity of nightlife participants in many of those areas, and the significant influence that nightlife areas can have on other aspects of life in the city.

In *Urban Nightlife*, I draw on ethnographic data gathered in downtown Northeast, Georgia (a pseudonym)—a city recognized nationally for its urban nightlife—to answer the question of what happens in this kind of shared public space. I explore the interactional dynamics occurring as diverse groups of nightlife participants move through the public streets and the nightclubs in pursuit of fun. I discover that despite the popular perception that diverse groups are engaged in harmonious interaction with one another, as some scholars have suggested, these groups are in fact engaged in ongoing social conflict on the streets and in the nightclubs. This conflict manifests in the ways that groups talk about, and act, on meanings of race; the ways that men and women pursue one another in games of flirtation and sexual innuendo; the ways that nightclub owners, bouncers, and patrons evaluate social class; and the ways that participants communicate their cultural sensibilities through consumption of particular clothes, venues, and music.

I introduce and develop the concept of *integrated segregation* to describe the nature of interaction occurring broadly in urban nightlife. A key conclusion from *Urban Nightlife* is that social tension persists in racially and culturally diverse contexts like urban nightlife, in part because many participants fail to draw a connection between tensions in the nightlife and the historical and contemporary institutional forces that support and perpetuate those tensions. Ultimately, *Urban Nightlife* tells a story not only about interaction in urban nightlife, but also about how people in cities manage the complexities of race, class, and culture in everyday life.

Acknowledgments

This book has benefitted from the feedback and support I received from a number of individuals during its preparation. I would like to thank Henry Louis Gates Jr. and his staff at the W.E.B. Du Bois Institute for African and African American Research at Harvard University. The institute provided computer equipment, an office, access to library materials, a community of energetic and diverse scholars, and a research assistant, Anthony Jack—who proved to be thorough, resourceful, and even inspirational. I was able to complete essential portions of the book while I was a fellow at the institute during the fall semester of 2009. The other fellows enthusiastically responded to my research and provided thoughtful comments and suggestions. To all of them, I am grateful. My colleagues and friends in the Boston area were extremely supportive during my time there as well. Special thanks to William Julius Wilson, Ray Reagans, Larry Bobo, Chris Winship, Michèle Lamont, Frank Dobbins, Abby Wolf, Vera Grant, Shelarease Ruffin, Rilwan Adeduntan, John Cassidy, and Carla, Jennifer, Tony, and Tony Jack.

In the fall of 2010 I was fortunate to be nominated for, and selected as, a Dr. Martin Luther King, Jr. Visiting Professor in the School of the Humanities, Arts, and Social Sciences at MIT. I had the opportunity to share my work with anthropologists, urban planners, and Business School students and faculty. Special thanks to Susan Silbey (Anthropology), Ray Reagans (Sloan), Roberto Fernandez (Sloan), Ezra Zuckerman (Sloan), Wesley Harris (Aeronautics), and Catherine Turco (Sloan) for their support.

I received feedback at the MIT-Harvard Economic Sociology Seminar that helped me to broaden my approach to describing observations in the nightlife. My colleagues in the Anthropology Department at MIT were welcoming and supportive. Thank you to Manduhai, Mike, Stefan, Jim, Jean, Erica, Graham, Heather, and Chris. I would especially like to thank Jean Jackson (Anthropology) for thoroughly reviewing an earlier version of chapter 3. Her comments helped me to substantially revise the chapter, and the book is much better for it. In the Department of Urban Studies and Planning Amy Glasmeier and Phillip Thompson were wonderful colleagues. I also benefitted greatly from the questions and feedback I received from the participants in the weekly seminar in urban planning.

Spending time in Cambridge afforded me the opportunity to share my research with a number of scholars at other colleges and universities in the area. In particular I would like to thank Steven Vallas (Sociology), Emmett Price (African American Studies), Wilfred Holton (Sociology), and their colleagues at Northeastern University, and Ashley Mears (Sociology), John Stone (Sociology), Julian Go (Sociology), and their colleagues at Boston University. Thanks to Richard Miller at Suffolk University for sharing his students with me as well.

As an ethnographer I have learned that completion of extended projects is difficult to achieve without the support of one's colleagues. I would like to thank my colleagues at Texas A&M University who supported my leave to complete the book. Special thanks to Ben Crouch, Joe Feagin, Mark Fossett, Antonio Cepata, and Jane Sell. My colleagues in the Race and Ethnicity Workshop at Texas A&M University have offered invaluable support. Thanks to Kim Brown, Joe Feagin, Sarah Gatson, Joseph Jewell, Verna Keith, and Wendy Moore. Our graduate students in the department are intelligent, energetic, and hardworking. I thank Chad Scott, Jenni Mueller, and Kenneth Sean Chaplin, all of whom read portions of previous drafts of the book. I give special thanks to Sean Chaplin who spent considerable time with me as a research assistant on the project. He proved to be an astute observer with the critical skills necessary to be an outstanding ethnographer. Brittany Hearne, my undergraduate research fellow, followed in Sean's footsteps and proved to be equally dedicated to the project. She read the entire first draft of the book, raised questions, and provided valuable feedback. I greatly appreciate her assistance in tying up loose ends, and I am certain that she will do exceedingly well in the pursuit of her Ph.D. in sociology. Thanks to Ed Tarlton, a doctoral candidate in the Urban and

Regional Sciences Program at Texas A&M University, for drafting the figures for chapter 1, and Jaime Grunlan, an associate professor of mechanical engineering, for providing occasional inspirational chats at the coffee shop.

Being an ethnographer takes a great deal of dedication, focus, and stamina over the long haul, and it helps to have colleagues near and far who can sympathize with the ethnographic endeavor. Thanks to Elijah Anderson, Mitch Duneier, Mary Pattillo, Sudhir Venkatesh, David Grazian, Omar McRoberts, and Cat Turco for being those ethnographers. I would like to give Elijah Anderson additional thanks for giving me the opportunity to speak at the Yale University Urban Ethnography Workshop. The workshop has inspired me to continue giving support to young ethnographers.

Given that ethnographers spend so much of their time with other people, it is important to have a supportive family for success. I would like to thank Lyndel and Regina for all of the support at home, and Tamarra for her consistent pursuit of excellence away from home. Thank you to my mother and "UnDad" and my brothers Khary and Tim and their families. I love you all. I send a special shout-out to Red Man, Vybz Kartel, T-Pain, Dysquo, KFJacques, and Dirty Projectors for the head nods they provided when their tracks were on repeat in my iPod during the writing of this book. Reginald S. Stuckey of VibePony Records is a recording artist deserving of more thanks than I could possibly render here. To keep it simple, I want to thank him for allowing me an opportunity to live in another space and time. I especially appreciate his creativity and his phenomenal success. He has been an inspiration. In fact, if I could be anyone other than myself, it's a good bet that I would be him. I know that Kristin, Tiffanie, Jessica, Shannon, Brittany, Kaitlin, Eniola, Sam, Vic, Sean, Myeshia, and the many devoted Stuckey fans can appreciate his brilliance.

I would like to thank Peter Mickulas and Marilyn Campbell and the other wonderful folks at Rutgers University Press for seeing the book through to its completion. Thanks to freelance copy editor Joseph Dahm for his outstanding review and edit of the book.

Chapter 4 derives most of its subject matter from a revised and significantly extended version of my article (with Sean Chaplin), "Cracking the Code: Race, Class, and Access to Nightclubs in Urban America," *Qualitative Sociology* 31 (2008): 57–72. I would like to thank Springer Publications for permission to reuse portions of this article.

Finally, I would like to thank the nightlife participants for revealing to me insights about race, class, and culture. Theirs is a story that reflects the increasing complexity of negotiating everyday life in urban public space. Although many people have helped to shape this book, I must accept sole responsibility for what is written and therein any shortcomings. Ultimately it is my hope that readers might gain useful insights about human interaction through the narrative that I share.

Urban Nightlife

Integrated Segregation in Urban Nightlife

● ● ● ● ● ● ● ● ● ● ● ●

"Tom, come back," I heard a woman's voice shout.[1]

I looked in the direction of the voice and watched as a tall White man left Kilpatrick's bar and stumbled his way through the crowd toward me. I had been standing in my usual spot with my back to the street surveying the comings and goings of patrons for a couple of hours. The yellow parking ticket box had become my leaning post for watching the street corner activity. This particular corner, the northeast corner of Reginald and Stuckey Streets, is usually alive with activity as patrons move between three popular bars—Kilpatrick's, Figaro's, and the Corral—and tonight was no different.

After a few steps through the crowd Tom stumbled to a stop just near the corner. He swayed a little as other patrons passed on either side of him. Several feet away I could see a young woman intently moving toward him. She pressed her way through the crowd using her forearm and called out again, "Tom, come back."

Tom looked disoriented as he turned to the sound of her voice. A few feet away now, the woman lunged through the last group of patrons and grabbed Tom by the sleeve of his white, button-down, Ralph Lauren Polo shirt. She gave it a slight tug as if to both restrain Tom from further movement and gather herself.

Tom turned to the woman with a look of exasperation on his face as he labored to regain his balance. After a few swaying moves he looked into her eyes and said in his best impersonation of someone sober, "Look, Allison, maybe we should take a break from each other. I just wanna have fun."

Allison frowned.

Other patrons continued to pass Tom and Allison but paid little attention to the two as they talked loudly.

"I wanna have fun too," Allison protested as she fought back tears, "but that doesn't mean you have to kiss other girls."

"We were only dancing and she kissed me," Tom replied.

Allison held tightly to Tom's arm and tried to pull him closer.

Tom resisted, nudging Allison back by extending his arm.

A young man, who was walking toward Kilpatrick's with a group of his buddies, bumped into Allison and caused her to sway. She could hardly keep her balance in her red high-heeled shoes. Allison pulled on Tom to regain her balance, and this caused Tom to teeter. As both swayed, I could see tears welling in Allison's eyes.

"Tom, we can have fun together," she said.

"Look, Allison, I'm leaving. I'm going to catch my friends. I'll call you tomorrow and we can talk."

Tom snatched his arm from Allison and began crossing the street with a throng of patrons who were heading to other bars along Stuckey Street.

Allison stood on the corner shaken and upset. Tom continued to walk away, as tears began running down Allison's face. She waited a few seconds before she cried out again, "Tom, Tom," but Tom did not stop.

Although many patrons passed her, Allison seemed to stand alone on the crowded corner. She began wiping the tears from her eyes with the fingertips of both hands and, after a few strokes, wiped her hands on her white miniskirt. I looked to see if Tom had decided to come back, but he seemed to be moving faster the farther he got away from Allison. It was as if he were now liberated to "have fun" the way he wanted.

I looked back at Allison, who had begun to quiver as her tears intensified. She stooped to the ground, as groups of patrons continued to pass on either side. They took little note of her, even as she crouched slowly toward the ground.

She would have been in a full crouch position if it had not been for another young woman who grabbed Allison by the shoulders and lifted her up.

"Allison, come on. It's okay. Don't worry about Tom," said the woman.

Allison stood to her feet slowly with the help of the woman. Tears were still streaming down her face. The woman, apparently a friend, placed her arm across Allison's shoulder. They almost looked like twins wearing their white miniskirts and polo shirts.

As Allison whimpered into her friend's shoulder, I turned my attention to the revelry of a group of young men leaving Figaro's bar next door to Kilpatrick's.

"You prick," a tall White man said as he shoved his shorter friend and laughed. The other three young men, all White, began laughing as they joined this impromptu drunken game of shoving one another back and forth. Each of them was wearing a variation of the khaki shorts/polo shirt combination. They bumped into other patrons who seemed to take their game as a minor irritant and continued moving on to the next place to "get a drink and have some fun."

Just a few feet away from the group participating in the pushing game stood two White men talking with a group of four White women. One of the young men, dressed in khaki shorts, leather flip-flops, and a green polo shirt, seemed to be doing all the talking while his friend stood making quick glances to the group of young women, and then out to the activity of patrons passing on the sidewalk. The man in the green polo shirt wore his brown hair closely shaved. He focused his attention on the woman standing closest to him. She was a slim blonde, wearing a yellow halter summer dress and high-heeled wedge shoes with cork bottoms and white uppers. The hem of her dress stopped several inches above her knees and accented her long tanned legs. As the two talked and exchanged flirtatious smiles their friends stood impatiently. Moments later the group of women, led by the woman in the yellow dress, began walking toward the corner where I stood. As they left the young men, the one in the green polo turned to his friend, who then mouthed the words, "She is so hot." The men shared a high five and laughed, then turned and walked into the Corral.

As I watched that group of young women walk to the corner, led by the woman in the yellow dress, I noticed two Black men sitting on the bench that faces Kilpatrick's. The bench is about ten feet in front of my vantage point, and it sits by the edge of the sidewalk where patrons pass between bars. Both of the Black men were wearing blue jean shorts and sat with their buttocks on the backrest of the bench. The one to my left was thin and dark skinned. His hair was cut low, almost bald, and he wore a red-and-black, loose-fitting polo shirt. His feet were adorned in red-and-black Nike basketball shoes. As the group of women passed, he tapped his friend on the shoulder. His friend had brown skin and wore a Michael Jordan North Carolina throwback basketball jersey and powder blue-and-white Nike basketball shoes. He shook his head in agreement as he said, "Damn she is fine."

This narrative represents the typical kinds of activities I observed while studying nightlife in downtown Northeast, Georgia. I first began this study as an examination of the idea of "having fun" in and around nighttime hangouts. Downtown Northeast is an area just north of Big South

University—a large, predominantly White university with a national reputation as a "place for fun" based upon its annual placement on various top party school rankings. My primary focus was on how people get along in the public spaces of Northeast, Georgia, as they go about "having fun" in the nightclubs and bars and along the streets. Based upon my general knowledge of this kind of atmosphere, I had expected there to be stories of excessive consumption of alcohol, flirtation, brazen sexuality, and hedonism on the part of college students seeking to enjoy themselves in a public place with a reputation for meeting those expectations. Indeed there were such stories; yet as I conducted this study it became evident that there was another story—a story about the dynamics of race, class, and culture—embedded within the idea of "having fun" in this urban public space. I observed the ways in which race-related issues became intimately tied to class and culture in downtown Northeast, and how these issues manifested unexpectedly or were coded in various ways. This book reveals those observations.

I became interested in the street corners and the immediate social context of the bars, nightclubs, drinking spots, and restaurants that pervade downtown Northeast's nightlife, due in part to my sociological training in the traditional Chicago School approach. Scholars associated with the Chicago School focus on the nature of human behavior within the context of urban life.[2] Writing in the early 1900s, these scholars, primarily from the University of Chicago's Department of Sociology, examined how institutions like schools and churches as well as physical layouts of neighborhoods and communities shaped the ways in which individuals and groups interact.[3] These scholars used a variety of approaches to gather information about urban life, including ethnography, wherein a researcher participates and observes the activities of everyday life.

My desire to learn about downtown Northeast was motivated further by my general intellectual curiosity about public life and everyday interactions of people in urban settings. Some readers might refer to this curiosity and observational activity as nothing more than "people watching" or what the sociologist Elijah Anderson calls "folk ethnography," wherein individuals "with an eye to sorting out and making sense of one another either for practical reasons or to satisfy a natural human curiosity" spend hours taking in the sights, sounds, and interactions in public contexts.[4] Although "people watching" is an accurate description of one essential activity of ethnography, this designation fails to capture the other laborious and complex tasks required of sociologists involved in formal ethnography—those tasks include systematic observations, extensive note taking, on-site interviewing, comparative analysis, and theory building. Hence, ethnographers are charged with greater responsibility for a more comprehensive approach to exploring the social world than "people watching" suggests. Furthermore, ethnographers, after documenting what they have observed, then attempt to draw connections to what other ethnographers have said about social interaction in similar public spaces.

In sharing what they have learned, ethnographers are also clear about how their own biographies might have influenced how they interpret what they have observed.[5] As an African American male who grew up in Chicago, I am certain that my interpretations of nightlife in downtown Northeast enjoy both the advantages and disadvantages of my personal biography. It is worth noting that others will have observed similar occurrences in the nightlife, but as with all knowledge that requires interpretation, our perspectives may differ. This to me is the beauty of ethnography—it offers an opportunity for alternative perspectives about shared social occurrences. From my perspective, I find a compelling story in how nightlife participants negotiate race, class, and culture as they share the public space. I draw on literature from urban sociology to frame this story around the idea that groups are consistently contesting one another for use of that space.

Contested Public Space

Urban public spaces are generally viewed as regions open and accessible to a variety of individuals.[6] Consistent with this idea of being "open," these physical locations, like the street corners I described previously, may be occupied by almost anyone who chooses to be present. According to this idea of public space, individuals and groups may go into, pass through, or depart from the location as they wish. The underlying assumption is that there is freedom of movement in and around urban public space, especially when compared to private spaces that are governed by strict rules about who may or may not use that space. And yet, according to sociologist Lyn Lofland, while urban public spaces "are generally understood to be more *accessible* (physically and visually) than private spaces," there also exists social constraints that specify who may occupy particular public spaces.[7]

These constraints—for instance, normative expectations about who is to be found in particular physical locations—transform what is theoretically a free and open site into a space that is fixed with ideologies about use. The French philosopher Henri Lefebvre argues that these ideologies most frequently reflect the desires of the dominant class, which is favorably positioned to exert control over that space.[8] Hence the social meaning given to urban public space rests on how those in power conceptualized that space. As social psychologists John Dixon and his coauthors suggest, this way of defining space is easily observed in most urban settings: "Even society's most accessible and civic-minded spaces, the public areas of our towns and cities, are suffused by the ideologies of class, age, gender, sexuality, and 'race.' In acknowledging this fact, however, one must be careful not to imply that public spaces have become uniform arenas of repression and exclusion."[9] Although those in power may invoke ideologies to define the social meaning of a physical location, individuals and groups who may be excluded from using certain spaces by class, age, gender, sexuality, and race may contest both the purpose and the use of that space. In such a context there will be conflict, especially when those marginalized others are strangers—that is, those who are neither culturally nor biographically known to one another.[10]

Conflict over the use of urban public space may arise from simple matters of passing or greeting strangers, or over more complex matters involving institutional control of urban public space. In this book, I am primarily concerned with conflict arising from small group or interpersonal interactions in nightlife. The outcome of these interpersonal interactions frequently depends on a person's ability to draw upon what Anderson calls "street wisdom."[11] In his ethnographic study of encounters between African Americans and Whites on Philadelphia's public streets, Anderson suggests "street wisdom is largely a state of mind" and "is gained through a long and sometimes arduous process that begins with a certain "uptightness" about the urban environment."[12] It is this uptightness that compels strangers to question what each potential encounter with others might entail. According to Anderson, as individuals gain experience navigating public spaces, they learn how to draw on "a developing repertoire of ruses and schemes for traveling the streets safely."[13] Chiefly, "street wisdom" manifests in an individual's confidence and comfort in knowing how to address everyday situations on the city streets.

Although Anderson focuses on the potential conflict that city dwellers have as they encounter one another on the streets during routine everyday activities, I have observed that urban nightlife participants also draw upon "street wisdom" as they go about having fun in the nightclubs and bars of urban areas. The assessments that participants make of one another in the nightlife seem to be heightened by the fact that the cover of night facilitates a number of illicit activities that pose significant threats to nightlife participants' safety.

Like Anderson, other urban sociologists suggest that given the heterogeneity and density of urban populations, users of urban public space must work consistently to decipher verbal and nonverbal cues in order to avoid conflict.[14] In some instances, deciphering these cues can be problematic and leave individuals confused. For example, the sociologist Mitchell Duneier, in his examination of interaction between African American men street vendors—some of whom are homeless—and White middle-class women in Greenwich Village, demonstrates that despite possessing "street wisdom" some women passersby are drawn into "entanglements" with African American men.[15] These entanglements occur when the men waylay the women into conversations that frequently end with women being rude since the "the men offer evidence that they do not respond to cues that orderly interaction requires."[16] Beyond the kind of conflict one might expect to occur among strangers in general, Duneier speculates that "race-class-gender differences on top of micro-level conversational trouble leads to a tension well out of proportion to any material or physical harm the interactions themselves might involve."[17]

Studies like Anderson's and Duneier's identify particular strategies used by individuals to make distinctions among strangers and manage their encounters. I pay particular attention to these kinds of distinction-making strategies in my analysis of nightlife in downtown Northeast. By making distinctions based on visual cues given off by strangers on the public street, nightlife participants are able to determine who should and who should not be engaged in interaction. This evaluation process entails reconciling the stranger's appearance with who is expected to be present in a particular public space.[18] In general, physical indicators like hairstyle, clothing, race, and the way an individual moves are key considerations when evaluating a stranger.

Despite the idea that strangers contest one another for use of urban public space, urban sociologists also recognize that diverse kinds of people can be unified in this space. For instance, in his most recent study of urban life in Philadelphia, Anderson complicates his prior observations regarding conflict on the city streets by proposing that public spaces such as terminals, malls, parks, and restaurants where diverse people gather can serve as what he calls "cosmopolitan canopies."[19] According to Anderson cosmopolitan canopies are public spaces "that offer a respite from the lingering tensions of urban life and an opportunity for diverse peoples to come together" and "engage one another in a spirit of civility, or even comity and goodwill."[20] They are neutral spaces that people view as belonging to all kinds of people, and where strangers who would not ordinarily encounter one another are given the opportunity to become better acquainted under an air of civility. For instance, Anderson identifies places like the counter at Down Home Diner, in Philadelphia's Reading Terminal, as a public yet intimate space that gives strangers an opportunity to share in verbal interchanges that help break down social barriers. Under this cosmopolitan canopy strangers talk to one another about topics such as sports and news while being attentive to norms of common civility. Although Anderson also concedes that public spaces are typically characterized by social distance and tension among groups, he is optimistic that cosmopolitan canopies can play an important role in improving relations among diverse peoples.[21]

While I agree with Anderson that cosmopolitan canopies exist where diverse groups have frequent contact with one another, I do not believe these canopies are widespread. Furthermore, I am less inclined to share Anderson's optimism about the role cosmopolitan canopies can play in improving race relations even when they do exist. I take this position based upon my observations of places like downtown Northeast wherein diverse participants congregate, generally practice civility, and avoid talk about potentially offensive topics like race, but still are unlikely to have substantive interactions across racial boundaries. The lack of meaningful interaction is due in part to the fact that few people in downtown Northeast are seeking the kind of intimate interactions with strangers that transform impressions of other people. Most nightlife participants prefer to spend time interacting with people with whom they share common sensibilities and background. Furthermore, although the nightlife spaces are theoretically open to the public, participants are constantly competing to lay claim to particular nightclubs and street corners. Hence, I argue that interactions within the nightlife produce publicly shared spaces characterized less by Anderson's cosmopolitan canopies and more by what I refer to as *integrated segregation*—the idea that individuals in public space, rather than experiencing unfettered interaction with others on the downtown streets, are socially bound to interaction with those social types like themselves.

Although Anderson's study of everyday interactions, along with recent studies that explicitly examine urban nightlife—for example, sociologist David Grazian's research exploring the "staging of" urban nightlife in Philadelphia and the research of sociologists Paul Chatterton and Robert Hollands examining corporate influence on urban nightlife and youth cultures in England—provide important insights into the use of urban public space, none of them explicitly focuses on the dynamics of race, class, and culture as they play out on the streets and in nightclubs of urban nightlife. This is curious given the existence of nightlife areas in most cities, the diversity of nightlife participants in many of those areas, and the significant influence that nightlife areas can have on other aspects of urban life.

In this book I undertake a nuanced examination of urban nightlife to explore the question of how nightlife participants negotiate, navigate, and contest use of urban public space. I reveal how diverse types of nightlife participants define urban public space by their use of it, and show, in part, that this space is defined by the kinds of preexisting relationships and expectations that participants bring to the nightlife. I demonstrate that despite the popular perception that diverse groups are engaged in harmonious interaction with one another, these groups are in fact engaged in ongoing social conflict on the streets and in nightclubs. Yet I also suggest in part that nightlife participants ignore the historical tension among groups, particularly racial and ethnic groups, and view their conflicts as isolated incidents. I propose that observations and analysis of interactions on the streets of downtown Northeast can tell us how core issues of race, class, and culture are being managed throughout a variety of urban public spaces in America. I tell this story through the conceptual lens of integrated segregation, but first let me share a brief description of downtown Northeast as a backdrop for my observations.

Northeast

Northeast is located in northeastern Georgia. It has an established reputation as a lively music venue and has spawned nationally acclaimed musicians. It is also known regionally and nationally among U.S. college students because it is home to Big South University. Indeed the university is a major drawing force for Northeast. Combining both the academic with the social, BSU is ranked annually as one of the top places to have fun in the country and among the top public state universities for its academic programs.[22] BSU and the city of Northeast have an entwined social history based on geography, cherished social associations, and the personal interactions that have occurred between the local community and the university population over several decades.[23]

Northeast has a population of approximately 105,000 residents. Some researchers might question the designation of Northeast as an urban area given its size relative to large cities, but I define it as such for the following reasons. Northeast County, which is the county seat for the city of Northeast, is a U.S. Census Bureau–designated metropolitan statistical area and has a combined population of approximately 170,000. According to 2000 U.S. census data, Northeast ranked approximately 200 out of about 350 metropolitan statistical areas in the United States.[24] When the local colleges and universities in the Northeast area are in full session, there is an infusion of an additional 40,000 residents. City residents are likely to encounter strangers in public spaces at times of such a drastic increase in population. There is also racial and ethnic heterogeneity among the population. Approximately 64 percent of the permanent residents identify as White, 26 percent as African American, 6 percent as Hispanic, 2 percent as Asian, and 2 percent as Other. Hence, to borrow the language of noted urban sociologist Louis Wirth, given the population size, density, and heterogeneity of the Northeast population, I take the living conditions in Northeast to be consistent with urban living rather than simply a "small town" or "college town." Furthermore, Northeast has the trappings of an urban environment that must consistently manage its share of panhandlers, transients, gangs, drive-by shootings, and other violent crimes. It is for these reasons that I designate Northeast as an urban area.

Most of the residents in the city are young, similar to the case in other metropolitan areas. The average resident in Northeast is twenty-five. Some of these young residents likely stayed following their college years, and their presence adds to the lore of downtown as an exciting party scene. The ratio of male-to-female population is approximately four men to every five women. Young men in pursuit of interaction with members of the opposite sex recognize this as favorable, and Northeast has a reputation among men for having attractive women. In fact, during the time of the study, a popular men's magazine ranked Northeast among the top ten American cities for single men looking for the best women.

According to 2004 Big South University statistics, the student population numbers about 32,500—25,000 of whom are undergraduates. Most of the BSU students come from the northeastern Atlanta area, and approximately 84 percent of the students identify as White, 5.5 percent as foreign nationals, 5.5 percent as African American, 1.5 percent as Latino, and 3.5 percent as Other.[25] These demographics significantly affect the interactions and relationships among individuals in shared public spaces like downtown.

Downtown Northeast is located on a grid of about twenty-one square blocks. There are approximately 220 businesses, 50 bars—4 with dance floors—and 40 restaurants.[26] During the day, downtown Northeast serves as a center of civic activity for local residents and students. At night, it becomes a densely populated area where diverse groups contest one another for use of urban public space across racial, class, and cultural boundaries. I examine this conflict through the conceptual lens of integrated segregation.

Integrated Segregation

The unknowing onlookers driving through the busy streets of downtown Northeast during the late-night party scene might view the throngs of patrons moving from block to block and see a diverse group of individuals sharing in the revelry of one of the most well-known party places for college students in America, all of this activity seemingly taking place in an ebb and flow of crowd movement that has "having fun" as its primary goal. This picture of different types of people engaged in integrated happiness, however, belies an alternative reality.

Upon closer investigation one can see that this view of harmony and balance is disturbed by an ongoing social tension that runs along and across lines of gender, race, class, and culture. Rather than being engaged in harmonious integration, we see interspersed groupings that are in fact operating in integrated segregation as they occupy the urban public space of downtown Northeast. This scattering of diverse groups within the same physical space and the underlying tension among them is not a recent social phenomenon. Indeed, urban sociologists have noted the ways in which different groups, particularly racial and ethnic groups, negotiate the use of urban public space.

For instance, the sociologist Gerald Suttles, in his now classic 1960s study of White, Black, Hispanic, and Italian populations living in close proximity to one another in the Addams neighborhood of Chicago, shows how social relations among ethnic groups in the slums become structured as these groups vie for the use of public space.[27] Suttles, describing relations both among different ethnic groups and within a single ethnic group, uses the concept of "ordered segmentation" wherein "age, sex, ethnic, and territorial units are fitted together like building blocks to create a larger structure."[28] Suttles articulates well the ways in which interaction among these segmented groups is based upon a hierarchical arrangement for the use of recreational areas, streets, and stores whereby certain groups are privileged to use particular spaces at particular times.

Suttles further demonstrates that among the residents in Addams there is a "mutual tolerance," whereby various ethnic groups tolerate the presence of others in the public space; a "mutual exploitation," whereby ethnic groups exploit one another in commercial relationships; and a process of "turn taking," whereby the same public space, for instance a public park, is understood to be used by different groups at different times.[29] Although downtown Northeast might appear to be an urban public space characterized by Suttles's notion of "mutual tolerance," I identify ways that nightlife participants, bar owners, bartenders, and local government take action that supports the use of downtown Northeast as a space primarily for White college students. Furthermore, despite the fact that the city is diverse, there is very little opportunity for "mutual exploitation," given that Whites are the primary owners of the bars and nightclubs in downtown Northeast. Finally, although "turn taking" may be a phenomenon characteristic of nightlife in large cities—for example, see the sociologist Marcus Hunter's examination of the ways in which heterosexual and homosexual patrons in Chicago alternate the use of a popular Black nightclub on Friday and Saturday nights—there is no explicit use of the nightclubs in this way in Northeast.[30]

Throughout my analysis in this book I draw on concepts like those advanced by urban sociologists like Suttles, Anderson, and Duneier to elaborate a notion of integrated segregation. I propose this concept as a way to further expand how we think about the subtle ways in which conflict occurs among groups from diverse racial, class, and cultural backgrounds that are competing with one another for the use of urban public space in increasingly diverse social contexts. Although the idea of integrated segregation might be easily thought of as applicable primarily to the case of racially and ethnically segregated groups, I intend a broad application of this concept to include diverse kinds of groups within the nightlife context whose interaction is focused primarily on members of that same group.

Before describing integrated segregation more fully, it is useful to talk about groups within the nightlife. The most commonly observed groupings in the nightlife are those that I refer to as *caravanning groups*. These groups usually comprise two to ten people who "hang out" together as they move from place to place seeking the opportunity to have fun. They are typically segregated by sex, and the members of the groups usually share some prior affiliation with one another that extends beyond the nightlife. Within downtown Northeast a common example of a caravanning group that is readily observed throughout the nightlife is "frat boys." Figure 1.1 provides an illustration of how frat boy caravanning groups may be dispersed on a street corner in Northeast.

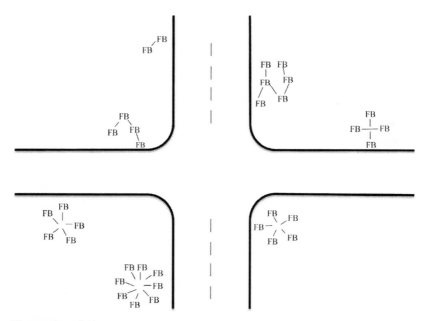

FB represents one frat boy
____: represents the connection of individuals together in a caravanning group

FIGURE 1.1 Frat Boy Caravanning Groups. This is an example of how caravanning groups of frat boys might be dispersed spatially on street corners in downtown Northeast. Prepared by Edward L. Tarlton.

Although caravanning groups may gain or lose members through-out the night, most caravanning groups remain intact until the conclusion of the evening. At the high point of the night, diverse caravanning groups may be observed sharing the densely populated street corners in downtown Northeast. Figure 1.2 provides an illustration of how diverse caravanning groups may be dispersed on a corner. Note that the figure represents male groupings without attention to race, class, or gender distinctions. The complexity of these distinctions is discussed at length later. For now simply note that diverse groups share close physical proximity on the street corners.

I find it useful, in thinking about the idea of integrated segregation, to draw out the analogy of social groupings as metaphorically encapsulated from one another within the same urban public space. These *social capsules* do not have physical boundaries in a literal sense, but rather symbolic and social boundaries that influence nightlife participants'

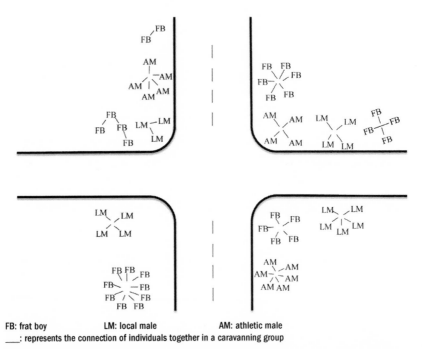

FB: frat boy   LM: local male   AM: athletic male
___: represents the connection of individuals together in a caravanning group

FIGURE 1.2 Diverse Caravanning Groups. This is an example of how various caravanning groups might be dispersed spatially on street corners in downtown Northeast. The groups are physically proximate to one another, but socially their interactions are focused on members within their caravanning groups. Prepared by Edward L. Tarlton.

direct engagement with others in the context of downtown Northeast.[31] According to the sociologist Michèle Lamont, "symbolic boundaries" are "conceptual distinctions that we make to categorize objects, people, practices, and even time and space."[32] The kinds of conceptual distinctions that nightlife participants make influence social interaction in downtown Northeast. For instance, as I demonstrate in later discussion, nightlife participants draw on characteristics like styles of dress and give those characteristics a distinct meaning, thereby creating a symbolic boundary. Such symbolic boundaries, claim Lamont and Molnar, become "social boundaries" when they are widely agreed upon and take on "a constraining character and pattern social interaction."[33] In downtown Northeast, participants use styles of dress as one marker of a social boundary and then engage or avoid people who are perceived to be inside or outside of the recognized boundary.

When we think of symbolic and social boundaries, it is easy to view them as limiting interaction between individuals and among small groups. Yet, I use the metaphor of a social capsule with boundaries to illustrate the ways in which numerous small groups are socially clustered with other caravanning groups, thereby giving their boundary enforcement against excluded groups a collective effect. For instance, a caravanning group of two to ten "frat boys," drawing on styles of dress as an indicator of status, might enforce boundaries against "local" males who do not wear the customary polo shirts like the frat boys. At the same time, similarly situated frat boy caravanning groups are also enforcing such boundaries against other local males throughout the nightlife. This boundary enforcement at the caravanning group level has the effect of boundary enforcement at the social capsule level. When these multiple caravanning groups undertake action to enforce boundaries against other caravanning groups, this activity helps to support integrated segregation in the urban public space. Figure 1.3 provides an illustration of how diverse groups may be spatially located as they enforce boundaries against one another.

I differ from Suttles, whose notion of "ordered segmentation" views groups as sociospatial units that come into contact and have conflict with one another at specific times and in specific spaces, in using the notion of social capsules as a more precise way to capture the collected sense of conflict that looms in an otherwise uniform public space for having fun. Using the concept of social capsule helps us to visualize downtown

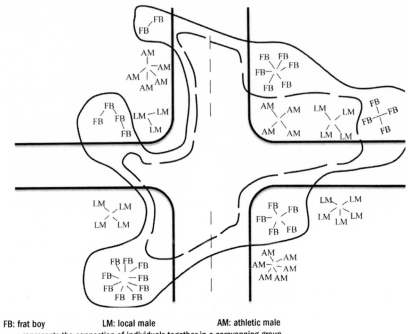

FB: frat boy   LM: local male   AM: athletic male
___: represents the connection of individuals together in a caravanning group
-----: the exclusionary boundary formed by caravanning groups practice of interacting with groups like themselves

FIGURE 1.3 Integrated Segregation. This figure illustrates how frat boy caravanning groups' enforcement of boundaries against non–frat boy caravanning groups creates a figurative social capsule. Frat boy caravanning groups may be physically proximate to local male or athlete male groups, but they are socially proximate to other frat boy groups that share similar class and cultural sensibilities. Hence, frat boy caravanning groups might have civil interactions with groups of strangers, but it is typical that those strangers will also be frat boys. Prepared by Edward L. Tarlton.

Northeast as a space involving a collection of groups who experience conflict in a more nuanced way than typified by "ordered segmentation." Ultimately, it is the recognition or lack of recognition of social boundaries by various nightlife participants that influences the overall nature of interaction taking place on the public streets.

How Groups Come Together

Given the significance of group activity for having fun in the nightlife, it is important to ask how caravanning groups and by extension the larger encapsulated groupings come together. One of the most important mechanisms in the formation of these groups is individuals' participation in late-evening gatherings usually between ten o'clock and midnight. These activities—also known as "pregaming"—are held at individuals' apartments or at fraternity houses, where friends and associates are invited to drink alcohol and socialize in small groups before they make their way to the downtown streets and nightclubs.[34] Typically invitees to these gatherings have received an invitation from the host, or someone who knows the host. It is rare that participants in these pre-downtown gatherings come to know of them by chance. Rather, these gatherings are characterized by the hosts' intentions to bring together "known" others for sustained interaction with people whom they know or whom they come to know more intimately within these kinds of settings. In short, these gatherings help to segregate downtown partygoers into groupings even before they have made their way to the streets of Northeast.

The gatherings may include from as few as three or four participants to as many as several hundred—all of whom are somehow at minimum loosely connected through social networks. For instance, the intimate gatherings typically may include coworkers from a local restaurant, students taking the same course, friends from high school now attending the same college, or people hosting out-of-town guests whom they want to "show a good time in Northeast." The large gatherings typically include individuals attending a theme party like "Pimps Up and Hoes Down Party" or "Pajama Party" as well as annual fraternity and sorority events like the "Spring Tea."

For those patrons who participate in the pre-downtown gatherings, reuniting with their group becomes a focal point as they move through public space. These groups of people who are focused on "having fun" with "the girl from the house party," "the guy from the fraternity," or "the people who had all the beer" means that individuals collectively seek to participate with people who are their desired social types. More important, they generally restrict their interaction or movement to places where mostly their desired social types congregate.[35]

The idea that people are seeking out social types like themselves is not surprising. Social scientists have consistently demonstrated how people self-select others like themselves based on a number of attributes and factors. For instance, the psychologist Beverly Tatum shows how youths attending a racially mixed school choose to sit in the school cafeteria with others whose racial identification is like their own.[36] The students are drawn to one another out of a sense of shared identity. Like the students in Tatum's work, nightlife participants in Northeast seek out those with whom they identify. Yet the nightlife participants are choosing their social types based on a number of characteristics beyond just race—a point I discuss later in detail. They spend the evening seeking out those others who are presumed to have shared tastes and sensibilities based on the idea that "people like me will know how to have fun like me."

In order to meet their desired goal of uniting with similar others, the patrons must pass individuals who occupy statuses unlike their own.[37] Thus, the street corners during the peak hours when people pass to and fro have the appearance of integrated public space where diverse individuals share social relationships. As I have observed, however, these streets are a physically integrated space, but socially they represent the clearest form of integrated segregation. Furthermore, this integrated-segregation masks ongoing social conflict among groups and has implications for how individuals interpret the place of race, class, and culture in their everyday lives. Ultimately, the participants' interpretations of nightlife in downtown Northeast suggest the complexities of contemporary race relations more broadly.

Race, Class, Culture, and Integrated Segregation

A key characteristic of the nightlife in downtown Northeast is that many patrons emphasize gathering with individuals with whom they have had some prior affiliation—as most readily observed by the patrons' indulgence in pre-downtown social gatherings. This emphasis gives public space in downtown Northeast the feel of a "parochial realm" that is based on the desirability of having fun with those acquaintances from "communities" that exist beyond the context of downtown Northeast—for example, "communities" like those formed at work, in school, or within organizations.[38] I have designated the collection of these groups that are based on shared similar social characteristics as social capsules. As indicated previously, social capsules consist of multiple caravanning groups, like frat boys, dispersed throughout the nightlife but that simultaneously enforce boundaries against groups or individuals perceived to be outsiders—for example, locals—thereby giving the boundary enforcement a collective effect. As an abstract concept, the idea of social capsules in public space can be used to designate groupings based on a variety of social characteristics in a number of social contexts. Yet within the context of downtown Northeast nightlife, social groupings are inextricably linked to distinctions related to race.[39]

The fact that nightlife participants in downtown Northeast form social groupings that are linked to race is interesting, given the prevailing conventional wisdom that American society has become "color-blind"— that is, that people are treated equally and with fairness irrespective of their racial and ethnic backgrounds, and that interpersonal relationships are increasingly formed without regard to race. A number of sociologists have questioned whether Americans do in fact operate from a color-blind perspective and whether American society has become what some commentators have identified as a "postracial society." For instance, the sociologist Eduardo Bonilla-Silva demonstrates the ways in which White respondents in his study employ color-blind rhetoric to evaluate or explain the experiences of minorities.[40] Although Bonilla-Silva recognizes this color-blind rhetoric, he argues that the use of such rhetoric in fact permits Whites to ignore the continued structural inequality and institutional racism that minorities face. Similarly, the sociologist Joe Feagin suggests that although racial attitudes among Whites have improved, the color-blind rhetoric masks systemic racism—that is, enduring and foundational racists practices that support the economic and political power of Whites.[41] For sociologists like Bonilla-Silva and Feagin, the rhetoric around race may have changed, but the structural evidence of racism and discrimination remains.

My own observations of interpersonal interactions within the nightlife suggest that rhetoric has indeed changed and that discrimination itself has become more nuanced for those taking part in having fun. In fact, I attempt to show throughout the book that despite the conventional wisdom that we are moving into a postracial era when the social significance of racial categories based on phenotype is substantially reduced, if not purportedly irrelevant, the public spaces of downtown Northeast continue to be characterized by integrated segregation that reflects historical tensions between African Americans and Whites.[42]

Despite the fact that social interaction in downtown Northeast's public spaces is characterized by integrated segregation rather than integration per se, I do not mean to suggest that most nightlife participants are explicitly incorporating avoidance tactics with the primary goal of excluding others from their social grouping based on race. Rather, I suggest that exclusion, to some degree, occurs as a by-product of everyday interaction wherein which individuals merely interact with those others who share similar tastes and sensibilities. In general, the nightlife participants are inattentive to the ways in which these tastes and sensibilities filter out others from their groups.

Furthermore, I argue that it is the patrons' overall inattentiveness to the nuances of their participation in downtown nightlife and the underlying issues of race that makes the integrated segregation of today's downtown Northeast far more problematic and difficult to confront than the legally sanctioned and explicit segregation of the Jim Crow era. A key reason for this problem is that integrated segregation reflects group dynamics that are considerably more nuanced and incorporate not only ideas about race, but also ideas about class and culture. Hence, the matter of negotiating public space is made more complicated, for instance, by the class distinctions between college students and the poorer local residents, and the subtleties of cultural cues used to distinguish those individuals, irrespective of race, who are legitimately permitted to take part in the nightlife. It is these kinds of distinctions that will be the subject of my analysis.

The complexities of race, class, and culture may be observed as individuals and groups pass one another on the streets of downtown, or negotiate each other's presence within the nightclubs. Although social markers of class and culture influence how individuals situate themselves, or how others situate them within various groups, it is clear from my observations that race is the most influential characteristic designating group composition in the nightlife of downtown Northeast.[43] Thus, beyond the occasional inclusion of one or two African Americans within a predominantly White caravanning group, most of these groups are segregated and cluster together socially with similarly composed groups to form social capsules. Yet the street corners, as the site of public space where caravanning groups pass, appear significantly integrated. Let us first turn to how these groups come to be racially segregated within the context of downtown Northeast, and then discuss the dynamics of interaction between groups on the street corner that give the appearance of integration.

Race

The ways in which Black and White patrons think about the public space in downtown Northeast may in part be influenced by the history that shaped downtown. After the Civil War, Union troops occupied Northeast. This allowed African Americans to establish their own public space on the outskirts of downtown. The corners of Farrell and Oak Streets became known as "the Spot," the cultural center for the Black community of Northeast. By 1910, the Spot was anchored by the Knox Building, which housed businesses for African Americans. At that time, both Blacks and Whites understood the demarcation of physical and social space for African Americans in downtown Northeast, the city of Northeast, and the South more generally. African Americans' attempts to gain access to other spaces were met with resistance from Whites in many places throughout the South.

For instance, in the early 1960s a major challenge to the notion of segregated space in the South came as African Americans attempted to desegregate public universities in states like Mississippi, Tennessee, Alabama, and Georgia. These attempts were often met with hostility and violence as Whites resisted the enrollment and attendance of Blacks to the states' White universities. White students at BSU threw bricks and bottles and shouted racial epithets at newly admitted African American students. Their responses illustrated the magnitude to which some southerners felt social boundaries among the races had to be maintained.

These social boundaries were supported by the ever-present threat of violence to African Americans. For instance, the lynching of three African Americans by local Klansmen in the early 1960s was a reminder to the Northeast Black community that violence could be easily perpetrated against Blacks. An all-White jury in the local court found the Klansmen not guilty, and their acquittal further supported the racial status quo. This local incident is consistent with others occurring throughout the South at this time and demonstrates what African Americans could be subjected to if they attempted to encroach social boundaries in the Jim Crow South.

Despite a history of racial segregation in the South and in Northeast specifically, few contemporary nightlife participants are consciously aware of the previously demarcated boundaries of use within the nightlife of downtown Northeast, or that African Americans had even established their own social space within downtown. Indeed, I was unaware of this rich history, and it was only through my desire to understand the context of downtown interaction that I further investigated. I discovered that those individuals who are most knowledgeable about the history of African Americans' participation in downtown social life tended to be older African Americans who were recalling narratives told to them by parents and grandparents. Hence, my observations suggest in part that today's nightlife participants' formulation of racially segregated groupings in downtown is based not on explicit acknowledgment of race and the history of race relations in Northeast, but rather on the social networks evidenced in the pre-downtown gatherings.

Thus, even if we start from the position that race is no longer explicitly relevant to the question of with whom individuals interact, we can still observe the historical manifestations of race in shaping the formation of these racially segregated groups in downtown nightlife. For example, as I have noted, the social character of downtown Northeast is influenced largely by the pre-downtown gatherings. Patrons who attend these gatherings do so at the beckoning of a host with whom they are familiar. In other words, you receive an invitation to participate in these gatherings if you are embedded within the social networks of the host. This is the simple idea of "who you know."

White, Black, Latino, and Asian students, as well as university athletes, fraternity and sorority members, coworkers, native Northeasterners, and college students from other local universities, host these gatherings.[44] Patrons who attend these gatherings typically share racial or ethnic background with the host irrespective of the host's other social characteristics. To be sure there were instances when the gatherings would include diverse kinds of people from different backgrounds, but in most of those cases, the individual host had social networks that were integrated based on her or his participation within the broader Northeast community. Since these gatherings are the foundation for late-night interaction within the context of downtown and they contribute to integrated segregation, it is important to ask how these racially segregated networks are formed. Furthermore, how might historical factors influence that formation?

I propose three main explanations for the patrons' racially segregated social networks. First, many social networks are based upon individuals' sustained daily interaction. According to the social network literature, individuals may develop ties with others with whom they have frequent contact, yet the strength and nature of these ties may be mediated by a number of demographic factors like gender, race, and social class.[45] For my purpose, I assume that individuals' frequent contact produces opportunities to exchange information that helps build social ties. These ties are the foundation upon which the pre-downtown gatherings are based in the nightlife of downtown Northeast. Thus, given the disproportionate representation of Whites at Big South University, there is a high probability, based upon chance alone, that Whites will have sustained contact with other Whites and thus form social ties.[46] So for White students in particular, their racially exclusionary selection of friends may result as a by-product of the overall population within which they have sustained interaction, rather than the purposeful exclusion of others by race.

Second, some patrons may simply choose to establish ties with others who share similar social status. For instance, there is evidence in the social networks literature that positive identification with a particular group produces some level of interpersonal attraction to that group.[47] Furthermore, this attraction is enhanced when a small number of people share that attribute—for example, racial or ethnic background.[48] It is thus conceivable that within the context of both the university and downtown nightlife that African Americans, Asians, Latinos, and other racial and ethnic groups, given their relatively small population sizes, would seek out social relationships with others who share their backgrounds. This self-selection may be predicated upon mere feelings of affinity for one's in-group, yet these feelings are often undergirded by distrust of members from other racial and ethnic out-groups.[49] This underlying distrust creates the potential for conflict, especially within the context of competition for use of the urban public space in downtown Northeast.

Third, given the level of residential segregation in America, it is likely that most of the college students who attend Big South University arrive in Northeast from racially segregated communities.[50] Furthermore, many of the local residents from Northeast also live in racially segregated communities. Thus, it is likely that both students and local residents have an established sense of comfort with interacting with people like those from their home communities who share similar racial and ethnic backgrounds. Consequently, individuals may choose others with whom to interact as a matter of comfort, while paying little explicit attention to either their own motivations or the broader implications of their choices.

It seems clear that these explanations in some combination help to account for the formation of racially segregated groupings in the downtown nightlife. Whether the patrons' choices for interacting with particular groups of people are based on implicit or explicit considerations of race, the end result is that clusters of groups that are racially segregated share the urban public space.

One of the arguments that I make throughout this book states that patrons' inattentiveness to their own motivations for social interaction regarding race make integrated segregation problematic. Furthermore, although the patrons may not explicitly consider issues of race regarding the formation of their social networks, these choices cannot escape the indirect influence of historical relations between African Americans and Whites. Hence, conditions like the history of African Americans' distrust of Whites resulting from racial violence, the structured inequality that continues to produce disproportionate representations of African Americans in institutions of higher learning—like Big South University—and the structural forces shaping residential segregation provide the backdrop for how these caravanning groups of Blacks and Whites interact within social capsules in urban public space.

Class

Beyond the influence of race, both African American and White patrons' interactions in downtown are complicated by the nuances of class and culture. Within the social sciences, typical ways of conceptualizing class include categorizing individuals into groups like "lower" and "middle" class based upon some threshold in annual income, years of schooling, or occupational achievement.[51] Within the context of downtown Northeast we might presume that college students, by virtue of the fact that they are pursuing post–high school education, are middle class, while those patrons who have completed only high school and work in the low-wage sector in Northeast are lower class. Although such categories are useful for understanding a broad view of social class, they are less useful for understanding a particular social context and the nuanced ways in which such categories might be employed within that context.

For instance, as I have demonstrated in *Talking at Trena's*, categorical ways of thinking about social class are made more complex when considering African Americans in particular, because many of Trena's patrons, despite attaining educational achievements comparable to Whites, were restricted to lower status jobs owing to racial discrimination in employment.[52] Thus, their occupational attainment, a key indicator of social class, did not reflect their status as college graduates. Although the setting of *Talking at Trena's* as a racially and gender segregated neighborhood tavern on the South Side of Chicago is much different from downtown Northeast, the analysis indicates the importance of being attentive to the context within which social class categories are utilized.

Similarly, the sociologist Mary Pattillo recognizes the importance of understanding the contextual ways in which individuals talk about social class. She suggests that Americans in general rarely talk about class per se in economic terms, but rather in terms of status and lifestyles: "Americans talk *around* class by using the vocabulary of status and lifestyles. Instead of referring to how much money someone makes, we describe their overseas vacations or their fancy cars. Instead of looking at a person's résumé to see if she or he attended college, we dismiss him because he has cornrows or her because she wears long press-on nails."[53] For my purposes, I find it useful to be attentive to the interpretive ways that individuals, in their everyday interactions, present themselves and assign others to social classes within the nightlife of downtown Northeast. In short, my focus is on how the patrons enact class. This analysis necessarily relies upon the language of meaning making typically employed in discussions of culture.

Culture

In this study, I use the concept of culture generally to identify "shared outlooks, modes of behavior, traditions, belief systems, worldviews, values, skills, preferences, styles of self-presentation, etiquette, and linguistic patterns" that influence nightlife participants' interactions with one another within the context of downtown Northeast.[54] These elements of culture are nonmaterial, so onlookers are likely unable to apprehend them simply upon passing on the street. Still, nightlife participants make distinctions by using symbols and objects as proxy for an individual's culture. In my cultural analysis I am most concerned with what symbols and objects have meaning for the nightlife participants, how the participants construct meaning in interaction, and how they convey codes about the use of public space.

Cultural theorists like Pierre Bourdieu are concerned with the idea that individuals convey implicit signals about status through what he terms "cultural capital." Both the conveying and interpretation of these signals are filtered through individuals' everyday practices or "habitus."[55] For Bourdieu, the conveying of implicit and explicit signals about one's status is most readily observed in educational systems where students are learning both the explicit knowledge content and implicit messages about tastes, styles, manners, and cultural sensibilities. For my purposes, I am concerned with how nightlife participants signal their status to one another, and how others receive these signals. I am curious about how signals of status within the nightlife are given meaning. For instance, what kind of status is conveyed through frequenting particular nightclubs? What status is being conveyed based upon the kind of drinks purchased? To what degree are these tastes and sensibilities related to an immediate nightlife culture or to experience outside of the nightlife? Furthermore, what are the social consequences for the use of particular kinds of status markers? These questions suggest a system of meaning making taking place as people go about having fun in the nightlife.

Implicitly, it is this kind of taken-for-granted meaning making that undergirds integrated segregation. As caravanning groups are passing one another on the streets, they are evaluating the statuses of others and acting based upon the meanings accorded to these groups. These actions help to enforce boundaries among caravanning groups and broader social capsules. My goal is to uncover the nuanced ways in which nightlife participants interact and to reveal what these interactions tell us about the complex relationship among race, class, and culture on the city streets and in the nightclubs. For instance, one common means of conveying one's status is through styles of dress irrespective of one's race. Hence my analysis of culture necessarily takes into consideration the kinds of meanings that nightlife participants give to clothes. Social anthropologists like Mary Douglas and Baron Isherwood suggest that evaluating one's appearance is part of a broader goods information system wherein individuals purchase and display certain kinds of goods as a means of making real the distinction they already make among one another.[56] I undertake the goal of teasing out such important cultural distinctions throughout the book. Uncovering these distinctions helps to explain how race, class, and culture become nestled together in everyday life.

Conclusion

One primary goal of sociological research on interaction in urban public space is to articulate the implicit and explicit rules that individuals and groups employ as they interact on the city streets.[57] Key among studies employing this analytic perspective has been the consideration of racial or ethnic tension among groups in close physical proximity.[58] For instance, some scholars examine how Blacks and Whites navigate passage on the city streets where issues of race and class are an important part of how passersby assess one another. These scholars take into consideration matters of "greetings," "respect," and "passage" both within and across racial groups with the goal of explicating the rituals of interaction.[59] This tradition of research builds on the work of the sociologist Erving Goffman, who was concerned primarily with two fundamental aspects of social life: the systematic ways in which humans interact in face-to-face communication and the social, supraindividual rules that govern such behaviors.[60]

Following this tradition of elaborating on rituals of face-to-face interaction within urban contexts, I articulate the taken-for-granted understandings that patrons have in their interaction with one another as they pass on the city streets and socialize within the nightclubs. I identify specific markers of distinction upon which individuals evaluate others within the context of downtown Northeast—like the clothes that patrons wear, the music to which they listen, the bars they frequent, and the corners on which they congregate. I show how this distinction making among patrons supports patterned interactions on the streets and in the nightclubs that result in *integrated segregation*.

As a theoretical concept, integrated segregation helps to explain how individuals and groups use urban public space. In the context of downtown Northeast, integrated segregation reflects broader tensions around race, class, and culture. As I demonstrate, these tensions—to which most patrons are inattentive—are the basis for conflict in urban nightlife. It is by examining interaction in this context that we might glean how issues of race, class, and culture play out in everyday life and are suggestive of broader issues in contemporary race relations.

2

What Is Having Fun
and Who Has It

● ● ● ● ● ● ● ● ● ● ● ●

Nightlife participants seek out, as their primary goal, the opportunity to have fun, but what does that mean? For most of the participants having fun necessarily involves moving through downtown in caravanning groups that consist of two to ten participants who come together around particular social identities—for example, "athletes" or "sorority girls"—and consuming alcohol in the revelry of nightlife. As these participants move through downtown engaging in ritual games of alcohol consumption, their collective behavior enhances the lore of BSU and the reputation of downtown Northeast. It is not so much the outcome of the ritual games that is important for the participants, but rather the collective enjoyment they experience with members of their caravanning groups and others they find acceptable. These experiences become the basis for what some nightlife participants describe as an "epic night"—a night of drinking, partying, and fun of legendary proportions that usually ends with someone intoxicated and passed out.

The majority of nightclubs in downtown Northeast are dedicated to the entertainment of twentysomethings who are looking to have fun drinking and socializing with one another. Although there is some variety in the kinds of entertainment offered—including a gay bar, a strip club, a few alternative rock venues, and a dance club—most of the drinking establishments are nightclubs that cater to the musical tastes and social atmosphere of the college students from BSU. The students who attend the university are from primarily White, suburban areas of metropolitan Atlanta, and the late-night entertainment largely reflects the tastes of these students in variable ways.

Beyond the goal of having fun through the consumption of alcohol, nightlife participants also seek interaction with members of the opposite sex—engaging them in games of sexual innuendo and flirtation, with alcohol as the medium through which they lay aside their inhibitions. The underlying desires that drive the interactions between these young men and women are sexual. Hence, according to the sociologist Amanda Coffey, Northeast may be described as a "sex setting"—a place where sex is "part of the vocabularies and routines of the setting."[1] Despite this characterization of downtown nightlife as a sex setting, there are few explicit sexual acts that occur, save the occasional groping, "make out" kiss, or "girls gone wild" breast exposure.

Although occasional small groups of male and female nightlife participants who pass through the streets of downtown might be identified or self-identify as homosexual or lesbian, there is limited interaction among such groups on the streets of downtown, except near Whitey's, the only explicitly gay bar. Based on its location in a lightly populated area of the nightlife, its patrons do not happen upon it by chance, but rather are seeking it out explicitly. Even those heterosexual participants who have patronized Whitey's recognize its location as providing a measure of privacy for lesbian, gay, bisexual, and transgender nightlife participants. Sociologists also recognize the importance of gay and lesbian nightclubs spaces in nightlife culture. For instance, Chatterton and Hollands, in their study of urban nightlife in England, indicate that gay nightclubs were once exclusively for gays and lesbians as social safe havens, but because of pressure to generate revenue they are increasingly being marketed as "gay friendly" nightclubs that draw in diverse patrons.[2]

Still, although there is evidence of increasing social acceptance of gays and lesbians, many of these nightclubs, like Whitey's, remain physically and socially distant from central nightlife activity or part of a collection of nightclubs that make up "villages" unto themselves. Downtown Northeast remains largely a heteronormative space wherein the majority of patrons understand exchanges of flirtation and sexual innuendo to be heterosexual.

Generally, having fun in downtown Northeast consists of individuals in caravanning groups consuming alcohol and engaging in flirtatious interaction with members of the opposite sex. As caravanning groups move from place to place, they are evaluating other nightlife participants in order to distinguish those with whom they might have fun. Although the clearest distinctions drawn in the nightlife are among members of caravanning groups based upon race, it is the subtle distinctions based on class and culture that are frequently at play in the nightlife, particularly since White students from BSU are the predominant users of the nightlife space. Thus, before discussing the explicit distinctions that arise related to race, and their basis for competition for the use of public space, it is important to understand how class and culture play out in the types of nightclubs that participants frequent.

Nightclub Types

Many nightlife participants categorize nightclubs using identifiers to classify them based on the kinds of people who patronize the nightclub, the kind of music played within the club, or the stylistic atmosphere maintained. Although many categories for various nightclubs exist, I discovered that there were five main types of identifiers that patrons use to group downtown nightclubs and hence the kinds of participants who frequent them: "frat bars," "freshman bars," "regular bars," "alternative bars," and "dance clubs." These identifiers are not mutually exclusive types but rather rough indicators that are used based on a number of factors including who is making reference to the nightclub.[3] In addition, nightclubs might share similar characteristics and yet be designated differently. My goal here is to present general characteristics of nightclubs to facilitate understanding of how individuals and groups negotiate public space in downtown Northeast. Indeed, it is the identification of particular nightclubs that has implications for how caravanning groups move throughout the night and how nightlife participants experience integrated segregation.

Frat Bars or Fratastic Bars

Although members of fraternities and sororities make up only about one-fourth of the undergraduates at Big South University, they have a significant impact on both the university and downtown social scenes. In fact, many patrons consider frat bars or fratastic bars as the prototypical down-town nightclubs. These nightclubs are characterized as such because their typical clientele consists of members of fraternities and sororities from BSU. The term "fratastic" is disparaging and typically used by individuals who are not members of a Greek-letter organization to highlight the self-important "fantastic" attitude associated with being a fraternity member. In other contexts fraternity members themselves might use the term "fratastic" to emphasize the quality of fun they are having at a fraternity social event. Irrespective of the specific use, the term generally refers to members of Greek-letter organizations.

It is important to note that despite the fact that there are Black fraternities and sororities at the university, both Black and White nightlife participants use the term "frat" in "frat bar" to reference only White fraternities and sororities. The use of "frat" to reference only White organizations is consistent with the historical racial segregation out of which Black Greek-letter fraternities and sororities were created.[4] Today there are a total of nine national Black Greek-letter organizations, collectively called "The Divine Nine."[5] These nine organizations have chapters throughout colleges and universities in America, but remain regulated by an entirely different governing council than those that oversee predominantly White fraternities and sororities. This fact suggests the entrenched nature of de facto racial segregation in at least this aspect of college social life.

Fraternity members who frequent downtown can be identified by some version of typical "frat boy" clothing, which includes a polo shirt, khaki shorts or pants, leather flip-flops or running shoes, and a well-worn baseball cap. There are variations on this style of dress that are dictated by the particular social occasion, but their attire is much less variable than clothing worn by young women.

Sorority members are often considered by non-Greek-letter nightlife participants as little more than the female counterpart created in social support of the male fraternities. They also may be identified by how they dress. These young women are sometimes pejoratively referred to as "sorostitutes" to suggest presumed frequent sexual liaisons that "sorority girls" have with "frat boys." Their styles of dress are consistent with those of typical college students; however, they emphasize "dressing up" as a hallmark of being a "sorority girl." Skirts, high heels, and jewelry even on casual occasions in downtown Northeast are essential indicators of their social status to one another and to those fraternity members whose attention they are presumed to seek. Their styles of dress, like those of other female college students, are influenced by annual fashion trends.

Although individual nightclubs in downtown Northeast may be known for particular music, the music played in a frat bar is generally a mixture of top forty pop music, old-school rock (for example, music by Bon Jovi), and country (for example, songs by Hank Williams, Jr.), with a dash of hip-hop. On some occasions these drinking establishments also provide live musical entertainment—most often a guitarist playing covers of old country favorites or contemporary rock. Most of these establishments also host theme party nights with drink discounts for members of particular fraternities and sororities. On occasion, Thursday evenings are set aside for the exclusive use of a nightclub by a fraternity or sorority until a designated hour. Nightclubs identified by patrons as frat bars include places like Hunter's Perch, Mutineer's, River Run Tap, Javelina Ranch, and Labador's.

Membership in a fraternity or sorority is considered high status among many nightlife participants. Hence, fraternity and sorority members who patronize frat bars typically exude an air of exclusivity in their social relations. They often seek to interact only with those who share their status. Since patrons who frequent frat bars include participants who are not members of fraternities or sororities, a great deal of time is spent assessing and sorting out those who should be engaged based upon cultural cues like clothing style, one's friends, and the conspicuous consumption of alcohol with little attention to cost. The result of these distinctions being drawn within frat bars is integrated segregation among those who are fraternity and sorority members and those who are not. Tensions arise as nightlife participants attempt to navigate the social boundaries within the nightclub and are most readily observed as young men pursue women within the nightlife. I explore the ways in which these tensions play out in my discussion of interaction between men and women in the next chapter.

Freshmen Bars

The legal drinking age in downtown Northeast, like in most other U.S. cities, is twenty-one. There are, however, some nightclubs that are "eighteen to get in, twenty-one to drink." In these nightclubs patrons who are at least eighteen years old are permitted to dance and enjoy the nightlife with older patrons who are of legal drinking age. When serving alcohol in these establishments, bartenders differentiate between those who may and may not purchase alcohol by looking for a distinguishing mark on the hand or a wristband administered to the patron by the bouncer at the nightclub entrance. This mark or wristband indicates to the bartender whether the patron "is legal." Although the title "freshmen bar" might seem an appropriate reference for this kind of nightclub because freshmen would likely be present, most downtown patrons use the term "freshmen bar" in a different sense.

A freshmen bar is commonly a nightclub that has a reputation for permitting underage drinkers to both enter the establishment illegally and engage in underage drinking. Patrons' explanations for why particular nightclubs are known as freshmen bars include the assertion that these nightclubs have lenient standards for fake identification cards (IDs) or that bouncers know several freshmen from the university and therefore permit them to enter. Some patrons suggest that nightclub owners who seek to maximize profits encourage a freshmen bar atmosphere, and at the same time law enforcement officials, who fear the influence that bar owners have on local politics, ignore the illegal admission of underage drinkers.

Based on my observation, the bouncers most frequently guilty of permitting high proportions of underage drinkers to gain entry to nightclubs dubbed freshmen bars are those individuals who themselves are socially linked to fraternity members. This means the bouncer may know underage drinkers through social networks that include friends who are fraternity members, or the bouncer is a fraternity member himself and knows young men from other fraternities. Thus, the density of freshmen in a particular nightclub is likely due to the bouncer's willingness to give admission to those underage drinkers he knows loosely through fraternity ties.[6] It has been my observation that young men or women who frequent freshmen bars are typically socially linked by fraternal or sororal relationships that illustrate the age-old adage, "It's not what you know, but who you know." Consequently, it is clear why downtown patrons would identify a bar like River Run Tap as both a frat bar and a freshmen bar.

To suggest that freshmen bars exist should not be taken to mean that underage drinkers are blocked from entering other nightclubs in downtown. In fact, most nightclubs, on any given night, will have underage drinkers who are able to evade detection and gain access to the nightclub. This is because beyond the conspiratorial suggestions about owners' and bouncers' motives for permitting underage drinkers to enter nightclubs illegally, there is also the reality that underage drinkers seek to gain access to drinking establishments both for the opportunity to drink alcohol and as a rite of passage. In fact, underage drinkers have become quite adept at gaining access to nightclubs. For instance, underage drinkers purchase elaborate and expensive fake IDs. Others use the IDs of their friends who are of legal drinking age. Some patrons arrive at a nightclub and then telephone a friend inside who smuggles an ID outside for the underage drinker to use. Still others, who know the bouncers working the door, simply flash an ID and gain entrance, even though the birth date on the ID clearly indicates the patron is underage. Finally, when all else fails, those longing to gain entrance to a bar telephone a friend who props open a back door. I witnessed this kind of activity firsthand one night at the Corral.

I stood in line for the restroom in the back of the Corral. The restroom is about ten feet from an emergency exit (with no alarm) leading out to the alleyway behind the nightclub. The restroom area was crowded and the bar was packed. As I stood at the end of the line, I watched as a White male in blue jeans and a button down, blue, collared shirt spoke on his phone. He held the phone up to his left ear, and plugged his right ear with the forefinger on his right hand. The music was loud but I could still hear him shouting, "Are y'all there now?" After a pause he said, "Okay, I'm coming. Get ready." He walked passed me a few steps to the emergency exit door. He paused at the door and then looked quickly to his left down the stairs of the bar. Then he turned back and looked to his right where I was standing. Satisfied with what he saw, he quickly, but discreetly pushed the emergency door open and moved away. Someone from outside the door snatched it open and in a matter of seconds, six guys moved quickly into the door and began trotting down the stairs. I was curious about what they were doing so I followed behind them. Once downstairs, they walked quickly into the basement and went in separate directions throughout the bar. I stopped at the foot of the stairs and leaned on the wall near the pool tables. It was densely crowded at the bar and throughout the basement area. I watched as each patron who had entered the back door walked individually to the bar. After a few minutes I spotted the patrons, each with drink in hand, moving toward a corner of the bar together.

Since there is no cover charge to enter the Corral, I surmised that the patrons were underage and entering through the rear door to bypass the bouncer who would check IDs. Several underage drinkers who had also gained access to the nightclubs in this manner later confirmed my assessment of occurrences like this.

Whether one is able to gain access to one of Northeast's many nightclubs or attends the commonly understood freshmen bar, underage drinking is a staple of downtown nightlife and the "place to have fun" reputation of the university. This fact has been a topic of consideration for Big South University president Rick Armstrong and Northeast's mayor Carmela Devine. Furthermore, law enforcement officers have conducted sting operations to arrest workers in drinking establishments who sell alcohol to underage customers. Although these efforts were highly publicized, it is not clear whether a threefold increase in arrests for underage drinking between 2004 and 2006 actually stemmed the behavior.

Regular Bars

Some patrons believe that frat bars pervade the nightlife in downtown Northeast, but the reality is that there are far more "regular bars." Unlike frat bars, regular bars are spaces where multiple subgroups of college students, including fraternity and sorority members, go to interact. In effect, regular bars represent a broader college student culture than frat bars. It is within these regular bars that one can readily observe the social tension related to different kinds of individuals and groups navigating their social space.

Inside regular bars the music played is much like the top forty music in frat bars. Also like the frat bars, most regular bars do not have any significant dance floor space. Yet many patrons choose to dance, and music is an important determinant of who dances in the crowded regular bars. Music thus becomes part of the distinction-making process for groups inside of these nightclubs.

Since the established social identities that maintain frat bars as largely socially segregated spaces do not exist in regular bars, music is also an important means of controlling the flow of particular kinds of patrons in and out of the nightclub. For instance, those regular bars that play mainstream pop music likely draw more socially and racially diverse groups of clientele than nightclubs that typically play more rock and country. Hence, nightclub management needs only to shift the genre of music from hip-hop, for example, to country to alter the patron composition. When this happens, groups of patrons exit regular bars like Kilpatrick's, Figaro's, and the Corral as the deejay dramatically shifts his playlist from one genre of music to another.

The use of the term "deejay" here suggests that there is an individual responsible for music exclusively. In reality, the bartender or bar manager selects the music through a computer program from a variety of playlists. The bartender can set the playlist for multiple songs and hence shifts in music may be preprogrammed. Most bartenders prefer to program five to six songs at a time so that they can control the social atmosphere in the nightclubs. This becomes important when the semipublic space is encroached upon by otherwise undesirable clientele.

On Stuckey Street, the strip with the most popular regular bars, one can see the greatest diversity of downtown patrons. Groups of athletes, fraternity and sorority members, and locals intermingle as they pass one another. Occasionally small groups of gays, lesbians, and racial and ethnic minorities can be seen moving through the crowded street. All of these groups are negotiating the public space, attempting to navigate their way to another desired location. Along the way, they make distinctions among one another, giving rise to a shared space that is characterized by integrated segregation.

Alternative Bars

Downtown Northeast is so closely associated with Big South University that one might get the impression that frat bars and regular bars are the only drinking establishments that downtown Northeast has to offer. Yet another category exists, what many downtown patrons identify loosely as "alternative bars." These nightclubs are part of a subgroup of drinking establishments in downtown that cater to a specific clientele or have become associated with particular subgroups that fall outside of the mainstream clientele in downtown Northeast. Included among these alternative bars are those nightclubs associated with the music scene in Northeast and host both locally and nationally known bands that play original and cover music and attract a variety of music enthusiasts. Included among these clubs are the well-known music venues Illuminati, Bedrocks, and Swirlyville.

Most of these alternative bars are located just outside of the densely populated areas of downtown Northeast. In a sense they are miles away, though they are only one or two blocks west of Maxine Street, which serves as an imaginary dividing line for those who wish to escape the college atmosphere. Around the Illuminati on Farrell Street between Oak and Dayton Streets are located a number of drinking establishments that accommodate the styles of the alternative crowd. Here patrons are often dressed in goth attire or wearing the latest thrift store outfits as they hang out in places like Cash's, O'Neal's, and Origami's. Many of the patrons hanging here seek good conversation rather than being mostly motivated to pursue drunkenness or liaisons with members of the opposite sex.

Counted among those nightclubs where conversation is the central theme is Universal Tap, a drinking establishment recognized by a popular magazine as one of the top ten bars in the nation for its atmosphere, microbrews, and imports. Here professors, graduate students, and locals gather for drinks in the early and late evening and share in intellectual discourse. Similarly Chillers on Chesterwood Street and Stillwater's on Farrell Street provide places for conversation and tend to have older crowds until about eleven in the evening, while Blocker on Chesterwood Street and Hot and Cold on Leslie offer similar atmospheres for those folks who just want to relax and "chill." Those who would rather gawk at women than talk to them pay the cover charge to enter the Scene, a gentlemen's club on Reginald Street between Chesterwood and Stuckey Streets. All of these alternative bars serve a variety of patrons who wish to have entertainment outside of the typical party scene.

Dance Clubs

The downtown party scene is largely a place for drinking alcohol and socializing, but five nightclubs in downtown boast space large enough to be labeled dance clubs by patrons. They are Club Sleepless and Be Happy on Chesterwood Street, Club Connections and the Bounce on Stuckey Street, and Whitey's on Woodard Avenue.

Like other nightclubs in Northeast, these clubs have experienced various transformations over the years, and some have closed for good. For instance, the Bounce is now Round Up but does not cater to the same musical taste (that is, hip-hop and dance) as its predecessor. Club Sleepless closed in 2007 and has not reopened. Be Happy, a dance hall complete with a stage, was rented by several organizations including some BSU Black student organizations for parties but was converted to Lucky Number, an elaborate upscale dance club reminiscent of clubs found on the strip in Miami Beach.

In general these dance clubs create an interesting dynamic for interaction in the public space of downtown Northeast since they attract diverse kinds of patrons. One dance club in particular, Club Sleepless, has had significant impact on the ways people negotiate public space downtown.

Club Sleepless began in 2000 as a juice bar and dance club that served no alcohol but was the only downtown nightclub to stay open beyond two o'clock. Diverse groups of patrons danced to club, hip-hop, and top forty deejay music mixes until about three. Although alcoholic beverages were not served, the nightclub owners who also owned Mickey's Sports Bar and Grille, a drinking establishment adjoined to Club Sleepless, provided access to Mickey's through a side door and offered discount drink specials to Club Sleepless patrons. In May 2001, the Northeast County government, citing the need to prevent the reoccurrence of "early morning crime waves previously experienced," passed an ordinance prohibiting public entertainment facilities like Club Sleepless from maintaining hours of operation beyond the two o'clock hour.[7]

Club Sleepless adopted the common "eighteen to enter, twenty-one to drink" policy when it began selling alcoholic beverages. After this transition, it began to draw greater numbers of Black patrons from both Northeast and the university. As a result the White college students who frequented downtown labeled Club Sleepless "the Black club." This moniker took on greater significance when William Ernest Moore, a twenty-year-old White male and out-of-town visitor to Northeast, was shot and killed shortly before three o'clock on the northeast corner of Chesterwood and Maxine Streets near Club Sleepless. It was purported that words had been exchanged between Moore and a group of African American males standing on the corner. This group allegedly included George Martin, a twenty-nine-year-old Black male and Northeast resident who was arrested and tried for the shooting but acquitted. By then Club Sleepless was not only "the Black club" but also "unsafe," despite the fact that there was no evidence that either Martin or Moore had been inside of Club Sleepless before the street corner shooting. The corner near Club Sleepless became a place where White college students passed with caution if at all.

Although the other dance clubs do not have an established reputation as being "a Black club," they typically receive greater patronage from Blacks than do the frat bars and regular bars. Indeed, the entertainment, music, and events provided by these dance clubs make downtown attractive to local African Americans who would otherwise avoid downtown Northeast since they generally perceive it as a place with "hick music," "rock and roll," and "drunk White people."

Beyond these nightclubs, Whitey's, the only gay club, provides a social space for lesbians and gays to go and dance with a sense of freedom. Although self-identified lesbians and gays may patronize alternative bars and regular bars, most identify Whitey's as their party venue. Rachel, a twenty-two-year-old White female and self-identified "lipstick lesbian," said, "I like to go to Fun and Folly, but Whitey's is the only place where I can really feel comfortable being me." Whitey's serves as a venue where patrons can take respite from the hyper-heterosexuality and pursuit of attention from the opposite sex that takes place in other nightclubs.

Dance clubs in combination with frat bars, freshman bars, regular bars, and alternative bars make downtown a place where different types of individuals may encounter one another as they move through the streets headed to their desired destinations. Once patrons arrive at their destinations, they must pass through the entryways of the nightclubs. These entryways are "protected" by bouncers who play an integral part in how integrated segregation takes form in urban public space.

Bouncers

Bouncers are nightclub employees hired to exercise the will of nightclub owners with respect to who should and should not gain access to the nightclub. Bouncers have the power and authority, supported by the owner and police officers working on the streets outside of the nightclubs, to deny access to underage drinkers and potential troublemakers and eject patrons who cause trouble once they have gained admission. Given the symbolism of the bouncer as "protector" of the nightclub gateway, women are rarely posted in this position as anything more than ticket or cash collectors, while the men provide "the muscle."

It is also rare that bouncers in downtown Northeast are members of a racial or ethnic minority group. Given the fact that racial or ethnic minorities are rarely used as bouncers and that the majority of the patrons are White, some scholars, like the sociologist Wendy Moore, might suggest that downtown Northeast is in fact a "White space" wherein White racial norms and values as well as the tacit justification of White power, privilege, and wealth are being reproduced.[8] Even so, I show later how the racial and ethnic minorities' presence challenges these spaces and how conflict occurs along racial and ethnic lines. Indeed, some African American nightlife participants suggest that nightclub owners use African American bouncers as a tactic to deflect accusations that the nightclub's dress codes are racially discriminatory against African Americans. In such cases, dress codes are perceived to support nightclubs as the privilege of White college students. For now, it is simply important to recognize that the bouncers are the key authority at the thresholds of the nightclubs and that racial and ethnic minorities generally do not have such responsibility.

Although their authority is limited to the entranceways of the nightclubs by law, some bouncers step beyond this threshold to escort troublemakers from the nightclub. In rare cases, a bouncer may improperly cross the threshold to engage in physical confrontation with a patron who has verbally antagonized the bouncer. When this occurs, few bouncers are reprimanded for their behavior because they are able to conjure up an account of the events that satisfies nightclub management and law enforcement authorities who might have been called to the scene.

Bouncers may also be responsible for a number of manual tasks related to running the nightclub. For instance, many bouncers remove trash from the nightclub at closing time and some are responsible for helping to replenish the alcohol supply from storerooms. In addition to their wage pay, there is typically an implied or explicit arrangement by which bartenders share a portion of the nightly tips. Hence, bouncers benefit significantly by making certain that they admit patrons who will spend large sums of money on alcohol and tip well.

Unlike the usually large bouncers who work in the downtown nightclubs in major cities like Chicago and New York, the bouncers in downtown Northeast tend to be of average physical size. In fact, many of the patrons who frequent the nightclubs, for instance college football players, have greater physical stature than the bouncers working the doors of Northeast's nightclubs. Although they are not physically imposing, some of the bouncers have an air of authority and power.

Recall that those bouncers who work freshmen bars are typically socially connected to regular patrons in some way outside of the nightclubs. Thus they are willing to admit "friends" en masse even though their friends might be underage. In addition to this type of bouncer, who is rare, there are two additional types of bouncers.

The second type of bouncer is easygoing and considered civil by most patrons. These bouncers have a laid-back personality that conveys to patrons that the atmosphere inside of the nightclub is easygoing and "chill." Interestingly, these bouncers tend to be thinner in size than the third type of bouncer and work at nightclubs that are usually socially homogenous.

The third type of bouncer exudes an air of brash confidence and authority. His persona often leads patrons to describe this type as an "asshole" or "dick." He takes his responsibility for "protecting" the nightclub entryway as a personal responsibility, meaning when a patron complains about some nightclub policy the bouncer takes the complaint as a personal affront. These bouncer types tend to be individuals who seek physical confrontation with patrons whenever possible. They testify to other bouncers and friends about spending a great deal of time at the gym weight lifting and are generally preoccupied with getting big. The rapid increase in their body size brings some patrons to aver that the bouncers "are on steroids," especially after one has thrown a patron out of the bar without justification. These bouncers tend to work in establishments that draw the greatest diversity of patrons.

As "gatekeepers," bouncers play a key role in influencing the composition of the nightclubs. They sift out potential patrons using guidelines provided by nightclub owners for desirable clientele. Implicitly, their responsibility for admitting particular nightlife participants places them in position to influence the extent to which participants experience integrated segregation within the nightclubs. The importance of their role manifests particularly in tensions between them and Black patrons around the dress codes that some nightclubs have implemented—a point I address in chapter 4.

The Police

The Northeast Police Department plays a significant role in maintaining public safety in downtown Northeast. The dense crowds using public space and consuming alcoholic beverages increase the potential for harassing and criminal behavior. During the weekend nights, approximately four to eight police officers can be seen patrolling downtown on bicycle. Working out of a police substation on East Farrell Street, the officers sometimes position themselves on corners where the greatest numbers of patrons are congregating. These corners include the northwest corner of Reginald and Stuckey Streets and the northwest corner of Leslie and Stuckey Streets.

According to some patrons, the mere presence of police officers curtails behaviors that might otherwise go unchecked on the public streets. Many of the patrons view them as "really nice," or "pretty tolerant." As one patron noted, "They all know everyone is drunk." The police working the downtown party scene basically balance the missions of maintaining safe passage between pedestrians and vehicles and preventing crime on the streets with allowing patrons to enjoy themselves. The police usually become actively involved only with those who violate standards of public decorum like extreme inebriation, vomiting on the public streets, or engaging in scuffles or fights with other patrons. Typical arrests in the downtown area include public intoxication and disorderly conduct.

Although the police working downtown are focused on the typical activities of downtown patrons, they are also aware of the broader criminal context of nightlife in Northeast. Like most urban areas, Northeast has its fair share of criminal activity including robbery, sexual assault, and murder. In addition to these general criminal activities, Northeast has a growing gang presence. These gangs are made up of predominantly poor Black and Hispanic youth from various areas in Northeast. The gang presence in Northeast has all of the trappings of gangs from big cities, including occasional drive-by shootings and an illegal drug trade.

Perhaps the impression of gang activity is the reason that many patrons believe the police in downtown Northeast are more proactive in breaking up groups of youth that hangout on the corner in front of Club Sleepless. Comparatively, groups of college students are permitted to hang on corners like Reginald and Stuckey Streets. Indeed, the northeast corner of Reginald and Stuckey is where I would spend a great deal of time leaning against the tree or the parking ticket box. The perceived discrepancy between the treatment of local Black residents and White college students is one of the underlying bases of conflict that might appear among different groups in downtown.

In addition to the uniformed police presence there are also police officers from special operations in downtown Northeast. These officers conduct undercover operations to arrest individuals for the sale of alcohol to underage drinkers. There is also an undercover drug unit working inside nightclubs to combat illegal drug sales. I first became aware of the illegal drug trade in downtown Northeast when, while standing on the corner of Stuckey and Reginald Streets, I was approached by a young patron who wanted to know where he could purchase drugs. Other individuals, mostly Black males with whom I became familiar, shared similar stories about being approached for drugs. I later came to know two individuals who had reputations as drug dealers, and whom I thought acted suspiciously on occasion, but I never witnessed them exchange drugs. It is evident from my discussions with patrons that drugs are part of the nightlife scene.

After the shooting of William Ernest Moore near Club Sleepless, police and the city government gave considerable attention to public safety concerns. In 2004, the Northeast County Commission adopted three measures to help police deal with mingling crowds, pedestrian traffic overflowing onto the streets, and drivers looping around the block. First, the Northeast County Commission purchased surveillance cameras and had them installed in downtown Northeast. Then they instituted a cruising ban, stemming from a proposal of top police officials. Finally they revised a loitering ordinance that gave police more authority to disperse lingering crowds.

The cruising ban in particular was found to be problematic by many users of downtown. The ban defined "cruising" as passing "the same traffic points within a no-cruising zone more than three times within any one-hour period."[9] University students protested the ordinance because it would make it difficult to pick up intoxicated friends from various locations in downtown during the late-night hours. Downtown residents protested the ban because it limited their access to street parking. Members of the local Black community protested it because they felt the ordinance would be unfairly enforced against African Americans. Ultimately, the ban was instituted and enforced between midnight and four o'clock on Friday, Saturday, and Sunday mornings. The police viewed these measures as important to maintaining public safety.

Conclusion

Downtown Northeast is a place with a reputation for an exciting nightlife. The density of nightclubs makes Northeast an ideal space to engage in late-night revelry. It is perceived as a prototypical place for White frat boys, sorority girls, and college students to have fun, but because it is a public space it also offers people from diverse backgrounds a place to come and socialize. The presence of individuals from diverse backgrounds means that patrons are constantly making distinction between groups of individuals interacting in downtown. These distinctions are made along racial, class, and cultural boundaries, forming what I suggest is a public space characterized by integrated segregation. In the next chapter I elaborate this concept by focusing on the ways in which men and women interact across gendered boundaries and how these interactions are complicated by race, class, and culture.

3

Gendered Interaction, Caravanning Groups, and Social Boundaries

● ● ● ● ● ● ● ● ● ● ● ● ●

As one might expect, caravanning groups are typically segregated into male and female groups. This segregation facilitates interaction within the nightlife between men and women seeking to have fun by consuming alcohol and engaging in flirtation and sexual innuendo with one another. Beyond the occasional interactions among nightlife participants on the downtown streets who might identify or be identified as members of a lesbian, gay, bisexual, transgendered, or queer community, interactions in the nightlife are decidedly heteronormative. Since it is the gendered interactions between men and women that define much of the nightlife activity, it is through examining such interactions that we might also readily observe how members of caravanning groups negotiate existing social boundaries.

In this chapter, I first discuss the nature of interaction between men and women generally and the role of caravanning groups in those interactions.

I then focus on how men and women in caravanning groups negotiate social boundaries—specifically those boundaries based upon differences in racial, class, and cultural backgrounds. The tensions that arise in these interactions provide further evidence of the constant enforcement and maintenance of boundaries that help to shape downtown Northeast as a place of integrated segregation rather than a place wherein diverse groups typically share in positive and meaningful interactions like those occurring under a cosmopolitan canopy.[1]

In Pursuit of Women

In everyday talk people generally use male and female as biological designations to refer to the sexes, but gender, or what it means to be a man or a woman, is socially defined.[2] For instance, according to Judith Lorber and other sociologists, men and women interact with one another following culturally patterned ways for how they are expected to behave.[3] Hence, as members of sex-segregated caravanning groups move through downtown, they participate in activities that help define what it means to be a man and a woman. Although these behaviors might be perceived as simply having fun in the nightlife in downtown Northeast, they have consequences beyond the immediate context of drinking and partying. Lorber suggests that it is through face-to-face interactions like those occurring in downtown Northeast that gender inequality is reproduced, because as individuals act out gender norms they reinforce gendered systems of dominance and power.[4]

In downtown Northeast, the men focus on pursuing women, who themselves work to attract attention from men. This pattern follows traditional gendered behavior—still held in high regard by most of the participants I encountered. Women may actively indicate to men their openness, but it is the general expectation among men and women that men actively engage women in interaction. In other words, men are given both the privilege and responsibility for "the first move," "walking over," "stepping," or "offering a drink" to women.

One explanation for why men continue to be expected to actively pursue women in the nightlife perhaps has to do with the fact that downtown Northeast is located in the southern United States. The South has a reputation for, if not pride in, adherence to a number of traditional gender role expectations, including ritualized courtship patterns that are passed down through generations. For instance, in their study of gender roles by region, sociologists Rebecca Powers and her coauthors found that both men and women from the South held more traditional attitudes about gender roles than did those residing elsewhere.[5] Adherence to these ritualized courtship patterns in downtown Northeast reflects nightlife participants' preoccupation with presenting gentlemanly and gentlewomanly behavior, much of which is articulated in the traditions of southern culture espoused by fraternities and sororities—a point I address later. For now it is important to simply recognize that men initiate interaction across gender lines and their pursuit of women has implications for interaction across other social boundaries in the nightlife.

Why are men in pursuit of women in urban nightlife? Grazian provides one explanation. In his study of urban nightlife in Philadelphia, Grazian shows how men engage in the "girl hunt," which is essentially a game "in which young men—particularly those of college age negotiating the gradual, yet erratic, transition from adolescence to adulthood—sexually objectify women in order to heighten their own performance of masculinity."[6] Grazian argues that for most young men, the stated goal of the "girl hunt,"—the "pick up"—is in reality a myth. He suggests that these young men simply engage in this collective behavior as a ritual means of affirming a set of cultural beliefs about what men ought to be like.

On the street corners of downtown Northeast, similar tales of the "girl hunt" are taking place as men pursue interaction with women. Like the men in Grazian's study, the men in downtown Northeast view this kind of interaction as a primary goal of entering into the public space of downtown. Mike, a twenty-one-year-old White male, explains,

> I think bar owners want women in the bar, just based on the fact that I think guys are downtown more anyway. But there's "Ladies' Night" and I feel like they [bar owners] are always trying to attract more women because that brings in the guys. I mean, it sounds unfortunate but I feel like that's just the way it is. Downtown, I think a lot of people are just looking to meet girls just to go home with them. A lot of people are just interested in meeting people in general, but I feel like bars are catering to people who are looking to meet girls to take home.

Underlying Mike's comments is the idea that women are objects to be pursued. Communications scholar Annette Markham suggests that this kind of perspective reflects the typical mind-set among college-aged young men who support a subculture that idealizes "the image of the stereotypical American male whose primary goal in life is to have sex with as many women as possible, using whatever means available."[7] Most men I have encountered in Northeast nightlife share the perspective that women are to be pursued. Irrespective of the actual outcome, this pursuit allows male patrons to build confidence in their "display of masculinity and heterosexual power."[8]

Men's pursuit of women in the nightlife reinforces gender expectations, placing men in a dominant position by their agency. Women sometimes employ strategies to subvert this unequal power balance. Some women challenge custom by aggressively pursuing men, but both men and women frown upon this behavior, which is seen as "slutty." The designation of women's aggressive pursuit of men as "slutty" might appear contradictory in a context where fleeting short-term encounters are emphasized.[9] Yet I discovered that many nightlife participants hold marriage as an important ideal to pursue even while in college.

Interestingly, there is some evidence that Georgians in particular hold marriage as more of an ideal at college age when compared to other Americans. For instance, according to a report by sociologists Tavia Simmons and Jane Lawler Dye based on data from the 2000 U.S. census, the estimated median age for first marriage in the United States was 26.6 for men and 25.0 for women, whereas the estimated median age for first marriage in Georgia was 26.1 for men and 24.4 for women.[10] These slightly lower averages place Georgians closer to college age at the time of first marriage and suggest perhaps normative support for the evaluation of potential marriage partners during college years. Further research on the age at the time of meeting first marriage mates would provide greater evidence of the purported social pressure on college students to evaluate their peers as possible mates. Still, given the overall average age of first marriage, it would seem that nightlife participants must balance having fun in fleeting encounters with the prospect of marriage shortly after college.

Irrespective of the tension between the ideals of having fun and marriage, men, because of their generally accepted active pursuit of women, remain in positions of power in nightlife interactions. Men may exert this power by harassing women. Behaviors such as catcalls, whistling, leering, or blowing kisses have been identified as harassing behavior regularly perpetrated by men against women in public spaces. For instance, the sociologist

Carol Brooks Gardner, in a study of women's strategies for negotiating public spaces, argues that women are situationally disadvantaged to receive public harassment. Furthermore, this harassment has psychological effects on women who are under social pressure to prevent being criminally victimized on the public streets.[11]

In downtown Northeast, the nature and intensity of leers, catcalls, and other such behavior depend upon several factors including the types of men and women in caravanning groups, the amount of alcohol consumed, and the overall party atmosphere—the more festive the atmosphere the less likely women are to employ strategies to directly address leering and catcalling. The hope for men, based upon the lore of the "pick up," is that their passing behavior will elicit interest from women, presumably as a start to more engaged interaction that will lead to some form of sexual encounter with a woman. Sociologist Kathleen Bogle, in her study of dating among college men and women, indicates that these sexual encounters, also referred to as "hooking up" among college students, might entail a range of activities from kissing and sexual touching to having sex, and tends to occur after a night of "hanging out" with members of the opposite sex.[12] Bogle argues that hooking up has supplanted dating as the major focus in relationships between college-age men and women. Although the kinds of encounters suggested by Bogle are a common theme in men's and women's discourse about nightlife, Grazian points out that the available evidence suggests that "one-night stands" and "hook ups" are manifestations of the popular media rather than frequent occurrences in urban nightlife.[13] It is difficult to evaluate the extent to which my nightlife participants have engaged in these kinds of sexual encounters, but it is clear from my observations that the idea of immediate sexual conquest looms large for nightlife participants.

A key source of having fun for nightlife participants in downtown Northeast occurs when individual men and women within their typically sex-segregated caravanning groups interact with one another across group boundaries. If individual men pursue women and women are receptive to their advances, the two groups may come together to interact in games of sexual innuendo and flirtation. Hence, the caravanning group is important for the collective experience of having fun in urban nightlife. The caravanning group is also the means through which broader social boundaries, such as those across racial, class, and cultural backgrounds, are negotiated, since interaction is initiated through members of caravanning groups. Before considering the complex ways in which broader social boundaries are negotiated, I turn to the following question as a means of highlighting the role of caravanning groups in men's and women's interactions when race, class, and culture are not explicitly considered: what strategies do women use to negotiate the advances of men whom they consider "undesirable"?

Negotiating the Approach from Undesirables

Whether a particular man or woman is considered desirable is doubtlessly a question of personal taste, yet I argue that these tastes are significantly influenced by the interactional contexts in which patrons' evaluations of others occur. When female or male patrons are asked to describe whom they think is "desirable," they often describe individuals using phrases that capture personal notions of physical attractiveness like "I like guys that are tall, athletic, with dark complexions" or "I like girls that are blonde, thin, and well-built." These characteristics indicate attractiveness rather than desirability. Desirability takes into consideration, to a greater degree, the social aspects of an individual's persona. Furthermore, evaluations of physical characteristics might vary, but these characteristics remain the primary basis upon which most patrons find others attractive.[14]

Given the custom that men approach women, how do women, resist, redirect, or otherwise handle advances from "undesirable" men who might approach them? Grazian suggests that the women in his study of urban nightlife in Philadelphia use individual and collective strategies to respond to approaches by men.[15] These strategies include tactics such as aggressively responding to approaches verbally or nonverbally, rejecting drink offers from men, accepting overtures but maintaining close contact with "girlfriends" in case the need arises to terminate the encounter, and giving fake names or phone numbers. The women in downtown Northeast use similar strategies to negotiate their interactions with undesirable men.

For instance, I observed Caroline, a White female patron, give a fake phone number and name to a male patron who was "creeping her out." Caroline's strategy illustrates ways in which women, although expected to be the recipients of overtures from men, take control of the situation and empower themselves. As Markham indicates, women may view these interactions as "a game" and proactively work to manipulate the situation to their advantage.[16] Markham provides an example from the literature that reveals the kind of thinking that may go into women's approach to bar interaction. In her self-reflections stemming from her ethnographic examination of men's pursuits of women at a local bar, Markham recognizes the power dynamic between men and women in the nightlife and sets out to compete against the men. She asserts, "As long as power moves are going to be made in this place [bar], let me make some and be equal. Let me play it better than they do. Let them want me. They'll never take me or have me. Let me be more powerful, more strong, more cunning, more wild, more outrageous, more of everything than they could dream of being."[17] Markham's recognition of "the game" empowers her to proactively engage the men that might approach her.

In addition to instances of deception like Caroline's, women have other strategies in their repertoire, sometimes relying upon the assistance of other individuals from within the caravanning group. For instance, some women develop a set of signals or code words to indicate to others that they need to be "rescued" from an encounter with a man. Misty, a twenty-three-year-old White female, indicated that she brushes her forefinger across the side of her nose as a signal to her friends that she needs their assistance to escape an encounter. She was quick to note, however, that this signal is rarely effective since few of her friends pay close attention to her once she has accepted the initial overture from a man. Still, it is the careful execution of collective strategies like this one that helps women thwart the approach of an undesirable man.

Interestingly, during my observations I noted that while women rely upon the strategy of caravanning group member intervention in men and women's interactions, men do not. Perhaps this gender-related difference is based upon two interconnected reasons.

First, given that interactions are taking place on public streets, a domain recognized by many as a male-dominated space, then female patrons are more likely to travel in caravanning groups, not only for sharing in the nightlife with friends, but also to support and protect one another from men.[18] As Duneier, in his study of homeless booksellers in New York, indicates, women are particularly disadvantaged in their encounters with men on the street:

> It is well known that streets and sidewalks are places where women are disadvantaged by public harassment. While the things we are witnessing are a case of the larger public harassments that occur between some people working the

street and pedestrians of both genders, perhaps for women it is a problem in distinct ways. . . . It is true that men, too, are often waylaid on the street, and the same lack of respect for the practical ethics of conversational closings exists in male-male encounters. But the nature of those violations is different. The sense of an entitlement to control another man is notably absent.[19]

Duneier suggests that the men attempt to assert control over women, but rarely make any such attempts on men. I observed similar efforts by the men to exert power in interactions with women on the streets of downtown Northeast. Hence, women in caravanning groups live by the adage of "safety in numbers" and take active roles in protecting one another from men.

According to the sociologist Laura Rivera, it is the perception of male dominance that drives nightclub bouncers' evaluation of male patrons. Rivera studied bouncers at an elite nightclub in Boston and found that they give closer scrutiny to male patrons because the bouncers believe that they can physically control female patrons should an altercation occur in the nightclub, whereas male patrons are presumed to be more difficult to manage.[20] If nightclub bouncers, as agents of social control within the nightlife, are making these kinds of evaluations of men's physical dominance over women, it seems reasonable to assume that male nightlife patrons are doing the same. Hence, I suggest the second reason for the difference in strategic use of caravanning groups by men and women is that men in downtown Northeast perceive members of their caravanning group to be capable of handling any potential threat posed by women. Thus, if a woman violates the customary practice of being approached and chooses to approach a man, the other men within the caravanning group presume that the approached man will not require intervention to terminate an interaction between him and the undesirable woman. In sum, male dominance in the nightlife partly explains why women strategically use caravanning groups to avoid undesirable men, and why men do not rely on other men to avoid approaches from undesirable women.

In gendered interactions, men and women may meet someone whom they consider attractive, but ultimately the caravanning group influences the degree of interaction between the two patrons. We have observed how men and women who share similar social backgrounds negotiate interactions, but what happens when outsiders penetrate these groups? Specifically, how do men and women respond to individuals with whom they do not share similar social or cultural traits? To address this question I first examine types of people who cluster together with one another to make up broader social groups, or social capsules as I refer to them. I focus on the ways in which different types of patrons represent themselves through their styles of dress. I uncover the nuanced ways in which viewers decipher the class, culture, and racial cues embedded in styles of dress and respond to these cues. I then examine how interactions between men and women, in particular African American men and White women, expose the underlying tensions and conflict between social capsules. I suggest how patrons' responses to outsiders' encroachments have implications for interaction among groups beyond downtown Northeast.

Frat Boys, Styles of Dress, and Gendered Interaction

When nightlife participants choose to go out with friends and associates they typically go to bars where they will meet people who are like them. As several clusters of these caravanning groups move about and interact with one another on the streets they form a broad social grouping that I call a *social capsule*. Specifically, social capsules consist of groups of patrons who affiliate with one another, or who are grouped by others, for the purpose of social interaction. These groups are usually based on individual social types.[21] For instance, "frat boys" as a collective group moving throughout all of the bars in downtown Northeast make up a social capsule. Although various caravanning group members of the frat boy type may not know members of other frat boy groups personally, they identify with one another. Furthermore, other patrons view frat boys as one group, even when they are interspersed in a bar or on the street corner with other social types like athletes or locals. They are presumed to frequent particular bars like Hunter's Perch, Mutineer's, River Run Tap, and Javelina Ranch.

Although patrons may frequent certain bars or listen to particular types of music to let others know they affiliate with a certain social group, it is styles of dress that are the key means by which patrons identify with a group. Patrons not only select styles of dress to identify with particular groups, but also evaluate others' styles of dress in order to assign them to social groups.[22] For instance, patrons consistently identify a polo shirt, khaki shorts, and flip-flops as frat boy attire, especially when White men wear this attire. Although the use of styles of dress to evaluate the social status of others can be complex—a topic I discuss at length in the next chapter—the key point is that patrons use basic knowledge of styles of dress to make initial distinctions that help them enforce otherwise intangible social boundaries among groups. There is an underlying tension in these negotiations that is seen most easily when men and women interact across social capsule boundaries.

Men evaluate not only women's physical attractiveness but also their styles of dress to determine if a woman is desirable before they approach. They expect women to dress in sexy or provocative attire, wearing the latest fashions, usually clothing that exposes legs, arms, and cleavage. Women also evaluate approaching men based on their physical attractiveness and styles of dress, although they expect less of men when it comes to dress. Despite the differences in expectations for men's and women's dress, it is clear that both men and women use clothing as a proxy for cultural and class sensibilities that may enhance or diminish the status of the wearer.[23] The process of assessing these sensibilities, however, is made more complicated by the fact that there is an ongoing presentation in mainstream media of the "hottest" and "most popular" clothing brands and styles.[24] These brands and styles of clothes are mass produced and broadly available to men and women from a range of cultural and class backgrounds. The implication, then, is that it is possible for anyone to appear socially acceptable in the nightlife.

Hence, after the evaluation of styles of dress, the initial verbal exchange between men and women is an important secondary means not only for determining attractiveness, but also for "placing" a woman or a man squarely in her or his particular social group.[25] In using the term "placing" I am referencing Lofland's ideas of "appearential" and "spatial" ordering whereby individuals take in a stranger's appearance and her or his spatial location to determine whether the stranger is "safe." This process amounts to stereotyping based on characteristics immediately accessible to the viewer. The viewer then uses additional information garnered through initial interaction to clarify the identity of the individual.

For instance, many women consider members of fraternities as desirable and enjoy being approached by men displaying frat boy styles of dress. Fraternity members are given this status because women presume they are among the wealthier students on campus, members of families who have some storied history at the university, and socially connected to powerful people beyond the university. These presumptions are important because despite the fact that students go out for fun, they also hold an underlying belief that marital partners are sought and found during one's college years and nightlife provides one social venue for meeting members of the opposite sex. Hence, for a woman, the approach of a man in frat boy attire may have implications for life beyond the immediacy of having fun.

Since non–fraternity members also wear frat boy attire, the initial interaction between men and women often involves assessing individuals' actual social status rather than status presumed by appearance. Men who are not fraternity members but wear frat boy attire often report that women attempt to assess fraternity membership early in the conversation. David, an avid participant in the downtown nightlife, is a White male who is not a member of a fraternity, but likes to "dress up in a Ralph Lauren Polo shirt and khaki shorts." He indicates his frustration with women's evaluations: "When you meet girls, uh, it's like the second question out of their mouth. It's unbelievable. Like I meet girls and like the second question is like, 'What frat are you in?' [David makes an ugh sound and frowns.]"

Being rebuffed because he is not a fraternity member highlights, for David, the separation of status between himself and fraternity members. He can look through the metaphorical veil and see frat boys having fun, but cannot fully participate. Many of the young men like David who are not fraternity members have similar experiences. They develop a heightened sense of frustration from the very fact that they can see what they are missing. This is particularly troubling to them given that women in general hold interacting with fraternity members in high regard, yet fraternity and sorority members combined make up only about one-fourth of the BSU student population. Hence, the average male patron is competing with other nonfraternity men for the attention of a small number of women who actually seek interaction with those not in a fraternity.

Although fraternity members are given significant status within the context of nightlife in downtown Northeast, there are some nightlife participants who hold bias against both fraternity and sorority members, referring to them as "people who buy their friends." This phrase is made to suggest that fraternity and sorority members, instead of interacting with a wide variety of people and exercising the mental and emotional energy to determine "true friends," simply select their potential "brothers" or "sisters" based upon the perceived wealth of the potential member, who is then required to pay membership dues. For nonmembers the perception is that each member who has paid dues is "buying" an association with other dues-paying members. Despite this connotation, or perhaps owing to it, fraternity and sorority members maintain significant social status in downtown nightlife.

Underlying the tensions between fraternity members and nonmembers are issues of class and culture. For instance, there are a variety of fraternities on campus, yet the most visible of them are those that recognize a history dating to the early days of the university. Several of the fraternities presently occupy antebellum homes that were built by southern aristocrats who wanted their sons who were attending the university to enjoy the comforts of home while in Northeast. In many of these homes African American slaves served the young men and their families. And so present-day fraternity members not only are thought of as wealthy to many patrons, but also are considered to be part of the historically wealthy or "old money." There is a significant class status distinction being drawn by a young man who can claim to be both a fourth-generation BSU student and a fourth-generation member of the same fraternity in which his father, grandfather, and great-grandfather were members.

A young man's participation in a fraternity suggests not only a class distinction from the average young man, but also a cultural distinction that is embodied in the notion of the "southern gentleman." Some fraternities take development of the southern gentleman as the explicit aim of their organization. For instance, one fraternity's aim is to remain southern in a significant sense and to develop the ideal character and attributes of true gentlemen emblematic of their Confederate forefathers. It is this emphasis on the idea of a "southern gentleman" that gives fraternity members appeal to a number of young women entering the nightlife, as one woman indicates: "That's why I like frat guys, they are real gentleman. They know how to treat a lady. They hold doors, give up seats, and even offer to buy you drinks just being friendly." Whether fraternity members are perceived as having better manners, more money, or greater influence than other men, it is clear that they are given high esteem by many women, a point that non–fraternity members are reminded of as their advances are rebuffed.

The tension existing along social capsule boundaries between fraternity and nonfraternity groups is just one example of several that exist. There are other social capsules that are typified by the kinds of individuals that affiliate with them, or are affiliated with them by others. Most patrons recognize the following general types: "fraternity-sorority" or "Greek," "college student," "local" or "townie," "alternative," and "athlete."

Using cultural and class indicators like styles of dress, patrons actively place themselves and others into groups based on these types. They go to bars or street corners where those whom they wish to associate with are known to frequent. Their movement, in caravanning groups, through downtown in this manner gives social meaning to the intangible boundaries of social capsules. A brief discussion of each general patron type helps to further demonstrate how gendered interaction patterns across groups bring out the underlying tensions and reinforce integrated segregation in urban public space.

Class, Social Types, and Styles of Dress

Many nightlife participants make nuanced class distinctions among the kinds of people that are patrons of downtown, but most associate "college student" types with those who have middle-class backgrounds. From a conceptual standpoint "middle class" refers to the middle position in the American hierarchical social class system.[26] In general, this position is associated with the pursuit of at least "some college" education. Hence, college student types, by virtue of their pursuit of a college education, are thought of as middle class by laypeople and scholars alike. Although fraternity-sorority types are also college students, they classify themselves and are classified by others as being from upper-middle-class backgrounds. In reality, the fraternity-sorority types possess many of the same social indicators as college student types, but are placed hierarchically higher than college students in a nightlife context that helps to further stratify these similar groups from one another.

Most patrons recognize "local" or "townie" types as being positioned hierarchically lower than fraternity-sorority and college student types. These patrons are often associated with families who have lived in Northeast for many years and work in occupations or industries that service the needs of the university students. These occupations most frequently include university custodial, maintenance, and food service occupations. There are also some local or townie nightlife participants whose family members have professional backgrounds and work in middle- or upper-middle-class occupations as teachers, doctors, lawyers, local politicians, and businesspersons. As the locals interact with others in the nightlife they begin to make important class distinctions among one another. Those patrons whose families are from professional backgrounds choose to associate with college student types and are generally integrated into the social scene, while those from working-class backgrounds face greater challenges to integrate into a social scene within which middle-class status is emphasized.

The local young men are well aware of the challenges they face as they attempt to engage young women in the nightlife. For those men whose families have professional backgrounds, they simply emphasize their middle-class status within the context of Northeast to reduce biases that women might have against locals. For instance, Matt, a local White male, said, "I try to work in early in the conversation that my father owns a business in Northeast and we support the football team. Girls like guys with money so if they think you have it then they are more likely to keep talking to you." Like the young men in Grazian's study, patrons like Matt craft identities around characteristics that attract the attention of women.[27] Other men from the local professional families try to emphasize their connections to the university. Perhaps they mention that a parent is a professor or administrator at the university. These young men themselves might be "just working right now" or "taking classes at a community college," but despite their lack of integration into the university campus life, they feel comfortable negotiating interactions in downtown with members of the opposite sex.

It is often difficult for working-class local males to find their place within downtown nightlife. When these locals do not don the clothing worn by frat boys or college students and attempt to approach women, they usually receive swift rebuffs to their advances. Rather than being discouraged by these kinds of rejections, however, the locals enthusiastically engage college girls as they pass on the streets of downtown. Women generally characterize the locals' approach as more aggressive than that of other male patrons, but I have observed a wide range of males behaving aggressively toward women, occasionally grabbing or groping them as they pass. Perhaps women simply have heightened perceptions of their encounters with working-class males whom they generally consider undesirable. Irrespective of the source of heightened perceptions, interactions between caravanning groups of local male patrons and college girls reveal underlying tensions between social capsules populated by college students and locals. It is rare that these tensions produce anything more than brief encounters within which women aptly utilize one of their strategies to avoid or terminate interaction.

Working-class patrons may have difficulty fitting into the social scene, but the "alternative types" avoid the public spaces where the majority of nightlife activity takes place altogether. They are an outlier group, easily identified by their "artsy," "goth," or "rocker" styles of dress, and choose to spend time at bars like Cash's, O'Neal's, and Origami's. Despite their status as alternative types, the men of this group approach women, who share their same social status, and experience rejection, but their rejections stem from an individual woman's evaluation rather than from a caravanning group's evaluation like that typical of fraternity or college males' experiences. Women from this group reject men as individuals, due in part to the general expectations that they have about going out downtown. As Liz, a self-described alternative White woman, explained, "All those people [general downtown crowd] want to do is get shit faced and 'hook up' with each other. I go where you can have a conversation with people. Basically friends bring friends to meet friends and talk." Individual face-to-face interaction like this makes it likely that rejection will come from an individual rather than a caravanning group. Given the limited interaction that alternative types have with fraternity-sorority, college student, and local types, it is rare that conflict arises among these groups.

Race, Styles of Dress, and Gendered Interaction

Thus far in the discussion regarding men's and women's interactions across social capsule boundaries I have mentioned very little explicitly about race; however, the last type of patron that frequents downtown, the "athlete" type, conjures up explicit ideas about race among the nightlife participants. Despite the fact that there are athletes from varying racial and ethnic backgrounds who participate in sports like swimming, baseball, softball, tennis, soccer, gymnastics, equestrian, and track and field, when patrons identify the athlete type who frequents downtown they are generally referencing those athletes who compete for Big South University in football and basketball, specifically Black men.

The use of the term "athlete" to designate Black males is similar to most patrons' use of the term frat boy to reference White male fraternity members—ignoring the presence of Asian, Hispanic, and Black fraternity members in the downtown nightlife. Some patrons also specify the athlete types as "the football players" and "the basketball players."

Irrespective of which of the terms are used, patrons are indicating a subset of athletes whose identity is squarely centered on their race, gender, and athletic participation. Although they represent perhaps the smallest proportion of patrons who frequent downtown, their presence has a significant impact on the dynamics of nightlife and the use of urban public space.

The athlete types are easily identified by their styles of dress that usually include some form of athletic wear like T-shirts, shorts, exclusive training warm-up suits, and jackets emblazoned with the words "Big South Football" or "Big South Basketball." It is easy to understand why athlete types wear their athletic gear given the overall success and popularity of these athletic programs at the university. The players are more readily identified by strangers as affiliates of the university and contributors to the team's success when they wear the clothes of a winner.

By wearing distinctive Big South University athletic gear, the athletes are attempting to assert an identity that will make them more positively received in the context of downtown. Their behavior is consistent with that of other African American men who have found it prudent to both draw attention to their athletic prowess and allay the fears of presumed African American male criminality held by others. Indeed, several studies have demonstrated how African American males are generally stereotyped as criminal threats and hence adopt certain strategies to disavow criminal intent.[28] For instance, Anderson demonstrates how African American males adopt the use of certain greetings and identification cards as a means of disavowing criminal intent on the city streets.[29] The use of such strategies seems necessary given evidence of racial profiling.[30] Beyond reducing others' fears by wearing athletic gear, the athletes in downtown Northeast also enjoy fan adulation, and a general sense of comfort from others—as one African American athlete said, "I put my gear on 'cause people just treat you better when they know you play for Big South."

Although athletes generally have success in their attempts to stand out from other African American men by wearing their athletic gear, some undiscerning or casual fans view any African American male in Big South athletic gear as an athlete. This stereotyping has consequences for interaction on the public streets. As indicated previously, both college student and local African American men frequent the nightlife in downtown Northeast. Their presence means that patrons must distinguish among athletes, locals, and college students rather than generally accept Black males present in the nightlife as athletes belonging to the context. This is often challenging for patrons, particularly White women, especially given that at various times athletes, locals, and college students wear hip-hop gear, in particular athletic wear.[31]

Since initial interactions across social capsule boundaries can be facilitated by styles of dress, the right combination of Big South apparel can provide an opportunity for Black men to engage White women who would otherwise rebuff their advances. Still, despite the fact that athletes are accorded greater status in the nightlife than other African American men, this status is significant for only a small proportion of adoring White male and female fans. Most White patrons remain preoccupied with making distinctions within race that advance "having fun" and creating the potential for developing extended relationships.

African American Women, Athletes, and White Males

The relatively small proportion of African American women who frequent downtown are better able to make distinctions among those Black male patrons who are athletes, college students, and locals than are White women. This is due in part to the fact that the Black women, typically college students, are part of a small Black community on campus wherein they share networks with others who know intimate information about individual African American men. This knowledge is useful for discerning who is a member of the university community and their status within that community. Hence for this subset of Black women, downtown Northeast is like a parochial realm, wherein they may not know all of the participants individually, but still share a loose connection to them through others. This is an important observation because the parochial realm is a context in which there is greater social accountability for one's behavior than there is within the public realm.[32] This accountability contradicts the idea of "free" interactions that characterize "having fun" in the nightlife.

It is also revealing that many of the African American women who frequent downtown complain that it is difficult for them to "have fun" because there are so few desirable men. Both White and Black men's interaction patterns contribute to this situation. First, much to the disapproval of African American women, most of the Black men spend their time downtown in pursuit of White women. They, like their White male counterparts, are focused on flirtation, chance encounters, and the pursuit of women. Even if African American men are not intentionally focused on pursuing White women, it is likely that their desire to interact with patrons of the opposite sex will result in encounters with White women based upon the disproportionate representation of White women in downtown. Second, although some White men may find African American women attractive, they rarely engage them in interaction. These White men are typically in pursuit of the attention of White women. Anita, an African American female college student who frequents downtown, made the following observation when asked about her interaction with White male patrons: "Most of these White guys are intimidated by Black girls. They might look at you and want to say something, and I've caught them looking, but they don't say anything. They get shy and afraid to talk to us. Besides they are usually chasing White girls and only want to talk to us when they are drunk."

Anita suggests that African American women intimidate White men. Implicitly, this intimidation is owing to stereotypes about African American women who are often characterized as obdurate, confrontational, and hypersexualized.[33] Some scholars suggest that racism and sexual politics affirm these kinds of negative stereotypes of both Black men and women in America. For instance, the sociologist Patricia Hill Collins, in her examination of Black sexual politics, asserts, "Whether depicted as 'freaks' of nature or as being the essence of nature itself, savage, untamed sexuality characterizes Western representations of women and men of African American descent."[34] Collins goes on to argue that perceptions of Black women as sexualized beings are based in a New Racism that uses mass media to "disseminate ideologies needed to justify racism."[35] Collins suggests that music videos, especially through their depiction of Black women, replicate the power relations of racism. Given Collins's argument, one might suggest that the "intimidation" of which Anita speaks is merely White men's avoidance of African American women rooted in racism.

Although purported intimidation may account for some of the White men's resistance to engaging African American women, my observations appear to support at least two alternative explanations. First, some White men may view African American women as attractive, but do not approach them because there is little support from their caravanning groups for such behavior. Since caravanning groups are composed of significant others, they determine not only who is perceived as desirable, but also who is undesirable. During my time in the field, I did not observe caravanning groups of White men seeking out interaction with African American women; however, I did observe occasional passing interaction between individual White men and African American women. These interactions included typical nightlife passing behavior like momentary stares, smiles, and flirtatious comments.

The second explanation for White men's resistance to engaging African American women is that despite the idea of "having fun," most patrons also recognize that passing encounters in the downtown nightlife have the potential for long-term relationships. Hence, it makes little sense for individuals to interact with patrons from other social capsules with whom they have no desire to establish long-term relationships. Irrespective of the specific reasons for White men's resistance to interacting with Black women, the fact remains that African American women are avoided in the context of downtown Northeast, and this avoidance produces frustration for these patrons.

African American Men's Pursuit of White Women

African American men fare much better in their attempts to "have fun" than do African American women, since the prevailing social norms for interaction in nightlife make men responsible for approaching women. Whether a man pursues this opportunity is generally a matter of personal initiative and group support for his initiative. Group support is usually forthcoming since, as Grazian indicates, young men pursue women in part to demonstrate their masculinity to other young men in their group.[36] Thus African American men, like their White counterparts, pursue women. Within the context of downtown Northeast that means pursuing White women. They do this despite the fact that they may experience more rejection than White men do pursuing the same women. Still, through their active pursuit of women African American men experience the thrill of having fun in the nightlife.

Although African American men may, and do, pursue White women, this pursuit is a source of significant tension across social boundaries in the nightlife. Of course tension exists across other social boundaries like that between college student types and frat boy types, but the most significant tension manifests when African American men attempt to interact with White women. These tensions are often reflected in White women's consistent rejection of African American men's approaches. More significantly, African American men sense disapproval from White men and African American women for their approaches. Despite this disapproval, it is rare that direct confrontation occurs between African American men and White men or African American women. Rather, those who disapprove rely upon caravanning groups as the most consistent means of enforcing boundaries in interactions between African American men and White women.

As discussed previously, women employ strategies to manipulate, divert, or prevent interaction with men they find undesirable. They often rely upon help from their caravanning group members to implement these strategies, including verbal and nonverbal rebuffs of approaching men, rejecting drink offers, and giving fake names or phone numbers. Although I have observed White women's general use of these strategies with White men, they seem to emphasize to a greater degree avoidance of direct interaction with African American men altogether. These avoidance tactics include sidestepping areas where African American men have congregated.

It was about 11:45 p.m. and I was posted up on the yellow parking box surveying the corner. . . . As I turned I noticed five female patrons, all White, walking in almost a single file line across Reginald Street. They appeared chained together, holding hands with one another, right hand to left hand. The leader, a tall, blonde female patron, guided them. As she began to approach Kilpatrick's she slowed down to let the human chain of her friends, dressed in short skirts, sleeveless tops, and high-heel shoes, catch up. There were other patrons on the corner but movement was unencumbered. As the leader walked closer, she noted the presence of three African American males dressed in hip-hop gear on the bench in front of Kilpatrick's. When she caught the appearance of the males she turned away quickly and tugged her right hand close to her body. The patrons in tow behind her snapped forward. The leader quickly diverted her steps from the center of the sidewalk to the edge close to the patio of Kilpatrick's and away from the bench where the Black males were gathered. She accelerated the speed of her walk, yanking the other female patrons forward. About fifteen feet past the bench in front of Kilpatrick's the leader slowed down again as the rest of the patrons in her group made it past the bench. The Black male patrons had been looking as the female patrons walked past but none said anything.

Although early in my research I was unable to determine the specific reason for this kind of behavior, I took note of it. At first, I simply categorized it as a tactic that women generally used to manage interactions with men in downtown nightlife.[37] I began to pay more attention to these kinds of passing behaviors in the nightlife. What I discovered was a consistent pattern of avoidance that seemed far more frequent when the White women were passing African American men than when passing White men. This perception was supported in interviews with White women who expressed the belief that African American men were more aggressive than White men in their approaches to women. As one White female patron stated, "Black guys aren't afraid to talk to you like White guys are. They'll grab your hand and say whatever they are thinking." My observations of White women's avoidance of Black men on the street, and the seeming freedom with which African American men approached White women on the corner, supported this assertion. Through prolonged observation, however, I was able to derive two important insights relevant to White women and African American men's interaction.

First, those African American men who choose to sit on the bench in front of Kilpatrick's bar select this area for its strategic location as a place where many patrons pass. They have as their explicit purpose to see others and to be seen by others, especially women, with the goal of engaging or harassing—depending upon one's perspective—passing women at both a high rate and more aggressively than do other White men and African American men who spend time around downtown moving from bar to bar. Given the limited contact that White women might have with African American men in general, and in the downtown context in particular, their interaction with African American men in this public space becomes representative to them of African American men's behaviors more generally.[38] Hence, the women may be generalizing about African American men's behavior from a limited group of young Black men who have this behavior as their explicit purpose.

Second, at various times during the evening several of the African American men who gather on the corner are locals or middle-class African American male college students who have been denied access to the nightclubs for dress code violations. They don hip-hop clothes prohibited in many of the nightclubs. As I discuss in the next chapter, many of these young men view wearing hip-hop clothes as an important display of their identities. They may also be firmly invested in some behaviors emphasized by hip-hop culture. For instance, they may subscribe to misogynistic views of women as sexual objects to be pursued aggressively—a theme presented in the lyrics and performances of many popular hip-hop entertainers. Hence, their approach to women is a culturally grounded, stylistic performance of aggressive masculine behavior reflected in aspects of hip-hop.

This aggressive pursuit of women may be further fueled by the fact that these young men are acting on their frustration from being rejected from nightclubs as social equals. Their participation in one central activity of the nightlife, entering the bars, has been limited by their failure to adhere to the dress codes, which some of the young men believe unfairly target clothes worn by participants in hip-hop culture, particularly Black men.

Irrespective of the specific reasons that African American men might be viewed as aggressive, the main point is that many White women view them as more aggressive than White men, and take measures to avoid them. This avoidance can be subtle, like the movement of the caravanning group of female patrons described previously, or explicit like that expressed to me by Misty, a White female patron. Misty is a BSU student.

It was about 12:30 a.m. and I was standing inside of Figaro's near the door. As I peered out the door to watch the crowds pass on the street I saw Misty handing her ID to the bouncer. When she looked up, we both smiled. Misty entered the door followed by two of her sorority sisters whom I had come to know through frequent interaction downtown. When they got into the bar we exchanged greetings and a laugh about the frequency of my visits to downtown. It seemed unusual that she was only accompanied by two sorority sisters because on previous nights I had seen Misty with anywhere from four to six of her sorority sisters.

"Hey, where are your other sorority sisters?" I asked.

Misty had a look of frustration. She turned to her sorority sisters and smiled, then she turned back to me and said, "They didn't want to come with us. We wanted to dance."

"I thought they liked to dance too?"

"Well, when I said we were coming here Jennifer said, 'I'm not going there. I don't wanna go there. I don't want to deal with all those Black guys.' So she, Liz, and Keri decided to go to Javelina Ranch."

"Really?"

"I got pissed off and told them, that I liked Figaro's 'cause I liked the music and that there was nothing wrong with Black guys. She said, 'I don't like them.'"

"Haha. Well, if there was anyone in your group that I thought had a problem with Black guys it was probably her."

"Oh well, it's true she doesn't like Blacks and has said it before. We basically had it out because she makes these kinds of comments about Black people. So we are here and they went elsewhere."

Although I was not frequently privy to direct conversations among White patrons about African Americans, I often received retellings and secondhand accounts that suggest Whites have a range of attitudes about the presence of African Americans in the bars and nightclubs. These attitudes range from displeasure at their presence to excitement for the purported energy that Blacks contribute to the nightlife. For Misty's sorority sisters, one in particular, there is a clear disdain for African Americans. She chose to avoid Figaro's because it attracts African American patrons, who are drawn to the bar since it is one of the few places in downtown Northeast where the deejays play hip-hop music. The sorority sister's avoidance further supports the notion that some White women are explicitly avoiding African American men. Furthermore, it is possible that one motivation for avoiding Black men in the bars includes these women's racist attitudes toward Blacks more generally. Yet I rarely observed any explicit expression of these attitudes within the context of nightlife.

Of course not all White women avoid interaction with African American men. Indeed some gravitate toward spaces and bars where they congregate and seek to initiate interaction. This is rare, however, given that such initiations violate underlying norms that support men making the approach, and usually only within their own social grouping. Furthermore, most interactions that White women initiate involve the pursuit of Black athletes who have significant status within the context of downtown. Although African American men generally view this as a favorable situation, African American women see these rare approaches by White women as problematic since, as one African American woman indicated: "All White girls wanna do is have sex with these Black athletes. They ain't trying to marry them." This observation is supported by some White women who have shared their fears that they would lose financial support from their parents if they were discovered to be "in a relationship" with an African American man. For one White woman, her "relationship" served a sexual function as part of "having fun" in her college years.

For most African American women, White women's approaches are motivated by the stereotypical notion of hypersexualized Black athletes, and take away from what otherwise would be African American men's serious interests in Black women. This situation further exacerbates African American women's frustration with social life in downtown Northeast. Furthermore, since White female and Black female patrons rarely share similar friendship networks with one another, African American men, especially athletes, are emboldened to manipulate multiple relationships simultaneously with female patrons from both groups.

The fact that it is normative for White women to avoid African American men within the context of downtown means that African American men and White women rarely hold extended conversations within the public context of downtown. Instead they discreetly arrange meetings for later, sometimes referred to as "booty calls."[39] Through consistent observation I discovered this pattern of arranged meetings. These meetings typically become public if either one of the women that the athlete is sharing his time with believes that she can make a public claim to a relationship with him. Still, given the separateness of the networks, athletes are able to claim an African American "girlfriend," while a White woman could make similar claims to her friends that she "was seeing" a prominent African American athlete. This is not to suggest that women are generally unaware of the existence of these external relationships, but rather many choose to ignore them because the relationships serve a function. Whether that function is social status from association with the athlete or purely sexual gratification, the women choose to ignore the fact that the athlete is involved in other relationships.

Conclusion

Interaction across gendered lines is a key activity in the nightlife. In general, men pursue women, while women utilize strategies to rebuff advances from undesirable men. This activity takes place through caravanning groups that influence the participants' ideas about who is and who is not desirable. It is through influencing interpersonal relationships between men and women that the caravanning groups ultimately influence how nightlife participants interact across broader social boundaries. One means through which patrons evaluate one another across social boundaries is styles of dress as a proxy for class and cultural backgrounds.

The patrons of downtown share a tacit understanding of the kinds of styles of dress associated with a variety of social types including fraternity-sorority, college, locals, and alternative types. These types constitute the basis upon which broader social groups, or social capsules as I have characterized them, function. As caravanning groups of two to ten individuals move through the nightlife assessing one another, social boundaries for interaction are recognized using styles of dress as one of the initial indicators of a patron's sensibilities. What one wears influences others' judgments as to whether one should be engaged or approached for interaction. Yet because styles of dress are not exclusive to a particular group, patrons must further assess status through verbal exchanges. Although men and women may manipulate these verbal exchanges so as to express their most desirable representation of self, attire remains a strong indicator of one's social status within the nightlife and is used to enforce intangible social boundaries.

The primary responsibility for policing social boundaries is left up to the caravanning group. In a sense, caravanning group members help to reject individuals from other groups, thereby providing an informal means for maintaining boundaries between broader social groups. Although caravanning groups are generally effective at maintaining social boundaries, some bar owners have adopted measures that go further in maintaining social boundaries. The most significant of these measures is dress codes that limit access to the nightclubs. In the next chapter I turn to a discussion of these dress codes to demonstrate how they bolster boundaries between social groups based on race, class, and culture.

4

Is It a Blackout?

● ● ● ● ● ● ● ● ● ● ● ●

Dress Codes in Urban Nightlife

While many passersby perceive nightclubs as urban public spaces accessible to all, these spaces are in fact privately owned and provide restricted access. Owners may limit access to individuals who meet specific criteria.[1] In practice most nightclubs are semipublic spaces where access is granted to anonymous individuals who demonstrate the willingness to comply with formal or informal rules for access.[2] In some nightclubs, for instance, dress codes are used to limit or grant access to particular kinds of individuals. Although Northeast is generally a social space where students can be seen wearing casual dress like blue jeans, sneakers, and T-shirts every day and evening, several of the nightclubs have dress codes. Interestingly, African American men are disproportionately affected by the dress codes used by some of the bar owners. Interpretation of these dress codes for those Black men denied access raises the following questions: Are dress codes that disproportionately impact African Americans racially discriminatory?

What roles do race and class play in patrons' interpretations of dress code enforcement?

In this chapter I explore the context of downtown as a threshold of public and semipublic space in which individuals negotiate dress codes, race, and class. Since African American men are disproportionately affected by nightclub dress codes in downtown, I first focus on their responses. In particular I examine the responses of those Black men rejected from nightclubs for dress code infractions. The majority of these men propose that race is the most significant factor for being rejected from the nightclubs. Second, I briefly contrast these responses to the general experiences of African American men who are granted access to the nightclubs. For these Black men race is less salient in their general experiences. I argue that there is a fluid relationship between race and class that influences African American men's responses and experiences in this context. I then turn to a discussion of groups who are not generally denied access to the nightclubs for dress code infractions: African American women and White men and women. Given that they are rarely denied access to nightclubs for dress code infractions, their experiences vary from those of African American men, particularly those men rejected from the nightclubs. I then consider nightclub owners' potential motives for implementing dress codes. I consider how their "good" business practice may in fact mask racial discrimination. Ultimately, dress codes in downtown Northeast help to support social boundaries between broader groups of downtown patrons. In short, they support integrated segregation in the nightlife.

Dress Codes, Styles of Dress, and Race

Dress codes are standards for attire employed by a variety of institutions to regulate what individuals wear in particular settings. These standards are easily observed in workplaces, schools, and restaurants.[3] Such codes allow institutions to establish status, order, and control with minimal conflict. In general, individuals recognize the authority of signs reading "No shoes, no shirt, no service" or "Coat and tie required." Although some individuals, because of their social status, may occasionally violate these codes without reprimand, the guidelines tell us who may make use of particular social spaces and how they should be dressed. Beyond their general use as a means of social control, dress codes are also embedded with cultural expectations about taste as reflected in style. For instance, the sociologist Georg Simmel noted the significance of dress in low-status groups' attempts to attain higher social status by adopting the clothing styles of the social elite.[4] Such practices have been documented as part and parcel of social class group identity formation in a variety of contexts.[5] Yet there may also be the rare appropriation of lower-class clothing styles by the upper class. In short, individuals and groups select styles of dress "on the basis of their perceptions of their own identities and lifestyles."[6]

According to Bourdieu, styles are also embedded in tastes as strong indicators of one's consumption patterns.[7] Particular objects of consumption are encoded with cues that have "meaning and interest only for someone who possess the cultural competence, that is, the code into which it is encoded."[8] For instance, the meanings that individuals give to objects of consumption, like "baggy jeans," are based on one's sense of taste—typically derived from background experiences or habitus, as Bourdieu suggests.[9] The selection of particular styles of dress then becomes a sort of cultural identity embedded with indicators for both the wearer and those viewing the attire.[10] This self-presentation is complicated by race for those Black nightlife participants selecting hip-hop styles of dress in downtown Northeast.

Fashionable among many young urban Blacks today are the clothing styles associated with hip-hop culture—a culture that grew out of the artistic articulations of poor, young Blacks and Latinos.[11] These articulations are much like the subcultures of resistance identified among punk rockers, working-class "lads" from Britain, and Puerto Rican drug dealers in the barrio.[12] In this hip-hop culture, athletic jerseys, baggy jeans, over-sized plain white T-shirts, sweatbands, do-rags (polyester head wraps), "wifebeaters" (tank tops), and thick gold chains are worn as a means of representing one's identification with that culture. These clothing styles are typically adopted by young Black men in urban areas. Although these clothing styles have made considerable inroads into mainstream consumer culture, they continue to be emphasized internally and externally as a way for Blacks to represent a collective Black identity.[13] Interestingly, these styles of dress are the very styles regulated by dress codes in several of the nightclubs in downtown Northeast.

Few Whites choose to wear hip-hop clothing, and even when they do they are viewed differently than African Americans similarly dressed. For instance, the sociologist Mary Pattillo-McCoy, in her discussion of oppositional styles of dress associated with gangsta rap, suggests that Whites' "stylistic displays are less harshly sanctioned relative to the surveillance of black youth who follow the same fashions."[14] The importance of such variance in surveillance is that "the race of the wearer affects the degree to which certain styles are criminalized."[15] Pattillo-McCoy's point is particularly germane when discussing clothing styles that are associated with young Black men in urban areas. These clothing styles, absent a viewer's intimate knowledge of those Black men passing on the streets, become a proxy by which others attribute criminal intent to Black men.[16] Despite rich alternative depictions of Black men and their lives, the prevailing public view of young Black men is that they are engaged in an oppositional culture that takes criminal activity and violence as its main dictates.[17] This culture is suggested in their styles of dress.

Thus far I have focused on the implications of wearing hip-hop clothing for young Black men. This is because although hip-hop clothing generally receives scrutiny in downtown Northeast, women's clothing is not subject to dress code enforcement. The dress codes are decidedly focused on the attire of men. As one African American female patron remarked, "The dress code is really for guys. I've never seen a girl dress code ever." A White female patron echoed this perspective when she commented, "I'm not all that familiar with dress codes because they just don't apply for girls. We could walk in naked and no one would care." There are a number of possible explanations for why women's clothing is not the subject of dress code enforcement, but the most prevalent is that men dominate the urban public space and must therefore be controlled. Indeed, Rivera, in her study of status distinctions at an elite Boston nightclub, found that bouncers believed women to be the least difficult types of patrons to manage, and thus worthy of less surveillance than men, particularly those men perceived to be potential "troublemakers" based on their attire.[18] Furthermore, bouncers generally accorded African American men wearing hip-hop gear the status of potential "troublemakers." Similar perceptions seem to undergird the implementation and enforcement of dress codes in downtown Northeast.

Dress Codes in Downtown Northeast

Most of the dress codes in downtown Northeast began appearing in 2002. Their appearance coincided with the closing of the only downtown late-night dance club, the Bounce, designated by the local Black population as a place to go out and have fun. The Bounce had provided a cultural milieu where African Americans could share in the styles of dress, dance, and interactions associated with hip-hop. When this club, which attracted the local and college Black population as well as a few White patrons, closed, its patrons sought entertainment in some of the downtown area bars and clubs that played a mixture of music that included hip-hop. Although other nightclubs had regular Black patrons, the closing of the Bounce brought greater numbers of African Americans to other downtown bars and nightclubs. One patron, Joe, a twenty-one-year-old African American who frequented downtown during the initial implementation of the dress codes, made the following observation: "As I kept going downtown, you know, the same time I was going, the dress codes were getting more strict. The first thing I noticed was like jean shorts. You couldn't wear a pair of jean shorts to the bars. I was like, 'What's the big deal with jean shorts?' I didn't realize it, but then I started noticing that all the White people downtown didn't wear jean shorts. They always wore khaki shorts." Whether nightclub owners were specifically responding to the increase in African American patrons to their downtown establishments is unclear. For Joe, however, what was clear was that dress codes were being implemented, and when they were, they seemed to be focused on a very specific type of clothing.

Today the dress codes in downtown Northeast are firmly in place and convey to potential patrons which clothing attire might be grounds for being denied access. Codes are posted at seven nightclubs that play a considerable amount of hip-hop music: River Run Tap, the Corral, Figaro's, Kilpatrick's, Insignia, Ernie's Cove, and Club Connections. Although these nightclubs have explicit dress codes, some of the other bars may have dress codes that are not posted because these bars do not play hip-hop music and do not attract patrons who have adopted the style of dress associated with young Blacks and urban hip-hop culture. As one African American female patron observed, "Honestly, every bar that I have been to in downtown Northeast has a dress code. Even the bars I won't go to have them except they don't feel the need to mention it because the people that violate that dress code don't even come."

Restricted items vary by bar, but garments and accessories consistently prohibited include all athletic jerseys, plain white T-shirts, sleeveless shirts ("wifebeaters" or tank tops), jean shorts, sweatpants, loose or baggy clothes, do-rags, caps turned sideways (other than forward or backward), sweat-bands, and large chains (necklaces). While this list is explicit, some codes leave room for a variety of interpretations. For instance, what constitutes baggy clothes to one individual might constitute "loose fit" to another. In addition to these generalized descriptions of clothing, the dress codes typically end with a phrase such as "We have the right to refuse anyone," "Clothes must fit the atmosphere," or "Any clothes deemed inappropriate."

Some nightclubs have neatly typed, laminated signs on plain white paper. The prohibited clothes are listed in regular twelve-point font. Most patrons entering the bars fail to see the posted dress codes because the loud music and flashing lights gleaming from right near the door offer a distraction. These dress codes, however, become fully visible when an infraction is noted by a bouncer, who then points to the sign. At River Run Tap, the code's placement is inconspicuous, located at the base of an iron gate surrounding the patio of the bar. There is an interesting phrasing of the prohibited jewelry listed on this dark green, typewritten, laminated sign. In addition to listing the other prohibited items, the sign reads, "absolutely no Mr. T starter kits."

The Mr. T notation makes reference to a Black actor who is most known for his role as Sergeant Bosco Albert "B. A." (Bad Attitude) Baracus in the 1980s television series *The A-Team*. On the show Mr. T played the role of a gruff, hypermasculine, aggressive member of a military special forces unit. Mr. T demonstrated irrational phobias and contributed little to the intellectual process of planning an attack. During his public appearances he wore several large gold chains around his neck. Thus, the sign indicating "no Mr. T. starter kits" suggests that patrons may not be permitted in the nightclub if they have a single gold chain that is presumed to be a beginning to subsequent gold chains. The use of the "no Mr. T starter kits" phrase on a professionally printed sign makes light of the serious nature with which some patrons view race as part of the cultural biases of the dress codes.[19]

It is within the context of nightclubs that play hip-hop music and that Whites frequent that dress codes are most consistently enforced. In the following section I examine instances in which Black males attempting to venture into the nightclub scene in downtown Northeast are denied access. Those Black males rejected from the nightclubs exhibit the greatest acceptance of the notion that nightclub owners are racist in their use of dress codes.

Interpretive Responses of Rejected African American Men

The dress codes employed by the nightclubs have particular meaning to various individuals who use the bars. The underlying theme for the African American males rejected from nightclubs is that the dress codes were put in place by White bar owners in response to the presence of Black males. In short, the Black men believe the dress codes are racist. This belief is further evidenced by the fact that the Black patrons fail to understand why their particular taste in clothing is subject to dress codes, when from a stylistic standpoint a white T-shirt or an athletic jersey conveys similar social status as the colored cotton T-shirts or polo shirts worn by White males.

Furthermore, considering the cost of clothing, according to the Black males, some African American men's clothing is more expensive than clothing worn by the typical White male. Indeed, in my own investigation I discovered that the average cost of the authentic athletic jerseys worn by some of the Black males was between one hundred and three hundred dollars, whereas the polo shirts, including brands such as Izod and Ralph Lauren, worn by White males cost between fifty and eighty dollars. Still, dress codes are enforced against only the types of clothing frequently worn by Black males, leaving many Black patrons believing that the codes are directed against Blacks. For instance, Joe, an undergraduate senior from BSU, responds to being rejected from Figaro's. He is from a largely African American metropolitan area in central Georgia.

I had been standing on the corner just after 12:00 a.m. The crowd had swelled. It was warm out and folks were dressed in shorts and short sleeves all about. I watched as Joe attempted to enter Figaro's wearing a red collarless shirt, blue jean shorts, and white tennis shoes. The bouncer, a White male, motioned to Joe's shorts. Joe turned around frustrated without even talking and walked toward the corner where a group of Black males had gathered. I was standing in front of the group wearing what Perceval [my graduate student] and I call "all access" gear. I had on a yellow, collared, buttoned-down, short-sleeve shirt, khaki shorts, and sandals. The group of Black males was standing just behind me wearing an assortment of hip-hop clothes. When Joe looked up and saw me I said, "What's up man?"

He looked frustrated, "Nothing, man." We shook hands as he continued. "They're tripping over at Figaro's."

"What do you mean?" I asked.

"They wouldn't let me in with blue jean shorts," Joe said. "You know a lot of places have their guideline, you know, the dress code. But to me it just seems like it's to exclude Blacks from coming in."

"Why does it seem like that?" I asked.

"The dress code policy or whatever is basically, no jean shorts, no athletic wear, no jewelry, no excessive jewelry. Anything that's like, in reference to the hip-hop culture is excluded. You know what I'm saying, it's excluded from downtown but at the same time they wanna play all the hip-hop music, you know what I'm saying. But they don't want Black people in the club. It's like a contradiction. They can play the music, but we can't dress the part. You know."

Joe observes that there is an apparent contradiction in the use of dress codes in the downtown nightclubs. According to Joe, club owners wish to play the music that originates from urban Blacks, but they do not accept urban styles of dress that are closely associated with African Americans. To Joe, this is a direct way to limit Blacks' access to the social spaces that play hip-hop music. There are many instances that appear consistent with Joe's assessment that the dress codes are about race.

For those Black male patrons rejected at the door for dress code violations, there is a heightened degree of humiliation and frustration associated with being rejected. These emotions are heightened when those Black men rejected witness that White men are given access even when their clothing does not fit the dress code. For instance, Harry recounts being humiliated and frustrated by being rejected. He is from a small town in west Georgia and grew up in a low-income area of that town. Harry shares his recollection of the previous night's events while talking to me on the corner in front of Kilpatrick's, the Corral, and Figaro's.

I stood on the corner talking to Harry about hanging out last night. He told me that he had come out and gone around to different nightclubs, but that he was wearing blue jean shorts and couldn't get in. He said, "I got so frustrated yesterday, man. Shit, these bouncers wouldn't let me in. I had some blue jean shorts, and I had been to a couple of places—Kilpatrick's, the Corral, and Figaro's. I couldn't get in the other places so when I finally got to Figaro's and they wouldn't let me in, I was like, 'Man this is it. I'm tired of this shit.' I was so frustrated that I stood right by the door counting the White boys they let in. They must have let about six White boys in with blue jean shorts. I was like fuck it and I just left."

For Harry, the dress code enforcement is clearly about race. His experiences throughout the previous night made him particularly frustrated that some White males were given access when they were also wearing prohibited shorts. Without intimate knowledge of why these White males had been accepted given their dress code infraction, Harry was left taking their admittance as prima facie evidence that dress codes were specifically enforced against African American men.

While Black men's claims that dress codes are being enforced in a racially discriminatory manner might seem unfounded to some, these complaints occur within a broader context in which Blacks must evaluate everyday slights that deal both implicitly and explicitly with race.[20] Thus, the Black men's adamant claims that they are being rejected on the basis of race are legitimate given their overall experiences with race.

Despite these examples of Black men being rejected from nightclubs, there are Black men who do gain access. The presence of these men within the nightclubs raises an interesting question: if the dress codes are strictly about race as some African American men interpret, then how is the presence of Black men within the nightclubs to be explained? In the following section I briefly discuss the experiences of those Black men who were granted access to nightclubs to illustrate Black males' varied interpretations of the dress codes. These varied interpretations suggest some of the ways in which Black men negotiate race in semipublic spaces. Furthermore, they question the notion of a Black cultural essence that would equate being Black with wearing urban styles of dress.

Experiences of African American Men Granted Access

The various caravanning groups of Black males standing out front of nightclubs clad in their hip-hop gear provide visual evidence that the dress codes are enforced against styles of dress typically associated with young Black men and hip-hop culture. These Black males generally protest to one another arguing that the nightclub owners are racists. Still, many African American men frequent the nightclubs that some have suggested are racially discriminatory in granting access. As one might suppose, those African American men who have gained access to the nightclubs have chosen styles of dress that are inconsistent with hip-hop dress. These Black men are dressed like their middle-class White counter-parts who have chosen polo shirts, khakis pants or shorts, flip-flops, and other articles of clothing associated with middle-class college students. Furthermore, these patrons typically view the dress codes as the prerog-ative of owners who have the power to make the decisions about who comes into the club.

Derrick, a regular patron of the nightclubs in Northeast that use dress codes, shared comments typical of these Black patrons. He also spoke as a person who frequents all-Black nightclubs in Atlanta where there are also dress codes implemented by Black nightclub owners and enforced by Black bouncers. He once commented about the dress codes, "The nightclubs are not racist. It's just insurance against letting the wrong kind of people in. You know the kind of people that start fights and stuff."

Terrell, another regular to downtown Northeast nightclubs with dress codes, views the use of codes somewhat differently. He also attends BSU and had previously been rejected from nightclubs because he enjoys wear-ing clothes that are part of the hip-hop style of dress. He said, "They might have come up with dress codes that target clothes worn mostly by minori-ties, but if you wanna get in, you gotta conform. You gotta put on your col-lared, buttoned-down shirts. That's reasonable." For Terrell, it matters little whether the nightclub owners are motivated by race because the owners have not asked the patrons to meet an unachievable criterion.

According to my earlier work with sociologist Kenneth S. Chaplin, African American men like Terrell who gain access to nightclubs with dress codes demonstrate the ability to "crack the code."[21] By "crack the code" we meant that an individual has a requisite understanding of the nuances of dress in this context based upon her or his own class socialization. It is an implicit and explicit set of skills regarding the creation of a "respectable" appearance in Northeast nightclubs and society more broadly. The ability and desire to crack the code is an important concept for explaining the cul-tural nexus of race and class. I use this idea to expose how urban styles of dress that have long been associated with being Black are in fact a matter of class sensibility for those young men who crack the code. First, to crack the code they must demonstrate the ability to perceive the nature of the dress codes. They must appreciate the taste sensibilities of the nightclub owners who are creating, implementing, and having dress codes enforced. Or rather than appreciate these taste requirements, they must be willing to discard the implicit notion that they as Black men are the sum of what they wear. In reality this is the central tension between those African American men who gain access and those who do not.

Perhaps those Black men who evaluate the enforcement of dress codes as solely about race fail to consider how a social class sensibility, as reflected in nuanced taste in clothing, may affect their ability to gain access. I suggest, following Bourdieu, that class in the context of downtown Northeast most frequently manifests as a matter of taste. One assumption regarding class differences is that those individuals from middle-class backgrounds share tastes quite different from those of the lower class. These subtleties of taste are conveyed both implicitly and explicitly and are made sharper through a variety of institutions that reflect one's social class experience.[22] Thus, the styles of dress that one chooses are a manifestation of one's social class background. For the African American men who wear hip-hop clothing—generally associated with the Black urban poor—they are knowingly or unknowingly subjecting themselves to nightclub dress code enforcement. Thus, their rejection from the nightclubs in downtown Northeast is based on the evaluation of both race and class.

Such evaluation is complicated by the prevalence of Black middle-class youth who adopt the hip-hop clothing styles associated with the "street" identity of the lower class. Like the cultural omnivores identified by sociologists Richard Peterson and Roger Kern, these Black middle-class youths become samplers of cultural styles originating with the Black urban poor.[23] Perhaps this phenomenon can be explained by the close proximity of the Black middle class to their lower-class kindred.[24] These communities become places where the nuances of race and class are hybridized through taste. According to Pattillo-McCoy, this creates a dynamic where "every generation of black youth has been influenced by some form (and usually many forms of ghetto-based cultural production)."[25] An additional explanation for Black middle-class youths' adoption of these styles could be related to what Peterson and Kern identify as an "increasingly ubiquitous mass media" that has "introduced the aesthetic tastes of different segments of the population to each other."[26] Thus, Black middle-class youths may have appropriated their styles from the mass media presentation of hip-hop culture.

Irrespective of the source, the Black middle-class youths' adoption of these clothing styles problematizes the presence of African American males in urban public space. Some onlookers are left wondering whether those wearing, for instance, athletic jerseys are part of the Black middle class, whose members are generally regarded as civil, or the Black urban poor, whose members are generally regarded as predatory criminals. Indeed, the conclusions drawn by observers in the city matter. A misreading of the cultural cues being conveyed can be merely embarrassing or have detrimental consequences for both the assessor and the assessed.[27] Yet in most everyday occurrences a reading of such cultural cues is important only for access to particular social spaces like nightclubs.

African American Women's Thoughts about Dress Codes

In general, women who venture into the nightlife do not have their clothing scrutinized by bouncers for dress code violations. There are two straightforward reasons for this. First, as indicated previously, the presence of women in the nightclubs enhances the social atmosphere and draws men. Nightclub owners are well aware that men who come out to have a good time rarely seek to participate in what some patrons call a "sausage fest"—a gathering where others in the bar are primarily male. Thus there is economic incentive to have female patrons. Second, since bouncers who are responsible for maintaining control in the nightclubs view women as less threatening than men, they are also less likely to examine clothing worn by women for dress code violations.

Yet if the dress codes are formulated to prevent African Americans from entering, as some patrons argue, why is African American women's clothing not scrutinized? The answer is simple. Since African American women's hip-hop styles of dress may consist of articles of clothing like dresses, skirts, tube tops, high-heeled shoes, and blouses that are worn by other female patrons, bouncers would be required to identify a nuanced collection of brands in women's clothing and take the time to engage women about their clothing. Although such scrutiny could be used to support practices in racial discrimination, it seems impractical since it would result in a number of problems at the threshold of the nightclub that ultimately reduce the profit margins for nightclub owners including extended lines and longer waits and frequent patron confrontations with bouncers about the specificity of the dress code. Furthermore, such meticulous scrutiny provides little additional advantage for regulating activities within the nightclubs. Still, if nightclub owners are being racially discriminatory in their implementation and use of dress codes toward African American men, then the dress codes are relatively effective in reducing the number of African Americans in the nightclubs, including African American women, since women generally seek interaction with men who are like them.

Although African American women are not subjected to scrutiny based on dress codes, their thoughts about the codes are consistent with those of their African American male counterparts. For instance, those African American women who are from the working or lower class, typically locals, tend to view the dress codes as racially discriminatory, despite the fact that they themselves are not prohibited from entering the nightclubs. There is little surprise in their response given that these women, who generally identify with urban hip-hop culture, appreciate men's styles of dress that include the styles prohibited at the nightclubs. Furthermore, these women are likely to be in attendance at nightclubs with African American men who are denied access and thus observe firsthand the frustration that their friends, boyfriends, brothers, and other associates experience when they are denied access. Hence, being rejected from a nightclub has a compounding effect not only for African American men, but also for African American women and those others who caravan with them.[28]

Whereas working- or lower-class African American women generally view the dress codes as racially discriminatory, middle-class African American women tend to acknowledge that racial discrimination may be in fact one of the motivations for the owners' use of dress codes, but that dress codes against hip-hop styles are not specifically about race. Rather they view the choice to wear hip-hop clothing as a matter of taste related to one's social class and thus view the dress codes as restricting nightclub access to those individuals who have middle-class tastes or sensibilities including the willingness to comply with the dress codes. Like those African American men who demonstrate the ability to "crack the code," these women observe that changing from hip-hop clothing does not equal shedding one's Blackness because individuals may still represent elements of an "African American identity" through dress while being in compliance with the dress codes. For instance, Lori, a twenty-two-year-old, middle-class African American student at BSU, acknowledges racial differences in the types of clothing brands worn by Whites and Blacks, but suggests that African Americans can still "dress up" in hip-hop-styled clothing. "How you dress up depends on race. But I mean for each race I guess it's considered dressing up. But like I said about the frat boys. They wear their polo shirts and khakis. . . . Blacks dress up another way. Like they usually wear like, Girbaud, but like they'll wear like the nice collared Girbaud shirt.[29] Sometimes, like now that they got the dress code, they dress a little nicer. Like instead of wearing a Girbaud T-shirt, they'll wear like the short-sleeve Girbaud collared shirt." Lori's comments capture the extent to which middle-class African American women recognize the class sensibilities embedded in the dress codes. For many of them, the dress codes are welcomed at the nightclubs because they help restrict the number of lower-class, local, or "ghetto" African American men who gain access to the nightclubs. As one African American female patron stated, "The dress codes keep the lokes [locals] out." These women recognize that the fewer lower-class or local male patrons in the nightclub, the less likely it is that they will receive advances from men with less social status in the nightlife and who are generally perceived as more aggressive in their advances than middle-class African American men. Like their White female counterparts who seek to have fun generally with fraternity members who have significant status in the nightlife, African American women seek to have fun with African American men who have middle-class backgrounds or some other valued status like athlete. The competition for African American men with status is significant given that there are so few available. The enforcement of the dress codes exacerbates this competition since it further limits the number of African American men present inside nightclubs. Given this condition, many African American women simply choose to hang outside where there are more African American men. For some patrons, the presence of African American men and women on the downtown street corners is another sign that dress codes are racially discriminatory because "all the Blacks are outside."

White Patrons' Perceptions of Dress Codes

White patrons experience dress codes in a significantly different way than African American men. Whereas African American men generally feel under surveillance and as though they must make conscious choices about their clothing for the purpose of gaining access to the nightclubs in downtown Northeast, White patrons, both men and women, rarely consider the implications of what they wear for access because their typical styles of dress are not subject to negative evaluations by bouncers. Given this, few White patrons are aware that some nightclubs in downtown Northeast actually have dress codes. For instance, in an interview I asked Eric, a twenty-two-year-old White male who frequents downtown wearing his polo shirt and khakis, what he thought about the dress codes. "What dress codes? They have dress codes for bars in downtown Northeast? I didn't know." Eric's response is typical, especially since the vast majority of patrons do not patronize nightclubs where dress codes have been openly implemented.

Although many White patrons are unaware of dress codes, there are some who have attended nightclubs where hip-hop music is played and thus know about the dress codes. They may have become aware of the dress codes after witnessing an anonymous Black male turned away at the door of a nightclub for a dress code violation. Some White patrons who know about the dress codes learn about them through their friendships with African Americans who dress in hip-hop style clothing. Their African American friends may talk about the experience of being denied access to a nightclub, and in some instances White patrons may witness the experience for themselves. For instance, when the White patron and his African American friend—usually an out-of-town guest who is also unaware of the dress codes—arrive at the entryway, the bouncer informs them that they cannot gain access to the nightclub because the friend is not in compliance with the dress code. Being notified in this manner is frustrating for both the regular White patron and the out-of-town guest, especially since there are few alternatives for enjoying hip-hop music and dance in downtown Northeast.

These White patrons not only tend to have a greater awareness of dress codes, but also tend to believe that the nightclubs are racially discriminatory for employing dress codes that target hip-hop styles of dress. For instance, Robert, a twenty-one-year-old White male BSU student, made the following comment: "I know River Run Tap has a dress code. It's like you know, unwritten. I think they are racially profiling. They don't allow shorts with like cargo pants and like necklaces and stuff like that." Unlike the view that style of dress is a matter of class, a view typically held by middle-class African American men who willingly change their clothing to gain access to nightclubs, Robert associates specific styles of dress to race. His view is consistent with that generally held by African American men who have been rejected from the nightclub for dress code violations. Perhaps what is more interesting is that Robert is unaware that the dress code for River Run Tap is actually posted at the base of the iron fencing around the patio at the entryway of the nightclub. Since the components of his typical outfit are not on the list of prohibited clothing, including "no Mr.

T. starter kits," Robert has not had a bouncer direct his attention to the posted list. Furthermore, if Robert is correct that the nightclubs racially discriminate, then he is probably less likely to receive scrutiny for his dress than is an African American male.

As indicated previously, White patrons rarely wear hip-hop clothing downtown. In fact, I have not seen White patrons inside of nightclubs wearing clothing in violation of dress codes. Furthermore, I have witnessed only one White male rejected from a nightclub for seemingly violating the dress code. The patron was wearing a white "wifebeater" and blue jeans. As he stumbled to the door, obviously intoxicated, the tall White male bouncer said, "You can't come in." As the man started to plead in slurred speech, "Cum'on man. Let me cum innnnshide," the bouncer took both hands and pressed them against the patron's chest causing the patron to stumble back from the door of the nightclub. Then the bouncer said, "No you can't come in, so leave." The patron gathered himself, turned, and walked away. Although his tank top was in violation of the dress code, it was not clear why the bouncer had denied him access. Unlike typical interchanges with African American men whose clothing may be in violation of the dress code, the bouncer made no explicit mention of the dress code in his interchange with the White male. Perhaps the patron was rejected not for a dress code violation but for being too intoxicated or for previously making trouble in the bar. Without an explicit exchange between the bouncer and patron regarding dress, it is difficult to know exactly why he was rejected.

Since I had observed only one White patron denied access to nightclubs for an apparent dress code violation, I was surprised when Will, a twenty-three-year-old White male, recounted being rejected from a nightclub. Interestingly, his comments during the interview support some Whites' and many African Americans' assertions that the dress codes have been implemented primarily to restrict the participation of African Americans in the nightlife.

MAY: Do you know if there are any other places that have dress codes?

WILL: Oh yeah. They're ridiculous.

MAY: So would it surprise you if, this new place [a nightclub targeting fraternity and sorority members] has a dress code?

WILL: It would. The only reason I would say it would surprise me is because, to me the reason that most of these places have dress codes anyway is to keep Black people out.

MAY: Any kind of particular Black people or . . . ?

> WILL: Just any, I mean, I went up to Ernie's Cove one time to go in. I had never been there so I was going to check it out. The bouncer [a White male] wouldn't let me in because I was in a T-shirt. And I said, "Why?" and he goes, "We have a dress code." And I go—and to me a dress code in downtown Northeast is just silly—"This isn't like Central Park Manhattan."
> MAY: Right.
> WILL: And I said, "Why is there a dress code?" And he said, I mean his response to me was, "To keep the niggers out."
> MAY: He didn't say that.
> WILL: Oh he did. He said that. That's an exact quote.

Some patrons like Will suspect that the dress codes are directed toward African Americans, but rarely have specific evidence supporting this suspicion. In fact, Will's rejection for dress code violation seems to suggest the race neutrality of the dress codes. Still, if Will had doubt about the target of the dress codes, the bouncer makes it explicit—"To keep the niggers out." The bouncer seems to presume that Will, given his race, would appreciate the stated goal. It is almost certain that had Will been an African American, the bouncer would not have made explicit statements harking back to a Jim Crow era when racial segregation in public accommodations was explicitly supported by custom and law. Certainly, the owner, even if she or he initiated the dress code policy for the explicit purpose of keeping African Americans out of the nightclub, would not support statements like this made to an African American patron. The potential for bad publicity or legal action would be a deterrent from using such explicit racially discriminatory statements in support of a policy regarding dress.

Nightclub Owners and Dress Codes

The nightclub owners are rarely present during the late evening hours. Instead, they leave responsibility for managing the nightclubs to their managers, typically White men in their late twenties or early thirties. The fact that owners are not present during the late night eases the managers' and bouncers' burden as they enforce the dress codes. When patrons question the use of dress codes, both bouncers and managers typically indicate that it is the owner's desire to have a dress code. They simply state some version of the common refrain "Sorry, that's our policy. The owner wants to attract a certain type of clientele. You have to talk to him." Some patrons suspect that the nondescript "certain type" is coded language for "White patrons," but since the owner, who is responsible for the dress code, is not present to be questioned, the rejected patrons simply walk away.

Given owners' limited participation in actual nightlife activities, I rarely had the opportunity to speak with them regarding many matters, including the dress codes. Furthermore, since I was focused on the ways in which patrons navigated the public streets "having fun," interaction with the bar owners was not essential. Still the few owners with whom I had the occasion to interact generally avoided specific discussions, particularly about dress codes. Perhaps my status as an African American influenced their decision to avoid discussions about dress codes that many African Americans viewed as racially discriminatory. Their typical responses, such as "We are just trying to create a certain atmosphere," also suggest that they perhaps received legal counsel advising them to avoid public conversations about the dress codes.

I had only one substantive conversation with an owner that deviated from typical statements regarding the dress codes. He was a former manager at a nightclub that had instituted dress codes, but he had become part owner of another establishment that targeted patrons looking to drink and converse in a more laidback atmosphere. His new establishment did not have a dress code. When I asked him about the dress codes at his previous place of employment, he said, "Yes, we had to institute dress codes, and to me the dress codes are discriminatory, but we started to have trouble with drugs and stuff. There were just too many problems going on there. That's one of the reasons I left."

The general statements attributed to owners that dress codes are meant to attract "certain types" of patrons or "create a certain atmosphere" seems important to interrogate since some patrons view the dress codes as racially discriminatory.[30] According to Grazian, urban nightlife enterprises impose racial and class barriers that "generally replicate the same structures of race, ethnic, and class inequality and exclusion found in the larger society."[31] Hence, based on Grazian's assessment, one might conclude that the implementation of dress codes in downtown Northeast is in fact intended to be racially discriminatory. Whether this is the case remains an empirical question that is difficult to answer without specific commentary from the owners. It is clear, however, that the owners intend for dress codes to be used to help make distinctions among various patrons with the goal of identifying those who should be given access. Are these distinctions based on race, class, or culture? I suspect that the importance of each particular distinction is different for each owner. Furthermore, it is likely that all three distinctions are important considerations in varying combinations. Although I gathered limited commentary from owners regarding the dress codes, I do have evidence suggesting that they may be aware of the complex issues associated with implementing dress codes. For instance, Liz, a twenty-two-year-old White female patron, an acquaintance of Richard, a White nightclub owner, describes the kind of thinking, from her perspective, that went into his implementation of a dress code in his nightclub.

MAY: The clubs we mentioned before, some of them have dress codes. Do you know which bars have dress codes?

LIZ: I know Kilpatrick's used to. Honestly, and I know Ernie's Cove used to. It's the Monsoon now and I don't think it does.

MAY: Why do you think Ernie's Cove had a dress code?

LIZ: I know I'll tell you. I know Richard, the owner. I mean I love Richard. Yeah, he changed it because he needed a different clientele. He was not happy with it. I could go into more detail if you'd like.

MAY: Oh yeah, absolutely.

LIZ: [She laughs.] Well, I mean it's bad. He worked at another bar, bar backing. The clientele was the overflow of another club with mostly Black townies. So when he opened Ernie's Cove, and named it something a little less than classy, his followers followed him over there. He played the bumping, the hip-hop, the rap and stuff. He tried to have a dress code, to try to keep out you know the white T-shirt, and you know pretty much the Black athletic wear, I guess. And that dress code didn't work. They still came in because any man can put on a polo shirt or whatever and take off their hat for a second. So he wasn't happy with the clientele.

MAY: Well, here is a question, though, because you make a good point. You say the dress code didn't work, because any man could put on a polo shirt. But is there anything about that particular dress that the dress code was suggesting?

LIZ: The dress code was suggesting, trying to keep, pretty much the Black man out. Although, I will say in Richard's defense, he has plenty of Black friends. It's not a racist thing. I don't think so. He's a businessman. He's trying to make money. He sees money coming from the fraternity and sorority crowd, which is what he is trying to get now . . . and it's sad that it is like that. And he said to me, "I don't mean to be racist." He goes "I hate to have to do it but it's like, I need to make money. I gotta change the crowd." So he's now playing more, it's not "Lean Rock" whatever. He's playing the music that will bring the frat crowd in. He painted it and he changed it around and it is a little less Georgia crummy-looking inside. He classed it up so he's doing better. His business is doing better.

Liz's commentary regarding Richard's use of the dress codes exposes three key considerations. First, it is clear that nightclub owners are focused on their economic interests. They seek to maximize their profit by attracting patrons to their nightclubs. The more foot traffic to the nightclub the more likely the owner is to sell alcohol. In addition, the more fun that patrons have while they are drinking alcohol, the more likely they will return to the establishment. Given their economic interests, owners consistently work to attract patrons who will have fun and purchase drinks in their nightclubs.

Second, Liz's comments suggest that owners like Richard must reconcile their personal feelings with good business practices in order to maximize their profit. For instance, she indicates that Richard maintains relationships with a number of African Americans and that his initial business venture included patrons from his previous place of employment. For Richard, this inclusiveness brought a set of problems that worked contrary to the goal of maximizing profit. He attracted local African American patrons, who are typically lower class, thereby creating a twofold problem. First, local, lower-class patrons, according to bartenders, tend to purchase fewer drinks and are less likely to leave customary tips for drinks than their middle-class counterparts. This is a problem of both simple economics and class sensibility, in that lower-class patrons are less likely to have discretionary income like middle-class college students, and they are also less likely to be aware of customary tipping practices. It is easy to understand why bartenders find middle-class college students more desirable as patrons. Second, as indicated previously, many women view local male patrons, in particular African American men, to be more aggressive in their approaches than their frat-boy and White male counterparts. Hence women are likely to avoid nightclubs significantly populated by local, lower-class patrons. Richard understands that these problems negatively impact his business establishment, and thus attempts to implement a dress code to limit access to patrons who will generate greater profit. Yet, according to Liz, Richard was unsuccessful since local patrons continued to patronize his business, largely because it was one of a few places that played hip-hop music consistently throughout the night. Using profitability as his motive, Richard changed the décor and music to attract the fraternity crowd.

Finally, Richard's modifications to his nightclub raise an interesting question. Why is it financially viable for owners to limit the access of African American patrons—especially locals—to nightclubs in downtown? Beyond the previously mentioned practical reasons, there is an additional unspoken reason. Implicitly, owners are responding to the proclivities of their targeted clientele—in this case White middle-class patrons—to discriminate against other patrons based on race and social class. That is, owners, in order to make profit, must respond to the needs and desires of their primary clientele. In short, they are responding to the racism and classism of their patrons. Hence if key clientele were willing to frequent nightclubs where class and racial distinctions were not important, nightclub owners would have little economic incentive to institute policies, like dress codes, that support exclusion of particular types of patrons.

Perhaps the White patrons' proclivity to discriminate in this way is based on a local history of discrimination that has reverberated over time. As the sociologist Gary Fine, writing about the ways in which local group history impacts local culture and contemporary interactions between groups, states, "Certain actions become treated as proper, and, unless special circumstances apply, these expectations hold sway."[32] Hence, the patrons' tendency to avoid nightclubs frequented by African Americans, particularly locals, may in fact be based upon local understandings about race that have carried over time. To be sure, Northeast, like many other southern cities, has its own history in which Jim Crow segregation was the order of the day.[33] Such a history would support Whites' avoidance of social gathering places where a significant number of African Americans congregate. More important, a considerable number of the nightlife patrons are also coming from communities with high levels of residential segregation, and thus may simply seek out others like themselves as a matter of comfort. Irrespective of the specific motivation for avoiding African Americans, it seems that these patrons are viewing the social context of urban nightlife through what Feagin calls a White racial frame—a generic meaning system that encompasses racialized knowledge and understanding that help shape action or behavior.[34] It is through the use of this framing that patrons privilege White spaces over those occupied by Black bodies.[35]

Interestingly, at the same time that owners' implementation of dress codes can be justified as an economic response to patrons' proclivities, such a response might actually mask nightclub owners' intentional and willful discrimination against African Americans. Owners may in fact be participating in what some scholars have identified as "color-blind" racism.[36] Essentially, this entails using measures that disregard a person's race to determine who will participate in a particular activity, yet these measures, given historical, cultural, or structural conditions, disadvantage particular categories of people.

For instance, within the context of downtown the dress codes are "color-blind" measures in that they simply focus on styles of dress. Yet because African American men in particular have adopted these styles of dress, they are disproportionately affected by the implementation and enforcement of these policies. In addition, White patrons who simply wear styles of dress reflected in their middle-class upbringing benefit in that they need not consider dress codes.[37] Indeed many of them are unaware that dress codes are implemented. Although some African American men are able to "crack the code" given their middle-class backgrounds, "color-blind" dress codes continue to affect African American men disproportionately. Thus some scholars indicate that "color-blind" racism is more pernicious than the overt racially discriminatory practices existing during periods in American history like Jim Crow.

Conclusion

Dress codes are used in the downtown nightclubs to indicate which individuals will be admitted to engage in the nightclub activity. These dress codes are presented as objective standards of dress. Yet, as we have observed, their implementation, enforcement, and interpretation are based on subjective meanings and understandings for those who enforce the dress codes and those subjected to dress code enforcement. As various caravanning groups move through the nightlife and attempt to gain access to nightclubs, bouncers scrutinize their clothing for compliance with dress codes. This scrutiny itself may be innocuous, but given the nightlife context where there is underlying tension across social capsule boundaries, the dress codes become a mechanism through which a broader system of integrated segregation is supported.

5

Knockout

● ● ● ● ● ● ● ● ● ● ● ●

Verbal and Physical Confrontations

In densely populated gatherings where alcoholic beverages are served and people pursue "having fun," confrontation is bound to occur. These confrontations might stem from strangers bumping one another as they pass, arguments between friends that begin elsewhere but pick up intensity in the nightlife where people are less inhibited, or an ongoing dislike among members of various groups. Most confrontations entail brief incidental contact followed by one patron calling attention to the incident with a verbal acknowledgment like "Hey, man, you bumped me."[1] These exchanges typically end with an apology or some gesture of reconciliation from the offending patron. Sometimes confrontations involve extended verbal exchanges that might include nonverbal communication like finger pointing and other hand gestures. These exchanges dissipate when one patron, usually at the beckoning of friends in the caravanning group, decides to "walk away," and the other patron and her or his caravanning group are

willing to "let it end right there." Still, there are incidents that involve fisticuffs between individual patrons, sometimes escalating into all-out brawls
involving several patrons and requiring nightclub bouncers or police
to intervene. Although these brawls are rare and occur among caravanning groups, they also occur across broader social capsule boundaries that
include groupings like frat boy, athlete, and locals. This occurrence raises
interesting questions: What, if any, is the broader social significance of verbal and physical confrontations in urban nightlife? Furthermore, how are
these confrontations related to integrated segregation in urban nightlife?

In this chapter I examine verbal and physical confrontations in the
nightlife, giving particular attention to the ways in which these events
occur, who is involved, and how the confrontations are resolved. I categorize these confrontations into the following four types: skirmishes,
fisticuffs, "being bounced," and brawls. I discuss each of these types of
confrontations in light of my previous observations regarding race, class,
and culture in the urban nightlife. I pay particular attention to the ways in
which the underlying tensions among groups manifest in verbal and physical confrontations. Ultimately, these confrontations influence how various
groups of patrons think about use of urban public space and help to define
boundaries that exist among groups, thereby supporting integrated segregation in the nightlife.

Skirmishes

As patrons move through the crowded space in the nightlife, on the city
streets or in nightclubs, it is likely that they will have incidental contact
with other patrons. This incidental contact may be followed by a verbal confrontation wherein one patron calls to the attention of another
patron the infraction of some tacitly understood standard for interaction. I characterize exchanges like this as skirmishes, in which patrons,
typically strangers, have passing interactions with one another resulting
in verbal confrontations about spilled drinks, stepped-on toes, and other
unwanted contact. These verbal confrontations are resolved without
physical confrontation and patrons negotiate them with the support of
their caravanning groups, who generally wish to keep moving in order to
maximize the experience of having fun. Typical interchanges include the
following.

As I stood in Figaro's talking to Misty Kirby, a White female, and Keith, a tall White male, I noticed a White male arguing with another White male. They were standing a few feet away, close by the bar. I couldn't hear the conversation over the music but the tall White guy wearing a yellow polo and khaki shorts was waving his hand in the air from side to side. The other male, wearing a white polo and khaki shorts, just kept staring at him. After the guy in yellow finished talking, he turned back to the woman standing behind him and embraced her. She was wearing a white dress with spaghetti straps on the shoulders. They both seemed pretty intoxicated as they started walking toward the door. The guy in yellow still seemed pretty upset by the interchange with the other guy. He pressed through the crowd, bumping patrons as he passed. Most of the patrons he bumped just leered at the couple as they kept walking. As he and his female companion stumbled toward the door, they came closer to the group standing with me. The guy stumbled a bit, then bumped Misty in the back as she sipped her drink. She spilled a few drops on the floor in front of where we were standing. Immediately, she had a frustrated look on her face, but she didn't turn and say anything to the guy until he stumbled into her again. Misty rolled her neck around and turned and snapped, "Hey, take that somewhere else. I'm trying to drink." I was shocked that Misty said anything. She had no way of knowing that the guy was agitated from his argument. The guy tried to compose himself as he lifted his hands up apologetically and said, "Shorry." Misty turned back to Keith and me as the patron and his female companion continued stumbling toward the door.

Most patrons seem to operate with the taken-for-granted understanding that incidental contact initiated by other patrons, usually intoxicated, is a normative part of the social experience in the nightlife, and thus simply ignore patrons as they pass. Still some patrons like Misty are impatient with other patrons bumping or shoving behaviors for a number of reasons and make verbal response. As in this case, the intoxicated patron usually makes an offer of apology and proceeds.

This interchange also suggests interesting insights about the differences in confrontations between men and women, men and men, and women and women. I have observed generally that men and women's verbal exchanges with one another are far more amicable than verbal interchanges that occur between women and women and between men and men. In fact, incidental contact among members of the opposite sex is often received as an overture for flirtation. When men and women come into contact with one another in the crowded nightlife spaces, their initial responses might include a smile accompanied by an apology, a focused stare indicating attraction, or perhaps an apology followed by a pickup line. Hence, incidental contact may be the initial basis for a verbal confrontation, but in a context where a significant part of having fun is interacting with members of the opposite sex, it sometimes becomes a conversation starter.

Whereas the interchanges between men and women are likely to be amicable, the interchanges between women are much less so. In these instances women are usually direct and sometimes insulting to other women. Perhaps their responses are based on the overall competitive nature with which they view one another. Their verbal interchanges are brief, with few women offering apologies for incidental contact as they pass. In fact, most passing interactions between women include terse verbal comments like "excuse me," "watch it," or "coming through," but some verbal confrontations, especially rendered by intoxicated women, may include scowls accompanied by phrases like "Watch where you are going, bitch." These statements are typically rendered among passing groups who rarely look back to engage one another further. Hence, although women may have catty interchanges, these interchanges are brief and rarely escalate into physical confrontations.

Unlike women, men are much more likely to include verbal responses or acknowledgments to one another that either diffuse or heighten the interaction. Furthermore, men seem to place greater significance on their interactions with one another than do women and are consistently prepared to make a response. Most verbal interchanges between men convey a measure of respect from one man to another as a coparticipant in the pursuit of fun in the nightlife. They include phrases like "excuse me," "sorry, buddy," or "my bad," to which a customary response is a reconciliatory phrase like "no problem" or "it's cool."

Still, some men respond as though incidental contact or verbal acknowledgment of that contact is a challenge to their masculine identity or what it means to be a man. Typical responses in these instances have men prepared to escalate a verbal confrontation to a physical confrontation. This is because many young men learn that physical confrontation is an appropriate response to challenges, yet their responses may be tempered by the cultural context within which they have been socialized.[2] A man's response also may be influenced by the immediate context. Within the context of nightlife, the consumption of alcohol seems to increase men's tendency toward responding to an initial interchange as though it is a challenge.

Perceived challenges between two men often draw in members of their caravanning groups who may act as a counterbalance to the aggressive behavior demonstrated by a member of the group, or the caravanning group members may join in supporting the aggressive behavior, thereby pressing the interchange into a physical confrontation. These physical confrontations include fisticuffs and brawls, which I discuss later. Suffice it to say that men are more likely to have involved interactions with the potential for violence when encountering other men than are women who encounter women or men who encounter women. Perhaps this is because, as sociologist R. W. Connell indicates, that underlying the idea of masculinity is "a widespread belief that it is natural for men to be violent."[3] This would further explain why nightclub bouncers scrutinize men as potential "troublemakers," reasoning that if average male patrons might escalate a verbal confrontation to a physical confrontation, then troublemakers are certain to engage in physical confrontations. Despite the potential for violence in interactions between men, most of the initial verbal confrontations are simply marked by an apology and patrons' departure from one another's presence.

Although most initial verbal confrontations between men stem from incidental contact, a few of these confrontations may result from conflicts over women. For instance, a man who is offended that another man has attempted to talk to a woman accompanying him might approach another man to ask "Why are you talking to my girl?" or to let the other man know "We're together." Unlike those occurring from incidental contact, these verbal confrontations are systematic and direct, but typically conclude in a similar fashion with one man offering a reconciliatory response, because as one male patron indicated, "There are too many women downtown to be fighting over one." The density of women within the context of the nightlife makes it easier for men to walk away from verbal confrontations.

Whether women are at the center of verbal confrontations between men or the confrontations stem from incidental contact, women may also intervene in these verbal confrontations and successfully prevent them from escalating into physical confrontations as in this example.

As Brad, Keith, Theo, and I walked down Stuckey Street toward Reginald, we saw Ashley standing at the southwest corner of Leslie Street. We stopped on the corner to talk to her. . . . As we were standing there an intoxicated guy backed full force into Ashley from behind. He apparently didn't see us there and seemed to be in a hurry. I put my hand on his back to keep him from continuing to collide into Ashley. He was a White male wearing an orange shirt, blue jeans, and a hat that read, "I'm 21 bitch."

He composed himself and turned to her and said, "Sorry," then turned to me and said, "Sorry, man."

"It's cool," I said as he turned, took a few steps, and stopped at the corner. He was now in front of us.

We all turned our attention to crossing the street. As the streetlight changed to green and we were about to begin walking across the crosswalk, we all stopped when two cars made right turns through the crosswalk. The first car, a "pimped out," purple-painted, 1980s Chevy Impala, with two African American males leaning back in the front seat, turned right.[4] A sedan with glistening black paint and shiny silver rims followed the first car. I couldn't determine the exact make or model of the second car because it also had been "pimped out." It looked like a car from the 1980s also. Both the passenger side and driver side windows were tinted, but down three-fourths of the way. The driver was a dark-skinned African American man with a cigar propped in the side of his mouth. He was wearing a green-and-white New York Jets jersey and appeared to be about twenty-three years old with broad shoulders. In the passenger seat snuggled next to him was a brown-skinned, African American woman wearing a black top.

The black car turned the corner in front of the intoxicated guy who was just about eight steps in front of us. He was startled by the turning vehicle and shouted to the driver, "Hey, watch the fucking light, you asshole." The White male continued across the street as the driver of the car finished his turn, hit the brakes suddenly, and shifted the car gear into the park position. The White guy who had made the comment had already finished crossing the street and was on the other side. He didn't even notice that the black car had stopped. When the car stopped, the driver moved the cigar in his mouth and cracked the driver's side door open and the interior light illuminated. All I could see was the woman's two slender arms wrapped around the driver's right forearm as he started to exit the car. She pulled at his arm forcefully, although the man, given his size, could have easily pulled away. Seeming to yield to his female companion's resistance, the driver sat back down in the car, pulled his foot back into the car, slammed the door shut, and eased the car into gear and pulled off. The intoxicated patron had stopped on the other side of the street to take a photograph for a group of people he didn't seem to know and was none the wiser that the woman on the passenger's side of the car had intervened in a potential fight.

Women have a significant role in reducing conflict between men in the nightlife. As in this case, they may offer a voice of reason or a calming gesture that helps to rein in a male companion who wishes to demonstrate his manhood through an aggressive act. Women have the ability to announce the consequences of a man's physical confrontation in an immediate manner with statements like "Don't fight, they'll throw you out" or "I don't have time to get you out of jail tonight." These kinds of phrases can often be heard over music, on the streets, and in the nightclubs as women shout them with a sense of urgency that alerts even those individuals who are not involved in the conflict.

Sometimes women intervene in a verbal confrontation even by standing between the two men who are in conflict. Neither man seems to be willing to take the chance of striking the woman on accident by throwing a punch. Her presence gives each man a moment to weigh the costs of demonstrating his manhood through an aggressive act. Furthermore, by having a woman intervene each man is able to walk away from a challenge with his manhood intact since other patrons perceive the men as being respectful of the woman's wishes and neither had to prove his manhood through a physical confrontation.

Beyond demonstrating women's ability to intervene in verbal confrontations between men, the interchange in the crosswalk also permits investigation of interesting race, class, and cultural dynamics taking place as patrons navigate the streets. For instance, among White patrons in downtown, one aspect of having fun centers on intoxication. Many of the frat boy and college student caravanning groups engage in games where the primary purpose is "to get drunk." These groups also seem to share a greater level of tolerance in their verbal confrontations than do other patrons, like African American locals, who are not specifically involved in games of intoxication. Hence whereas frat boy and college student groups might take the White male patron's comment "Hey, watch the fucking light, you asshole" as typical passing behavior in a public space with intoxicated patrons, the African American male driver seems to interpret the expression as a personal affront to be addressed by direct confrontation.

The specific social identities of both the White male and the Black male in this interchange are not clear, but their styles of dress, activities of choice, and responses to the situation suggest something of their statuses. The White male conveys status as a college student through his attire of a shirt, jeans, and hat with the bold declaration of being of legal age to consume alcoholic beverages. The Black male is wearing a sports jersey, suggesting an affinity for urban styles of dress. As demonstrated in the previous chapter, this Black male may have middle-class status, but other patrons, bar owners, and police associate his hip-hop clothing with the urban poor. Although attire may not clearly indicate one's social status, participants' activity of choice further suggests their placement within the nightlife. For instance, the White male demonstrates his full participation in the nightlife by caravanning through the streets on foot, whereas the African American male positions himself as an observer or outsider as he drives through the area. Interestingly, city officials, citing concern for potential accidents related to the high density of pedestrian and vehicular traffic, implemented the no-cruising policy.[5] Many local African Americans interpret these policies as racially discriminatory since they target a disproportionately African American activity.

The White male's response to the encroachment of public space by the driver is direct, but within the nightlife context it is generally taken by others who share fully in the nightlife as an innocuous response coming from a drunken patron. In short, it is expected behavior. Since I was unable to hear the African American male's immediate verbal response or his companion's statements as she held his arm, it is difficult to know how he planned to address the White male's verbal comments or what actually compelled him to return to the car. Yet his immediate response is suggestive of the kinds of responses that Anderson observes among young Black males in urban contexts where personal affronts require an immediate course of action that sometimes quickly escalates into physical confrontation.[6] Anderson demonstrates how a simple gesture like making eye contact with an African American male on the city streets may become the basis for physical confrontation. Furthermore, such responses are suggested as appropriate in some hip-hop music wherein listeners may be told stories of violence as a response for simply being "looked at wrong" or "mean mugged."[7]

Taking the contextual clues discussed previously into account, I speculate that the two men in the interchange were headed for a physical confrontation had not the woman intervened. Furthermore, although the physical confrontation was averted, it appears certain that race, class, and cultural differences heighten tensions between these two men, even if only in their individual interpretations of the meaning of their interchange. This tension is an ongoing theme among the groups in particular, African Americans and Whites, within the context of downtown. As these groups compete with one another for use of nightclubs and urban public space these tensions manifest in skirmishes. These skirmishes seem to take on greater significance than being merely matters of incidental contact between passing patrons, as in this example:

It was about 1:30 a.m. and I had been standing in front of the Oil Company talking to Peter who decided to leave. After he left, I hung around in front of the Oil Company leaning against the parking meter. . . . A Black male came out of the Oil Company and stopped on the patio. He seemed "tipsy" but not drunk. He was brown-skinned, short, clean-cut, with short twisty braids and he wore a multicolored T-shirt, jeans, and gym shoes. As he was standing on the patio talking on his cell phone, two White males were walking past. Both seemed intoxicated as they stumbled toward Reginald Street. The first guy, walking a few feet in front of his companion, wore khaki shorts, Nike low-top running shoes, and a powder blue polo shirt. He was tall and slender. The second guy, straggling behind his friend a few feet, wore a long white, button-down, dress shirt, untucked, khaki shorts, and flip-flops. He was tall and medium build and wore his sleeves rolled up to the elbows. As the second White male was walking passed the Oil Company, he put a stick of gum in his mouth and threw the wrapper in the direction of the Black male on the phone. Although I couldn't be sure, the toss looked deliberate. The gum wrapper floated about four feet and hit the Black male squarely in the chest.

The Black male, who was still talking on the phone, walked outside of the chains in front of the Oil Company and called to the White male who had thrown the wrapper, "Hey, what did you do that for?"

Both of the White males stopped and turned around saying, "What, what?"

"Throw that shit for?" said the Black male.

"What?" replied the White guy who had thrown the wrapper.

The Black male, still holding the phone in his hand and up to his ear, stepped closer toward the two White guys and said, "Why did you do that shit?"

The White male in dress shirt said, "Fuck you."

The Black male repeated, "Why did you do that shit?" as he brought the phone down from his ear. They were now standing about four feet from one another and appeared ready to begin throwing punches when two women, who were apparently inside of the Oil Company with the Black male, walked out.

"There he is," the tall woman, with long, dark, hair screamed. "Terrence," she called to him. The Black male did not look back, but it seemed he recognized the voice by the way he tilted his head. The two White males looked slightly to the left but kept their main focus on the Black male.

The two women began walking toward the group. The tall one that had shouted Terrence's name was White, with tanned skin. She was wearing a black skirt that hung right at her knees, a white sleeveless pullover shirt, and black heels. Her friend was blonde and also had tanned skin. She was a little shorter and dressed more provocatively in a short dress with colorful print and red high-heel shoes. The dress came several inches above her knees. Both women seemed a little giggly from drinking and unaware of the tension between the men. As the women got closer to the men, their appearance caused the men in conflict to pause.

The woman in the print dress wrapped her arm around Terrence, who was still focused on the guy who had thrown the paper and said, "Terrence, we're leaving." She hugged him a little tighter then the two women turned and started walking in the opposite direction.

Terrence turned and looked back as the two women began walking. The two White males also watched as the women began walking away.

"I'm coming now," said Terrence, as he seemed to forget about the gum wrapper incident and the two White males standing there. He started walking behind the two women. The two White males watched as Terrence followed the women away. After a brief pause, the White male in the button-down dress shirt said, "Bitch."

Terrence, now about fifteen feet away, either didn't hear him or ignored him and continued following the women. The two White males turned and proceeded on their way toward Reginald Street.

Although the women in this interchange did not specifically intervene in the interaction between the men with the purpose of circumventing conflict, their presence significantly altered the men's behavior. Terrence and his White male counterparts pause and gaze in such a way that suggests they are viewing the women as objects of attraction. The women are able to provide a diversion from the men's desire to rectify their interchange with a physical confrontation. This instance is consistent with others that I have observed wherein men are distracted by the physical appearance of a woman in their presence. Men might stammer or drop complete phrases from their verbal utterances or hold still in their movements as though their ability to act is disabled. Whatever the extent of influence that women's presence has on men's behavior, it is clear that men take note of women and this can change how men interact with one another.

As mentioned previously, most interactions between men on the streets or in the bars are focused on treating one another as coparticipants in the nightlife seeking to have fun. Hence, acts of incidental contact are usually excused and rarely escalate into physical confrontation, unless these acts are perceived as direct challenges to one's manhood. For Terrence, having a gum wrapper thrown in his direction constitutes a challenge. He interprets the tossing of the gum wrapper as an intentional act on the part of the White male. Rather than making a simple passing comment typical of skirmishes, Terrence fully engages the White men in a way that is likely to have escalated if not for the presence of the women. There is no indication that the White male's pitch of the gum wrapper or Terrence's response to being hit concerned an ongoing interpersonal conflict specifically between these two patrons. Given this, I suggest that the interchange is based not only on the predispositions of the individuals involved or their intoxicated state, but also on the ongoing tension between African Americans and Whites for use of the public space more generally.

Based on my observations, African American patrons, irrespective of social status, typically characterize the nightlife as a social space focused on primarily providing entertainment for Whites. Complaints from African American nightlife participants include statements like "Downtown is for drunk White people," "They really don't want Blacks here," and "They change the music so Blacks will leave." These statements are supported by African Americans' limited participation in the nightlife activities that White patrons take for granted. Whereas African Americans perceive downtown as a space where they are attempting to fit in, Whites' comments like "Downtown is the best party place in the Southeast" and "It's a great place to party" indicate the ease with which Whites identify with having fun in the nightlife. While African Americans are attempting to create a social space in the nightlife where they feel welcomed, Whites are enjoying the nightlife in its fullness. Although some African Americans, like those who are athletes, enjoy aspects of nightlife entertainment, most are frustrated by the limited opportunities for African Americans to have fun. I suspect that many verbal confrontations between African Americans and Whites have as a subtext African Americans' frustrations with having to claim a space and Whites' feelings that their space is being encroached. This is a point I return to later.

Fisticuffs

During my time observing interactions within the nightlife, I rarely noted physical confrontation between nightlife participants. Given my observations, I wondered if other patrons had also observed limited physical confrontations in the nightlife. Most of them noted that although they had witnessed many verbal confrontations, few skirmishes escalated into fisticuffs wherein patrons would push, shove, or throw punches at one another after an initial verbal interchange. Liz, a twenty-two-year-old White female responded this way after I asked her if she had ever seen any fights downtown: "I've seen like little guys getting all up in each other's face, 'You just bumped me, dude.' You know they're drunk and they're trying to save their ego or their woman or show off or something, but no, uh, knock-down-drag-outs."

Despite the fact that physical confrontations are rare, they do occur. These fisticuffs are usually brief in duration and are frequently terminated by members of a caravanning group, or by the participants who seem to mutually agree that further physical confrontation is not worth the trouble of dealing with bouncers or police. Furthermore, since one or both of the patrons are usually intoxicated when the physical confrontations occur, it takes little time for a victor to be determined. For instance, consider the following physical confrontation.

It was 2:30 a.m. and I was sitting inside Burgers Plus having a late-night snack with Theo, Keith, and Brad. Theo had been peering over my shoulder looking out the window when he said excitedly, "Man, look. It's a fight."

I turned around in my seat and looked over my shoulder out of the broad glass window. You could see about twenty-five feet of the sidewalk that was illuminated by the restaurant lights. There were two guys in front of the glass window that caught my attention quickly. Other restaurant patrons also turned their attention to the activities outside.

One guy was an African American male standing at about five feet, ten inches. He was dark-skinned, medium build, wearing a black polo shirt and blue jean shorts. He was pretty upset as one of his companions stood between him and the other guy. The other guy facing off and talking was a White male. He stood just a few inches shorter than the Black male, but looked to be heavier. He was wearing a gray colored T-shirt with lettering of some sort, khaki shorts, and a white Big South baseball cap. He looked to be accompanied by a female companion and a male companion. They seemed to be pleading with him to come on with them as they stood a few feet away calling back to him.

After a few seconds of jostling, the African American male's companions let him go and he stepped quickly toward the White male who was standing in expectation. A few patrons who were standing in front of Burgers Plus waiting to be seated watched intently as the Black male got about four feet from the White male and put his hands up in a boxing stance. The White male followed suit and they circled about three steps. It was at this point that I could see that the White male was intoxicated, but the Black male did not appear to be.

Keith, seeing that the White male was intoxicated, said, "This could get ugly."

"Right," Brad added.

None of the patrons around seemed to think they should intervene, but rather they seemed excited to see a fight.

As the two men eased around looking intently at one another, the Black male leaned forward in a swift motion and threw one quick punch with the left hand that landed on the forehead of the White male. He spoke as he jabbed, but I couldn't hear him from inside the restaurant. The White male stumbled back a little, but seemed to be awakened by the first punch. The Black male stepped in with a second punch, this time with the right hand. He hit the White male in the left temple.

By this time the White male was ready to go on the offensive himself. He quickly stumbled forward and pitched his right hand. The Black male was able to anticipate the slow motion of the punch and side stepped. The punch brushed lightly against the Black male's left cheek. In one motion the Black male took two quick steps forward and grabbed the White male by his throat with his right hand and began choking and shaking the White male and shouting at him. The only word I could hear through the glass was "bitch." As the Black male squeezed harder the White male seemed to succumb to the pressure of the grip and began to flop a little. After about three seconds the Black male released his grip while thrusting the White male back by the throat.

The White male stumbled a few feet back and gathered himself, but held his position as his male and female companion took him by the arms pleading with him. The White male took a deep breath and stood up straight. He began to straighten out his clothes. The Black male, seemingly convinced that his point had been made, turned and walked away with his friends while Theo, Brad, Keith, and I added our own commentary and retelling of the events to one another.

As patrons to the restaurant who witnessed firsthand the fight entered, I asked them how the incident began. Based on various witnesses' fragmented explanations, the Black male had accidently bumped into the White male and before he could apologize the White male responded angrily with a phrase like, "Watch the fuck where you're going" or "What the fuck, dude? Watch where you're going." Irrespective of the specific phrasing, the Black male took these initial comments as insulting and made his own verbal retort. The White male responded by halting and providing additional comments to the Black male, and from there the two engaged in the physical confrontation I observed.

Leaving aside for the moment the potential underlying racial tension, the White male's initial comments were inconsistent with typical occurrences in the nightlife wherein one man extends to another the opportunity to reconcile incidental contact. Furthermore, rather than merely making a passing comment, the White male turned and further engaged the Black male in verbal confrontation. His actions heightened the conflict, and the Black male likely interpreted them as a challenge to his manhood—a challenge that he felt should be addressed with physical

nfrontation. Members of the Black male's caravanning group seem to
iare the expectation that this challenge should be addressed with physical
confrontation and permitted the Black male to engage the White male in
fisticuffs. As with other physical confrontations involving an intoxicated
patron, the fight was brief.

One interpretation of this interaction is to consider the underlying tension between African Americans and Whites who pass each other on the
public streets. Like Reginald and Stuckey Streets, Leslie is a main corridor of
nightlife activity where many diverse groups of patrons and participants pass
one another. Not only frat boy, college student, local, athlete, and alternative types but also occasional street performers and homeless men soliciting
downtown patrons for spare change are present. In short, it is a space wherein
groups are likely to share verbal exchanges latent with tension related to not
only the specific interchange, but also existing social conditions for participation in the nightlife. As indicated previously, many African Americans, both
locals and college students, are frustrated by the limited spaces within which
they may gather and engage in activities for having fun. They are further frustrated by their general perceptions that the nightclub owners and city officials implement rules to curtail African Americans' presence. For many of
these patrons their verbal confrontations with Whites take on a greater symbolic significance. They become a rare opportunity to direct their frustration
toward Whites, or even press a verbal exchange into a physical confrontation.

Still, despite the underlying tension between African Americans and
Whites, verbal exchanges between them rarely escalate to physical confrontation. For instance, Danny, a twenty-one-year-old White male college student, indicates that fights occur, but when asked whether he has witnessed
those between Whites and Blacks, he responds this way: "I can't think that
I have. I see, I mean I see a lot of like scuffles when people yell at each other.
Um, there's always fights at Javelina Ranch. At the end of the night there is
always people fighting. But I have never really like paid that much attention
to their race. I feel like, I mean Javelina Ranch is mostly White people."

Since Whites frequent Javelina Ranch, the bar Danny mentions, it is
unlikely that he would have the occasion to observe African Americans and
Whites in direct interaction with one another there. African Americans
generally recognize Javelina Ranch as yet another space within the nightlife that is decidedly for White patrons. They are quick to indicate that frat
boys frequent there to listen to covers of country music played live.

Interestingly, although Danny uses the term "fights," it is likely that he is referring more closely to the skirmishes or verbal confrontations that I have described in the previous section wherein people "yell at each other." His comments further indicate the extent to which it is rare that patrons engage in actual physical confrontation.

Like Danny, Lori, a twenty-two-year-old African American student at BSU, has rarely observed physical confrontations between Whites and Blacks. She provides an interesting rationale for why she does not observe such physical confrontations.

MAY: Have you seen any fights between Blacks and Whites?

LORI: Those don't usually turn into fights. Like usually when the Black people are really, really, irate, like I guess when Black people are angry they tend to act the same, they each wanna fight each other. If a Black person wants to fight a Black person, the White guy is more likely to say, "You know what, forget about it, its not worth it" and walk away and just take the loss.

MAY: Why do you think that is?

LORI: I mean, it could be anything, like different environments that they were raised in, or stereotypes about how we're supposed to act. You know stereotypes, sometimes we act on those, even though we like to say it's a stereotype, it affects the way we act.

Lori observes the possible influence of social context on nightlife participants' behavior. Her comments reflect observations that have been made by social scientists. For instance, studies suggest that young ethnic minorities, in particular low-income African American youths, are generally exposed to greater violence than White youths.[8] This suggests that within such contexts young men learn that the appropriate response to a challenge or threat is to retaliate with violence. Indeed, this is the point that Anderson makes in his work on youth violence in the streets of Philadelphia. According to Anderson, many African American youth in Philadelphia learn a "code of the street," which in part emphasizes one's preparedness to engage in physical confrontation. Anderson states, "By the time they are teenagers, most young people have internalized the code of the street, or at least learned to comport themselves in accordance with its rules. . . . [T]he code revolves around the presentation of self. Its basic requirement is the display of a certain predisposition to violence. A person's public bearing must send the unmistakable, if sometimes subtle, message that one is capable of violence, and possibly mayhem, when the situation requires it, that one can take care of oneself."[9]

Such a presentation of self creates a context where readiness for violence can quickly move to actual violence. In addition, Pattillo-McCoy observes that young middle-class African Americans in Chicago, because they have experienced residential segregation and have grown up in communities that abut those inhabited by lower-class African Americans, must also adopt similar responses in order to navigate the public spaces they share with their lower-class kindred.[10] These observations would seem to support Lori's assessment that African Americans, especially when they are in conflict or "irate" with one another, are willing to engage in physical confrontations.

Lori's description of what happens to an individual choosing to walk away from a conflict is also quite telling. She suggests that individuals who "walk away" demonstrate weakness and concession since they presumably "take a loss"—the loss to which she is referring is the diminishing value of the loser's manhood. Implicitly, Lori suggests that for African Americans, onlookers interpret "walking away" as cowardice rather than an exercise in sound judgment and reason. Interestingly, the cultural mandate to address a challenge without walking away increases the likelihood that a physical confrontation will occur. These confrontations have further consequences for the participants according to a study on youth violence and victimization by sociologist Kevin Fitzpatrick. Fitzpatrick, analyzing data taken from three nationally representative, stratified samples of youth, suggests that for those persons "who believe it's impossible to walk away from a fight or confrontation put themselves at great risk to be victims of violence at that time or at some later point, perhaps through the act of revenge."[11] This study suggests that the adage "violence begets violence" is appropriate to describe how confrontations play out in contexts where individuals choose not to walk away.

Perhaps the emphasis placed on proving one's manhood through physical aggression is related to African Americans' perceptions and realities, especially among lower-class African Americans, that there are limited ways in which to demonstrate their masculine identity within broader social institutions in America.[12] For instance, according to sociologists Andrea Hunter and James Davis, African American men develop masculine identities that reinforce manliness and aggressive behavior as an appropriate response to conflict. Their responses in part are based on the limits of their immediate social situation wherein many "must survive in a context of economic and racial oppression."[13] Hence, African American men's perceptions of masculine identity are in part a response to their general social condition.

African Americans' responses to verbal confrontation may also stem from stereotypes, according to Lori. For instance, one implied stereotype is the idea that African Americans, in particular males, consistently perpetrate violent acts. This stereotype may be supported by mass media presentations in which violent criminal acts perpetrated by Black males are disproportionately reported and sensationalized.[14] Lori suggests that although African Americans might criticize individuals and institutions for supporting these kinds of stereotypes, their own behavior is consistent with these stereotypes and further works to support them. I would argue that if African Americans or Whites who are in verbal conflict with one another believe these stereotypes, they are likely to act on them within their encounters. Hence, such stereotypes have consequences for action within the context of downtown Northeast.

Although African Americans who frequent downtown may have been exposed to cultural contexts that emphasize violence or share a belief in stereotypes about the aggressive Black male as a basis for escalating verbal challenges to physical confrontation, White males within the nightlife also share a belief that challenges to one's manhood should be met with physical confrontation. In fact, based upon my reading of the research literature on masculinity, aggressive and violent behaviors are nearly universal aspects of masculinity.[15] Still actual fisticuffs resulting from verbal confrontation in downtown are rare. Perhaps this is because aggressive behavior is worked out through passing verbal confrontation, or within caravanning groups through roughhouse play.

For instance, caravanning groups of White men can often be seen engaging in pushing or shoving games with friends. On numerous occasions White males greet each other with a headlock or a bear hug from behind. The recipient of such a hold may be lifted off his feet and carried forward as the aggressor laughs with delight at his demonstration of playful aggressiveness and strength. Once released, the recipient responds with similar behavior and a verbal phrase like "What's up, bitch?" to which a common reply is "Nothing, bitch," as both men laugh. After this initial display of aggressive, physical behavior, the men exchange a handshake greeting. This kind of aggressive behavior is typical and seems to be intensified after a few hours of drinking.

As indicated previously, fisticuffs among patrons are rare. If they do occur they are brief in duration, with only a few punches thrown. These fisticuffs usually occur among men and may be the result of incidental contact, a disagreement about a woman, or ongoing tension between groups, but most typically they are the result of both men feeling as though they have been challenged in some regard and need to address the challenge with physical confrontation. One might expect that the underlying tension between African Americans and Whites regarding the use of the bars and streets in Northeast might create the context for a great deal of physical confrontations between Whites and Blacks, but these too are rare. Whether it is the overall atmosphere focused on having fun, Whites' and Blacks' beliefs in stereotypes about violence among the groups, African Americans' feelings of being the minority, or women's interventions, patrons simply opt to walk away before verbal confrontation escalates to fisticuffs. Beyond these informal incentives for avoiding fisticuffs, bouncers and police provide formal social control over downtown Northeast. This means that those patrons who do engage in fisticuffs or other unwanted behavior are likely to experience "being bounced" from the nightclubs or the downtown context.

Being Bounced

Bouncers exercise significant control and authority within the nightlife. They use their judgment to determine who is underage, complies with dress codes, is drunk, or is a troublemaker before granting access to the celebrated spaces of the nightlife. Bouncers must then monitor the admitted patrons for verbal confrontation, harassing behavior, pushing and shoving, and outright fisticuffs. When physical confrontations do occur, bouncers use physical force to separate belligerent patrons from one another and subsequently remove them from the nightclub. In short, patrons experience "being bounced." Bouncers' use of force is sanctioned by bar owners and supported by police officers, who typically wait for the bouncers to clear the "troublemakers" from the nightclub before they become involved.

Although bouncers may use force to intervene in physical confrontations, the typical physical stature of bouncers at nightclubs in downtown Northeast suggests that bar owners expect few physical confrontations to occur. Most of the bouncers in downtown Northeast are average in height and stature, and rather than presenting an air of force and intimidation, most demonstrate a laidback demeanor with a disposition toward making polite requests rather than demands. The bouncers' average physical stature and laidback demeanor is not lost on the patrons, who make the following observations about the bouncers: "They are just normal-looking guys," "They're all just, most of the ones I've seen are all just frat boys who need a job . . . I mean bouncers is kind of a joke to me most of the time," and "They're usually not that intimidating, half the time they are just sitting down with their friends." Even so, bouncers are still called upon to use physical force to preserve order and enforce rules within the nightclubs.

The Corral was packed. The deejay flashed the lights just after I entered at about 1:40 a.m. and shouted on the microphone "last call." He was playing the usual Saturday night medley of hip-hop songs to close out the night. As I pressed through the crowd toward the back wall across from the bar, the song "Baby Got Back" played in the background.[16] I turned around and faced the bar and watched a few intoxicated, eager, White women climb on the four-foot-high bar top to dance. Several more women followed them. Some of them appeared to be underage. The women were wearing an assortment of high-heel shoes, tight pants, short skirts, tube tops, and sleeveless shirts. As the music bumped, men began to press closer to the bar to get a better view of the women, or perhaps take a peek under skirts. The women seemed mindful of this but were uninhibited. Other men, who were further away from the bar but not dancing themselves with other women, also stood gawking at the women dancing on the bar.

　　To the right I could see one White male climb up on the bar top to dance with one of the women. He was gyrating vigorously behind a blonde in a white skirt and orange top. Her face revealed a sense of displeasure when she realized that he was behind her. She moved up a step closer to the girl she was dancing next to. In just that moment the man, dressed in jeans and a plaid shirt, seemed to lose his balance and tumble off the bar. He was able to use the bodies of the gawking men below to balance and land on his feet. As he made his way back up to the bar top, I realized why he had lost his balance the first time. There was a bouncer pulling him by the leg of his jeans as he tried to reach up. The bouncer, in his red bouncer T-shirt, pulled with force and the man lost his balance again as he tumbled down hitting several patrons.

　　Suddenly I heard a rush of feet across the floor toward the area where the man had fallen. I could see four more bouncers moving in. One bouncer sprung from the staircase where he had stood perched looking for trouble and the others came from various directions. As they circled the man, another man, seemingly upset from being hit by the falling man in plaid, took a swing. This started a chain reaction of flailing fists between the fallen patron and a few other patrons standing nearby. I heard shouts and crowd rumblings as the bouncers moved swiftly. One bouncer grabbed the fallen man around the neck in a chokehold and shoved him through the crowd. Even though he was shorter he could easily move the man who was obviously intoxicated. The force of the push seemed to open a way as the patrons recognized the bouncers' authority. Another bouncer grabbed the guy that had thrown the punch and shoved him through the crowd. The other bouncers just stood in the area as the men who were accompanying both followed their friends out of the bar. All the while the women continued to dance.

The bouncer confronted the man in the plaid shirt because he violated the generally understood rule in nightclubs like the Corral that bar-top dancing is restricted to women. Although I had seen men attempt to dance on the bar top previously, they were quickly alerted by bouncers with a tap on the ankle and a hand motion calling them down. Such a warning is usually sufficient, but in this case the patron seemed insistent on dancing with the women. Given that most of the bouncers in the nightclubs are of average size, they typically work in groups to resolve conflicts, as in this case. They are able to dispense with the intoxicated patron and his caravanning group in a matter of seconds.

Patrons' compliance with the bouncers' use of force is due in part to the fact that resistance to being thrown out of the nightclub could result in having to deal with the Northeast police. Most patrons want to avoid being ticketed, fined, or arrested, since these penalties have consequences beyond merely ending a night of fun. Additional consequences may include community service, a ban from the nightlife for a specified period of time, and jail time. The threat of these consequences is heightened with the arrival of the police, and patrons respond accordingly, as indicated by Lori.

LORI: When the police come the fight stops. Like the police don't even have to put hands on anybody. They stop quick.

MAY: So you mean like guys will be fighting and then somebody see the police come up and they'll stop fighting?

LORI: Yeah. But I mean it will be guys fighting and security is already trying to break them up, so it's not like they just mid punch and stop. [We both laugh.] Its kinda like they already been worked down a little bit and then the police come, and they see the badge and they are like, "Okay, it's time to chill out."

Whether the patrons have been engaged in fights, underage drinking, or other unacceptable behavior in the nightlife, once police confront them they rarely resist the officers' directives. Irrespective of their social status— for example as frat boys, athletes, locals, or alternative types—patrons view police authority as the ultimate power in the nightlife and bouncers' authority as an extension of police power. This fact is not lost on the bouncers, several of whom are excited by the opportunity to show their collective group force. Occasionally, they spend their early evening gatherings retelling their exploits to one another before they begin the night's work. For these bouncers, participating in a show of collective force provides an opportunity for group bonding, not only with specific bouncers at a particular nightclub, but also with bouncers working in other nightclubs in the immediate area.[17] As one bouncer indicated, "We all kinda know each other and look out for one another." Irrespective of their individual goals, the bouncers have a collective sense of purpose, and that purpose is maintaining the nightlife as a place to have fun.

Although most of the bouncers who work the nightclubs in downtown Northeast are of average physical stature, there are some who are above average in height and weight. They stand at the nightclub entrance displaying their broad chests and well-defined shoulders and arms as they evaluate patrons seeking access to the nightclubs. Patrons' overall impression of these few bouncers is that they spend a great deal of time working out in the gym. Some patrons have even speculated that these particular bouncers use supplements or steroids to add muscle bulk with the goal of "getting big" or "swole." Rather than demonstrating a laidback demeanor like most bouncers, these "hothead" bouncers are perceived to be confrontational and look for if not create opportunities to use force. For most patrons, such bouncers take their jobs far too seriously in a context like downtown Northeast where little use of force is required and intimidation rarely necessary.

For instance, Austin, a White male who stands at about six-feet-two and 230 pounds, with a well-defined upper body, has developed a reputation as a "hothead" among the patrons. Since his first night as a bouncer at the Corral, he has demonstrated the propensity to use force with patrons who, by most observers' accounts, were compliant with his demands for them to leave the nightclub. His quick-tempered and aggressive responses to situations make speculation of steroid use believable to many patrons, as Austin makes an example of all patrons he escorts through the bar by shoving them into tables, chairs, and other patrons, leaving behind a wake of toppled furniture and drinks. He is aggressive toward any male patron he thinks to be a "troublemaker" or resists his commands. In fact, male patrons in general call Austin a "dick" or a "hothead" for his treatment of people, but both Black and White male patrons note that Austin is particularly aggressive with African American males. As one White male patron stated, "He really gives Black guys a hard time." Whether or not the owner intends for Austin's behavior to represent his sentiments, patrons take this to be the case. Hence, Austin's disposition toward African American men only heightens African Americans' feelings that downtown "is a place for Whites" and that "Whites really don't want us around."

Although patrons are generally respectful of the bouncers' authority, some patrons become disgruntled with a particular bouncer, as in the case of a confrontation between Austin and a group of African American males.

I was standing in front of the Corral when Mike Golden, an athlete, and some friends, all African American, arrived downtown. They were just chilling out front talking to each other. They decided to go into the Corral. I stayed out front observing folks on the street as the group of four African American men made their way into the bar, each showing Austin their identification cards. Mike was the shortest of the group, but all of his friends were thinner than Mike. Since I wasn't inside the Corral I did not see the initial incident. I heard later that Mike and his friends had some drinks and the bartender pushed Mike and then had Austin escort Mike's friend, Rick, out of the club. Rick is about six feet tall with a thin, wiry build. Austin escorted Rick out in usual fashion. I saw him with his arm around Rick's neck from behind, and his other forearm in Rick's lower back. He knocked him against chairs and finally against the wooden patio railing, dislodging the railing from its base. As Austin pushed Rick through the club onto the patio, Mike and his friends followed saying stuff like, "Man, you don't have to push him like that. We're leaving." They all stepped off the patio and stood on the sidewalk in front of the Corral looking disgruntled.

Mike was upset but wanted to just walk it off. Austin returned to his post at the patio entranceway checking IDs, as Mike turned to his friends and said, "Let's just go, man."

"That's fucked up what he did, man," one of Mike's friends said. Mike turned to Rick to calm him down. He could see that Rick was angry about the way he was handled. Rick was still gathering himself from Austin's shove. Mike tried to talk to him but Rick walked back up to the gate a few feet and stood about six feet from the opening yelling at Austin. Mike just stepped back as Rick's other friends step forward, standing a few feet behind Rick.

"You bad up in the club, but bring your ass out here," Rick shouted. Several patrons around the doorway waiting to go in took note. Austin ignored Rick's first comment as he looked over a woman's ID. He waved the woman in and then looked up at Rick and said, "Get the fuck outta here."

"You bad. Just bring your ass out here," Rick shouted. "I'll whip your ass you come out here."

Austin stood up, stepped passed patrons at the patio waiting to enter, and walked right outside the railing onto the sidewalk. Rick took a step back seemingly surprised, but still ready. He put his hands up in boxing position. Austin, seemingly confident in his ability to handle Rick, just took a step forward.

Rick said, "Come on, bitch."

Other patrons who had been standing around chatting turned their attention to the two men who had squared off.

Austin, who was clearly bigger than Rick, took a quick step forward, brought his right hand up, and took a rapid roundhouse swing with massive force. The force of his punch suggested that he wanted to end the fight in one swing. Rick, to my surprise, successfully ducked Austin's punch in a smooth motion. I was certain that Rick would have been floored if Austin's punch had connected. Before I could process this thought, Rick continued lower to the ground and swiftly grabbed both of Austin's ankles and snatched them forward with force greater than one would have expected for Rick's thin build. Austin was surprised as he lost his balance and fell backward landing squarely on his back. When Austin's back hit the ground two of the other men who had been with Mike started kicking Austin all over.

As the crowd moved forward to see Austin taking the kicks, Frank, a White bouncer from the neighboring Figaro's nightclub, rushed to Austin's aid. Frank stepped in and pressed one of Mike's guys aside. Bouncers from the Corral stepped from the patio and pushed people in the crowd back as the police, who were stationed at the corner, quickly pedaled their bikes to the street area outside of the Corral. As Frank pushed the other guys away, and the other bouncers made their way through the crowd, Rick and his friends saw the police on the curb and instantly stopped. Austin rushed to his feet. He was unscathed but red with anger.

"I'm gonna get you. I'm gonna get you," Austin shouted.

Frank pushed Austin back behind the railing and onto the Corral patio, pleading with him to calm down. Once he was behind the railing, two of the Corral bouncers grabbed him and pulled him back into the doorway of the nightclub, while another took Austin's seat working the door at the front of the nightclub.

The crowd murmured as Rick, Mike, and his friends eased away. The police seeing that the situation was under control simply stood near the curb, straddled over their bikes.

Frank walked over to the police and said, "Oh, it was nothing. Just a guy mad that he was thrown out." Frank then walked back toward the front door of Figaro's as the patrons reassembled in line to get into the Corral. The police got on their bikes and rode back to the corner as Mike and his friends started walking up the street. The guys that had gathered near where I stood began talking about the fight. As the crowd dispersed, a White male that had been standing a few feet away from me said, "Shit, I'm glad somebody finally got his ass. He's a dick." The guy's friends laughed.

This particular confrontation was fueled not only by the incident between Rick and Austin, but, I would argue, also by the underlying discontent that some African American males have felt, especially when interacting with Austin, who they say "flexes" or demonstrates his power. For instance, rather than using the language typical of other bouncers enforcing the dress code like "I'm sorry, man, I can't let you in, the owner has a dress code" or "We have a dress code," Austin uses phrases like "I'm not going to let you in. You're violating the dress code." When enforcing the dress code, Austin positions himself as the authority, rather than as a representative of the owner's authority. The result is heightened interpersonal tension between bouncers like Austin and African American males who are disproportionately impacted by the dress code. Although some observers might view such tension, when it occurs, as a singular incident, many African American patrons view the occurrence as consistent with Whites' collective attempts—for example, through the implementation of the cruising ban, dress codes, and the playing of particular genres of music—to limit African American participation in downtown nightlife. As I have suggested elsewhere, such occurrences have a compounding effect, as they are retold to other African Americans and become the basis upon which African Americans build a collective memory of negative racial encounters with Whites.[18] Austin's confrontation with the African American males becomes an additional story to be told among African Americans in support of this collective memory.

As in the incident described previously, Austin has demonstrated a proclivity for using unnecessary force. Not only does he use unnecessary force to escort Rick from the nightclub, but he also violates the taken-for-granted understanding among bouncers that they manage situations within the nightclub and let the police manage situations on the streets. Whether this understanding is linked specifically to a legal mandate or simply common practice, bouncers understand their role to be limited to activity within the nightclub. Hence, Austin's behavior exceeds the bounds of his authority. Fortunately for Austin, Frank is able to intervene. In effect, Frank's actions work in Austin's interest and provide further evidence that bouncers view themselves as sharing a collective sense beyond that established among bouncers within a particular nightclub.

Police rarely become involved in situations within the nightclubs, but instead focus on managing the activities on the street. For most patrons, the mere presence of the police is enough to curtail certain kinds of behavior. Other patrons require engagement from the police. Simple police commands like "Stay on the sidewalk," "Let me see your ID," and "Clear the area" are sufficient to bring patrons into compliance. The authority to arrest patrons in violation of such commands is rarely needed. Still, there are occasional instances in which patrons, especially while intoxicated, become obdurate and question or challenge police authority. These situations are the street equivalent of patrons' "being bounced," but with far greater consequences than simply being escorted from the nightclub. The end result is that a patron may be arrested, as in the case of this incident between the police and a patron.

As I exited the bar, I saw a White man, who looked to be in his late thirties, standing about six-foot-three and weighing 220 pounds. Officer Jack was standing in front of him and pointed in his face. The man shouted something as if to state his case. At that point, Officer Jack, standing at about six-foot-one and 200 pounds, circled around behind the man and pulled out his handcuffs and took the man's right arm behind his back. The man began to twist and flail around trying to escape Officer Jack's grip. Jack quickly moved in tight and tripped the guy. Another officer jumped off his bike and dove into the fray. The guy was strong and continued to struggle with the officers, as one climbed atop his back and drove his knee right between the man's shoulder blades and held it there. The guy continued struggling as Officer Jack worked to get the cuffs on the man's wrists. The officers had the man face down but he wouldn't stop moving. Officer Jack leveled two quick punches to the man's side. A White woman in her thirties, apparently with the guy, winced at the punches and then shouted, "Hey, don't do that. Don't do that."

Officer Jack shouted to her, "Stand back, ma'am. He's resisting us." She took two steps back and Jack punched him a few more times and got the cuffs on him. Even as they were standing him up he was resistant. He seemed to stop resisting when he was on his feet but began shouting, "I'm hurt. I'm hurt. You're going to get sued."

Officer Jack took his hand and rammed it into the man's pocket and pulled out the contents, while the other officer held him by the arm. Officer Jack checked the man's other pockets and looked at the contents and then returned them. He patted the man's legs down and then the two officers walked the man to the car with the woman following behind a few steps. They put him in the car with the woman now pleading. Officer Jack shook his head and then walked around the driver's side and got in. He talked on the radio for a minute and then drove away leaving the woman in the street upset.

Such arrests, although rare, make it clear to the nightlife participants that police are willing to use force when necessary. Still, as demonstrated previously, patrons will engage in physical confrontations like fisticuffs, running the risk of arrests. Occasionally, these fisticuffs spin out of control and involve groups of nightlife participants fighting. These brawls require the intervention of bouncers and sometimes police.

Brawls

The archetypical bar brawl is exemplified in the saloon fights of Western movies wherein the star cowboy is involved in a confrontation with his antagonist. The star throws a punch, hitting the antagonist with such force that he tumbles into a table or a number of other patrons, who then push him back into the fight with the star cowboy. Almost instantaneously a melee erupts. Patrons begin punching and smashing chairs and bottles indiscriminately over one another. Some patrons stand back and watch the fights taking place in all directions, while other patrons push and shove, trying to exit the saloon to safety. These brawls last until there are only a few men standing with the remaining few exiting the saloon as quickly as possible. Although such extended conflicts make for good entertainment, they are not representative of the typical brawls that I have observed occurring in urban nightclubs where there are bouncers, or in some instances armed security, standing out front of the nightclub. In general, these brawls are brief, with bouncers assuming control before the fight can cause the club to close for the evening.

In downtown Northeast, brawls typically begin with a verbal confrontation between two men. As indicated previously, this verbal confrontation may stem from incidental contact. When one patron fails to acknowledge the incident or accept an apology, the verbal confrontation escalates into a physical confrontation with pushing and shoving. Most of the time cooler heads prevail, but in some instances patrons may begin throwing punches. These fisticuffs are heightened when members of each of the conflicting men's caravanning groups join the fight, creating a brawl. These brawls remain self-contained among those patrons in conflict and usually are limited to four to six men, as opposed to the all-out melee depicted in Westerns. As the men from the caravanning groups push, shove, and throw punches at one another, the bouncers and sometimes other patrons intervene quickly. These brawls typically last less than one minute and conclude with the offending patrons being escorted from the nightclub by the bouncers.

Despite the fact that brawls occur infrequently, most patrons view frat boys and athletes as the types of patrons likely to engage in brawls. Perhaps these perceptions are based on the commonplace understanding that fraternity brothers and teammates come to the aid of one another, so that when one brother or athlete becomes involved in a confrontation, they all do. Furthermore, patrons hold the impression that frat boys are predisposed to seek out conflict when they become intoxicated or are "full of liquid courage" and that athletes walk the streets of downtown with an air of self-importance looking for the opportunity to demonstrate their physical prowess. Interestingly, both of these patron types share high social status in the downtown nightlife. Some patrons indicate that such status empowers frat boys and athletes to engage in fighting. For instance, Joe, an African American male, shared these thoughts about athletes during a discussion of fights in downtown: "But the thing about it you know, the people that usually cause the chaos downtown is football players. . . . Most of them, a lot of them, that's out there on that field playing, most of them Black anyway. They are the ones that mostly everybody knows. But when you think of it, they can skate sometimes you know. If they have to you know—if something happens then they'll get banned for a while, but not for too long."

Joe's comments are especially interesting in two related ways. First, like most other patrons who frequent downtown, Joe uses the term "football players" to more specifically reference African American male athletes. So his suggestion that football players are the source of chaos is profound since it implicates African American men as the primary perpetrators of aggressive acts in downtown. Such an assessment is consistent with broader perceptions of African American men as a threat.[19] Furthermore, since many White patrons are unable to make distinctions among anonymous African American men downtown, the football players' behavior becomes a proxy for African American males' behavior more generally. Based on Joe's observations, then, White patrons' general fears of African American males vis-à-vis other patrons follows a logic based on broader media presentations of African Americans as a threat, as well as patrons' own limited observations of African American men's behavior in downtown. Although Joe is attempting to draw a distinction between those African American men who "cause the chaos" and himself, other patrons making quick assessments of caravanning groups of anonymous men fail to make such distinctions.

Second, Joe suggests that football players' status is a distinguishing characteristic that affords these particular African American men the opportunity to avoid serious punishment for fighting. Despite Joe's contention, some scholars suggest that African American athletes actually undergo more surveillance than their White counterparts and are more likely to be prosecuted relative to White athletes. For instance, sociologists Bonnie Berry and Earl Smith argue that African American athletes' experiences with the criminal justice system mirror those of African American males in general. Hence, they are likely to experience racial profiling and bias in a criminal justice system that criminalizes and targets African American men.[20] Assuming for a moment that Joe is correct in his contention that African American athletes can "skate," the privilege of avoiding punishment for engaging in a brawl is limited to a specific subset of African American men, namely those whom "mostly everybody knows," while other African American men in the nightlife receive additional surveillance and scrutiny without the purported benefit of such status.

Interestingly, one characteristic of the brawls occurring in the nightlife is that they typically occur among members who share similar racial status, but differ in some other social status. For instance, frat boys, generally recognized as White men, will engage in fisticuffs with other White male college students or locals, while athlete types, generally recognized as African American men, will engage in fisticuffs with Black college students or locals. These fisticuffs may escalate into brawls. The fact that they occur among patrons sharing similar racial status is based on the very specific use patterns of racial groups within the nightlife. For instance, patrons from different racial backgrounds frequently share the public streets, but only in rare instances do they share the same nightclub space in significant numbers. Recall that nightclub owners and managers help to facilitate these specific use patterns through the implementation of dress codes and the type of music they play. Nightclubs that play hip-hop music tend to draw diverse groups of African Americans who share an affinity with urban culture, while those nightclubs that play country music tend to attract diverse groups of White patrons who have an affinity for southern culture. Hence, if fisticuffs and brawls do arise in these contexts, they are likely to be among members of the same racial group.

Although brawls are rare and typically occur between caravanning groups of the same racial background, there are instances in which Blacks and Whites do engage in brawls with one another. In fact, the Black and White nightlife participants in such brawls seem to demonstrate greater levels of hostility and aggressiveness toward one another than do participants in brawls with other patrons who share similar racial backgrounds. It is as if the confrontation reflects hostilities beyond those arising from the initial incident. Perhaps these hostilities are grounded in African American patrons' feelings of being excluded or White patrons' feelings that their social space is being encroached. Irrespective of the source of increased hostility, it is clear that these brawls intensify quickly and require the intervention of both bouncers and police officers. For instance, in the following incident involving football players, all of whom were African American, several patrons became involved in a melee that apparently started with a remark made to a football player by a White male. In the following narrative I describe the events from my vantage point outside of the nightclub. I later garnered information from a patron who was inside the nightclub at the time the brawl began. This particular incident was also reported in the local news, although with fewer details.

It was about 1:45 a.m. and I was standing outside on the corner of Reginald and Stuckey when suddenly I saw the police rushing into the Corral. I turned my attention there. I started moving closer. As I moved closer, guys were rushing out of the bar. It seemed like an endless chain of Black patrons pouring out of the Corral, which was unusual. As I got closer, I recognized a few of the Black football players just walking out of the bar. From where I was standing I could see that there was a big fight on the patio of the Corral and just inside the doorway there was more going on. It was hard to tell exactly who was fighting but I saw groups of various Black men trying to get back into the nightclub. The police stood outside spraying pepper spray on the crowd of patrons who were on the patio pushing and shoving. As soon as the pepper spray hit, the crowd began to disperse quickly. The police began grabbing patrons who continued to demonstrate aggressive behavior. They were holding one Black male. It was Dontonio Wilson, a tall and muscular football player, standing at about six-foot-two. His dreadlocks flopped across his dark-skinned face as he kept shouting and trying to get toward the entrance. The police officer placed Wilson in handcuffs as he struggled. I stepped back from the scene as the pepper spray began to drift out from the patio.

The crowd continued to pour out of the Corral as the police stood shouting directives. The crowd coming from out of the club seemed to have calmed down considerably. There were more White patrons than Black patrons exiting at this point. A few minutes passed and I received a phone call from Perceval, who had been inside the nightclub. I had already overheard patrons say that a few football players had been fighting "White guys," but Perceval gave a few more details.

"May, the football players were fighting. It just broke out when this White dude said something to X [Xavier] and X just punched him. They say he called X a nigga. People started throwing punches all over. White dudes started swinging at the football players and they all started punching. The bouncers tried to get in there, but they couldn't really get it under control. It was like fifteen people fighting."

"I know I saw the police rushing to the entrance," I said. "That's when I knew the bouncers couldn't get it under control. I'm standing right outside. I'll see you when you get outside." We hung up.

I waited for Perceval to file out of the bar as the police stood out front keeping the peace. This was a big football recruitment weekend and they had about three hundred high school football players visiting the school. The Corral was packed since it is one of the few places that play hip-hop music and Blacks go. I saw a lot of Black patrons that I didn't recognize. I'm guessing they were football recruits. As people continued to file out I noticed that the police now had Wilson and another Black football player in handcuffs.

I finally saw Perceval. He walked out and said, "I don't know what that dude said to X, but X just started punching the shit out of him. Then all the other football players just started hitting any White boy they could see. When that happened I jumped on the bar so I could see. It was wild, man. When people started smelling pepper spray they started trying to get out the club."

As the crowd continued to file out, Winston, a Black college student that I knew, walked past talking to his friend. He had been inside the Corral and said to his friend, also a Black male, "Man, niggas always find a way to fuck shit up."

"I know that's right," his friend responded.

I surveyed the area a little longer and then stepped out into the street. I looked inside the police van and saw Victor Patterson, another football player, in the back of the van in handcuffs. The police had pretty much cleared the crowd out. Patrons from the other nightclubs were also coming out since it was closing time.

I was unable to verify whether the initial exchange between the football player and the White male involved racial epithets. The football players, probably at the urging of their coach, generally avoided the nightlife scene for the last few weeks that school was in session. When they were asked about the incident they chose not to discuss it. The police also were unable to ascertain the source of the initial conflict. Still, conversations among Black patrons after the brawl suggested that the White male patron had used a pejorative term referring to African Americans, and this is what provoked X to fight.[21] X was never questioned by the police, but for the next several weekends rumors among African American patrons generally emphasized that "X punched the shit out of that White dude," while White patrons emphasized that the "football players were causing trouble." This event resonated with many African Americans, because they viewed the White male patron's purported remark as representative of Whites' general attitudes toward them.

The brawl and the subsequent discussions seem to capture the underlying tension existing between not only African Americans and Whites vying for use of the public and semipublic space of downtown, but also the tension existing among African Americans from varying social class backgrounds. For instance, Winston, a middle-class African American college student and member of a Black fraternity, commented, "Niggas always find a way to fuck shit up." Implicitly, Winston draws a distinction between himself as a middle-class African American and the African American football players and locals whom many patrons perceive to be from lower-class communities. His comments characterize behavior, like fighting in a club or on the streets, as associated with poor urban Blacks or "niggas." Although the use of this term "nigga" is a hotly debated topic because of its history as a pejorative term for Blacks, some African Americans, particularly those from predominantly Black urban communities, embrace the term.[22] African Americans from all walks of life may also use the term as a means of claiming an "authentic" Black identity or as a term of endearment for close associates. Irrespective of the broader debates about the use of this word, the propriety of its usage remains a matter of context and is negotiated between the user and the audience. In this particular context, Winston uses the term derisively to identify patrons who engage in negative behavior, specifically fighting.

Winston conveys a sense of frustration, particularly with African American participants whose behavior limits his own opportunity to "have fun." His statement indicates not only frustration for having the night's activities ended, but also the added frustration that the football players' behavior, because they are African American, will be taken as representative of Black patrons' behavior more broadly, and hence African Americans will receive even greater scrutiny from bouncers and police. Furthermore, because of the conflict, nightclub owners and managers will implement additional strategies, albeit subtle, to make the nightclubs less welcoming to African Americans. Indeed, based upon my observations, Winston's frustration is warranted. After such rare events as this brawl, police presence increases and African Americans generally complain about negative treatment at nightclubs whether it is slow bar service or a change in music from hip-hop to country when they arrive.

African American college students find this treatment particularly problematic, perhaps because they consider themselves generally compliant with nightclub owners' expectations regarding dress codes and overall nightclub behavior. They feel as though they should be able to count on their middle-class status to distinguish them from lower-class African American patrons, but they are in fact being made to suffer the consequences for the actions of their lower-class kindred. In short, they are frustrated that their middle-class status does not permit them to escape the stigma of race. They are experiencing what Anderson refers to as a "nigger moment"—a situation in which middle-class Black people experience a dramatic failure of White people to treat them with the respect they have come to expect given their class status.[23]

Brawls like the one discussed here reveal interesting tensions across a number of racial, class, and cultural boundaries, and further reveal the ways in which different types of patrons perceive events based upon their social location within the nightlife. This is a point I return to explicitly in chapter 7.

Conclusion

Crowded streets and nightclubs, consumption of alcohol, and movement from bar to bar in caravanning groups mean that patrons are likely to have incidental contact with one another. This contact is the impetus for verbal confrontations between two patrons who then usually put forth the effort to deescalate the situation by offering acts of civility including simple phrases like "excuse me." The prospect of negotiating an encounter with bouncers or the police provides patrons further incentive to just "walk away." Although men and women engage in verbal confrontations, men are more likely to escalate verbal confrontations into fisticuffs, with a sense that their masculinity has been challenged. These fisticuffs rarely draw members of each man's caravanning group, but when brawls do occur, they usually occur among patrons who share similar racial status, albeit differing social statuses like frat boy, college student, or local.

Still, there are brawls across racial lines, and these brawls help to reveal the underlying tension among different groups. For instance, as these occasional brawls manifest across racial boundaries, some African Americans share a collective sense that Whites do not want them to participate in the nightlife. For these African Americans, the brawl itself is a representation of the hostility with which they are met within the nightlife more generally, especially when Whites have used or are purported to have used racial epithets during the physical confrontations. African Americans' collective sense that they are less than welcome is fostered under conditions of integrated segregation whereby caravanning groups, seeking to interact with others like themselves, exclude groups that are not like themselves, even when these groups stand in close physical proximity to one another. Although this exclusion—which may be intentional or unintentional—happens to a number of groups within the context of downtown nightlife, it is most clearly apparent among racial groups, particularly Whites and Blacks.

Brawls across racial boundaries may help to reinforce the boundaries among broader social groups in urban nightlife based upon how onlookers and participants alike interpret them, but these encounters are often defined based on nightlife participants' readings of what is implicitly communicated. In the next chapter I explore the meanings given to interactions when issues of race are explicitly communicated.

6

When Race
Is Explicit

● ● ● ● ● ● ● ● ● ● ● ● ●

Like other Americans, urban nightlife participants have a well-established
practice of using physical characteristics like skin color to assign others to
racial categories like White, Black, Asian, or Hispanic. The tendency to
identify others by physical characteristics is so engrained that persons of
mixed ancestry find it difficult to claim identities other than those associated with their skin color—for instance, consider the difficulty that professional golfer Tiger Woods has experienced around his racial/ethnic
identity. Despite the complexity of biological backgrounds, humans continue to rely upon simple racial classifications.[1] Such simple classifications
are the basis upon which nightlife participants manage interactions across,
and within caravanning groups. The fact that race plays a central role in
negotiating interactions in urban nightlife raises interesting questions: Do
nightlife participants explicitly talk about race on the streets, and in the
nightclubs in urban nightlife? If so, what is the nature of this race talk?

Nightlife participants rarely explicitly talk about race, despite their
common practice of assigning individuals to racial groups. When they do
converse about race explicitly, their discussions are usually with friends
or associates within their caravanning group. Although these conversations are rare they are important to examine, given the ways in which race

surfaces as a consideration in other aspects of urban nightlife—for example, in dress code enforcement and police surveillance. In this chapter, I turn my attention to interactions in which I observed patrons' explicit race talk, wherein racial difference, sameness, or hostility was expressly communicated. I focus on race talk as it occurs in situ among members of caravanning groups as well as across social boundaries. I also consider the ways in which my own identity as an African American might have influenced the kinds of conversations about race to which I was privy. This reflexive examination highlights the significance of race in urban nightlife. I conclude by suggesting ways in which these exchanges among nightlife participants support integrated segregation by reinforcing social boundaries among groups.

Race Talk and Civility

Nightlife participants are often in conflict with one another for use of the streets and nightclubs in downtown Northeast. This conflict manifests in boundary enforcement between caravanning groups, but because of enforcement by multiple caravanning groups at the same time throughout downtown, the collective effect creates boundary enforcement among broader social groups. For instance, caravanning groups of local males may come into conflict with caravanning groups of frat boys as the local males attempt to carve out a space of their own within downtown Northeast. Stories like this may be playing out throughout the nightlife as members in each of these groups use indicators of social class and culture, like styles of dress, to determine whom they should engage or avoid. Hence, unlike Anderson's cosmopolitan canopy wherein diverse groups are interacting with civility, members of caravanning groups of different identities may engage one another in conflict that simply reinforces existing boundaries among the groups.[2]

Despite the ongoing conflict among groups within the nightlife, civility does occur in downtown Northeast. Among the participants in downtown, common civility occurring across racial boundaries might include patrons exchanging passing greetings, sharing an occasional drunken high five with someone in another caravanning group, apologizing for incidental contact, or engaging in brief conversations at the bar as they wait to purchase alcohol. During my time in urban nightlife, I observed, experienced, and shared in these kinds of acts of civility on various occasions. One experience I had stands out as particularly interesting.

I decided to visit downtown at 9:00 p.m. rather than my usual arrival time of about 10:00 p.m. Most of the other nightclubs were occupied by a few patrons, but Figaro's bar was hosting its weekly Thursday, Friday, and Saturday night "Turn It Up Hour" with reduced drink prices from 9:00 p.m. to 11:00 p.m. . . . I stood talking with Misty and Cheryl, two White women.

The crowd continued to swell as "Turn It Up Hour" was nearing its end. At about 10:45 p.m. I decided to make my way to the bar to purchase a drink before the drinks became regular priced. . . .

There were about twelve African Americans scattered throughout the bar of mostly White patrons. Lots of folks seemed to be tipsy or getting there. There was an overall festive atmosphere as hip-hop music blared out in the background.

I continued to the bar. There were patrons crammed all the away around the bar about two rows deep. I was able to press my way up close and stood behind a short, White woman with blonde hair waiting to order a drink. She was wearing a white top and leaned with her elbows on the bar as the bartenders were trying to handle the rush of people. It seemed that everyone had the same idea of getting a drink before eleven. After the woman in front of me got her drink she turned around and squeezed between myself and other patrons, smiling as she passed. I replaced her and stood next to a White man who had just fought for a space at the bar himself. He stood about six feet tall and wore a white Big South cap frayed on the brim. He glanced at me once I moved in, then turned his attention back to the bartender who was standing closest to us taking drink orders.

As the crowd behind us pressed us closer to the bar and the bartenders were scrambling, the White guy turned to me and said, "Man, it's crazy in here."

"Yeah. I'm just trying to get me a drink before the prices go up."

"Me too. I wish they'd hurry up," he said as he turned his attention back to the bartender who was moving closer to our end of the bar. Before the bartender could make it to us, a woman a few feet away stopped him. She had blonde hair and was wearing a blue, sleeveless tank top. She seemed tall, but it was hard to tell because she was leaned on the bar with her breast noticeably "placed" on the bar top. The guy in the cap turned back around and looked at me and we both smiled.

"You can't blame him, can you?" he said.

"Naw," I said in agreement.

"She knows how to use those to get attention," he added.

We both laughed. He then turned his attention back to the bartender. When the bartender looked up, the guy wearing the cap made eye contact with him.

"Whatcha having?" the bartender shouted over the music.

"Two Blue Motherfuckers," the man shouted back.

The bartender turned and busied himself making the drinks as the man intently watched. I wasn't sure if I had actually heard the name of the drink right. After about thirty seconds and many splashes of alcohol on the bar, the bartender pounded two drinks down and the man paid the bartender. I looked down at the glasses that were filled with a bluish, transparent, concoction and then back to the man.

"What is that drink called?" I asked the man.

"Blue Motherfucker," he responded.

"What? That's a crazy name. What does it taste like?" I asked as I smiled.

"It's good. It's the shit that will get you fucked up and it's only a dollar."

"It looks like it will," I said as I laughed.

He picked up one of the glasses from the bar, moved the straw to the side, and began easing it up toward my mouth and said, "Taste it."

I lifted my right hand and blurted out, "No." I paused for a moment staring at the glass before me.

"It looks good," I said with a smile. "I'ma just get one."

"They're good. These Blue Motherfuckers will get you fucked up," he said with a laugh. He lifted the other glass and turned and moved through the crowd.

When patrons share close physical proximity with one another an opportunity is created for them to have at least passing interaction. As Anderson demonstrates, even people from diverse backgrounds who would not ordinarily engage one another can be drawn into conversation in such contexts.[3] Simmel identifies this kind of interaction among strangers as *sociability*, wherein participants emphasize superficial aspects of everyday life to achieve smooth interchanges. Accordingly, strangers in interaction renounce "both the objective and the purely personal features of the intensity and extensiveness of life in order to bring about among themselves a pure interaction, free of any disturbing material accent."[4] Strangers engaged in sociability in downtown Northeast draw on shared themes of nightlife like the consumption of alcohol or the pursuit of members of the opposite sex to facilitate conversation. Since patrons adhere to topical discussions that the vast majority of nightlife participants are presumed to know, it is likely that their attempts at sociability will be successful even across racial boundaries.

Although some patrons may find nightlife topics about alcohol consumption or pursuit of members of the opposite sex to be offensive, few indicate this in their conversations with strangers. They simply endure the brief interactions with hope that the offending patron will soon depart. Hence, I argue that few meaningful conversations occur across racial boundaries in urban nightlife since patrons are generally preoccupied with upholding the social order, including the ideal of sharing in common civility. Given this, nightlife participants are rarely willing to share personal opinions that might prove disruptive to the flow of nightlife activities. For instance, I speculate that if I had contended with the White male that his suggestion regarding the woman's attempt to get the bartender's attention by "placing" her breast on the bar top was offensive because it objectified women, I might have moved our interchange from a polite passing conversation to an involved exchange of hostile words.[5] Furthermore, other patrons are likely to have taken my challenge as a violation of the collectively shared goal of having fun in urban nightlife.

Like the urban dwellers in Anderson's study, nightlife participants recognize greetings, apologies for social mishaps, and deference to others' use of a particular space as important acts of civility. When patrons fail to demonstrate civility, verbal or physical confrontations like those outlined in the previous chapter might occur. Although patrons have established responses for acts they view as falling short of the standard of civility, it is unclear how they respond to overtures that seemingly go beyond civility, perhaps because so few such invitations occur in urban nightlife. Furthermore, since civility is not inherent to a particular physical space but rather socially defined, participants' evaluations of acts of civility are complicated by their personal backgrounds.

For instance, in the interchange at the bar I was surprised by the man's offer to taste his drink because I had learned growing up that such an offer was to be made only to those with whom one had an intimate relationship, particularly a familial relationship. Thus, his overture seemed to move beyond civility, and I was immediately confronted with a question: why would a stranger make such an intimate offer to another stranger? Setting aside for a moment the possible issues presented by our racial backgrounds, there are several potential explanations for his overture. Perhaps the man was intoxicated and thus less careful about with whom he shared drinks, yet his general comportment did not indicate that he was intoxicated. He may have wanted to proposition me using the taste of his drink as a lead in action, but his prior acknowledgment of the woman at the bar seemed to affirm his heterosexuality, and the nightclub itself was not characterized by open exchanges between homosexual men. He may have simply wanted to share the taste of a Blue Motherfucker with someone who had not had what he deemed to be an enjoyable drink. Or perhaps, unlike me, he had grown up in a community in which it was normal to share food or drink with someone who made a request no matter the relationship. Irrespective of his personal motivations for sharing the drink, I perceived his overture to be beyond common civility because of my own upbringing.

My belief that the man's actions moved beyond civility was complicated further by our racial difference. Although I had witnessed White and Black nightlife participants share in acts of civility, engage in interracial interactions, and even occasionally caravan together, I had also observed that the prevailing interaction patterns in urban nightlife were characterized by integrated segregation. Hence, I found the man's overture contradictory to the established patterns of interactions between Whites and Blacks. I was left wondering, what would compel someone to break this established interaction order? As I have demonstrated in previous chapters, the answer to such a question is clear when Black men pursue White women or White sports fans pursue the attention of Black athletes. It is difficult, however, to ascertain the man's goals in this instance. Although my evaluation of the man's conduct is partly based on my own upbringing, I suspect that given the established interaction patterns among nightlife participants, had other Black or White patrons had this experience they would have also viewed the man's overture as a questionable act—if for no other reason than the potential health risks related to drinking after a stranger. It is the shared understanding of the potential complexities of interactions like this one that generally dissuades strangers from engaging one another in exchanges that go beyond common civility.

In summary, when diverse groups of nightlife participants share close physical proximity, they are likely to engage in common civility. Yet the perfunctory nature of conversations characterized by civility suggests that nightlife participants are unlikely to have discussions that alter relations between diverse groups in any substantial way. Furthermore, if and when explicit conversations about sensitive topics like race do occur, they typically occur among nightlife participants who share the same racial background and who participate in the same caravanning groups. This observation is consistent with the insights uncovered by the sociologists Leslie Picca and Joe Feagin, who demonstrate the ways in which White students have moved their racist commentary from the front stage or the public arena to the backstage or the private arena.[6] In their study, Picca and Feagin analyze 626 journal entries documenting racial events that were written by White college students at twenty-eight colleges in the United States. They found that while students are civil in their discourse about race publicly, they are more likely to convey racist attitudes privately. In addition, not only did students make racist comments, but also even those students who disagreed with such comments tolerated them from friends and family members.

Similarly, in a previous work I demonstrate how African American men within a racially homogeneous tavern use the tavern as a backstage and freely express their views regarding race.[7] Given these observations, it makes sense that nightlife participants would also confine their explicit discussions of race to conversations with members of their caravanning group. The backstage, in the nightlife context, is not necessarily a private room in a distant location or some homogeneous gathering place, but rather may also be created by acts of discretion like whispering in public places. Although these kinds of conversations are rare, it remains possible to observe backstage interactions where people talk about race explicitly in the public space. I now turn to an examination of instances in which such race talk was explicit.

Race Talk and Caravanning Groups

I begin this discussion of conversations in which race is explicit with the acknowledgment that although I was able to gain access to both White and Black participants on the streets of downtown Northeast, I was rarely privy to explicit comments regarding race made by Whites. Perhaps this is because both Whites whom I knew personally and those who were strangers to me were hesitant to talk about race in my presence or the presence of other African Americans. In other words, they may have been practicing common civility by avoiding talk about race. It might also be the case that explicit discussions of race were not important considerations for those nightlife participants whom I encountered. Yet based on the few interactions among Whites in which I observed that race was an explicit topic, and the other behaviors that Whites exhibited around issues of race, it was clear that some White nightlife participants had strong opinions regarding race.

Although few White participants tended to have conversations explicitly referencing race, the African Americans I encountered seemed more willing to engage in such conversations both with me and with other African Americans. Perhaps these participants were willing to share racial commentary as a means of bonding with one another within a predominately White setting. Perhaps they were attempting to offend White nightlife participants who might overhear their racial remarks. Or perhaps they were engaging in race talk because race is simply a salient topic of discussion among African Americans. It is difficult to know the specific reasons why they engaged in race talk, but I am confident, based upon my observations of African Americans in other contexts, that my racial identity was an important consideration for those African Americans who demonstrated a willingness to share explicit race talk with me or with others in my presence.[8] Despite the possibility that these conversations may have been intensified by my presence, I believe they reveal an interesting aspect of how nightlife participants negotiate race as they go about having fun in the nightlife, especially with members of their caravanning groups.

In previous chapters, I have shown how caravanning groups set the terms of interaction in urban nightlife. For instance, the caravanning group influences whether one of its members perceives someone of the opposite sex as desirable, guides the movement patterns of participants through the downtown area, and is the means by which broader social boundaries of integrated segregation are enforced. Caravanning groups also provide an immediate context for people who usually know one another intimately to converse about a number of personal or sensitive topics like race. Since members of a caravanning group typically have preexisting relationships they are likely to share similar sensibilities, backgrounds, and opinions with other members of the group. Hence, when nightlife participants engage in explicit race talk wherein racial difference, sameness, or hostility is communicated, they are unlikely to be questioned by other members of the caravanning group. In fact, caravanning group members might support or encourage this kind of talk.

Most race talk includes singular statements made in passing about a racial group like jokes that pejoratively emphasize racial difference or stereotypical comments about a group's nightclub behavior. Rarely does race talk include serious and engaged discussions about racial problems, not even among those Black males who attribute racial discrimination to nightclub owners who have implemented dress codes. Rather race talk generally consists of pithy comments made in jest and shared among members in a caravanning group as they go about having fun. These comments tend to take on little significance among the members of the caravanning group, yet outsiders who hear explicit racial comments may be surprised, disturbed, and offended. One example of these fleeting kinds of comments occurred one evening during my visit to Gotham's—a nightclub where participants' conversations can be heard just above the sound of the soft background music.

There were only about twenty people sitting in Gotham's as I sat at the bar alternating my gaze between the football game on television and the rest of the nightclub. A few groups of men and women sat talking to one another on the lounge chairs at the front of the nightclub, while a few more groups were standing in various places talking. I was sitting between two White males who both seemed to be intently watching the football game. The man to my left was wearing a blue button-down shirt and the one on my right was wearing a yellow polo shirt. The guy to my left started talking on his phone and I overheard him say, "Yeah, I'm at Gotham's. Come meet me here."

. . . A few minutes later a White male came through the front door of Gotham's. I watched from my periphery view as the man who had entered walked toward the bar looking at each man sitting on the barstools. He spotted his friend sitting right behind me to my left and walked up to him. I lost sight of him but I could still hear their exchange as they stood directly behind me.

"What's up, man?" said the man sitting at the bar.

"What's up, man?" Responded the guy who had entered. They gripped hands as I turned my attention back to the football game.

"Man. It's hot as a nigger's balls outside."

"Yeah, it's hot as fuck out there," they both laughed and continued into their conversation.

"I got sweaty just walking from the car. . . ."

As they continued to talk I was immediately lost in thought as I wondered to myself if they had noticed that they were sitting next to the only African American in the bar. They had shared a greeting of familiarity with one another as one man casually makes reference to African Americans using the pejorative term "nigger." Although only one man makes the comment, the other man seems complicit in the use of this term. Given the overall emphasis on civility in the nightlife and my presence in the bar and close proximity to the men in conversation, their exchange raises an interesting question: Why would the men use the term "nigger" on the "front stage" in my presence? I suggest three possible explanations for the men's behavior.

First, the man making the actual statement might well have used the term freely because he was unaware of my presence in the nightclub. This seems unlikely given his initial examination of each man sitting at the bar stool before finally resting his eyes on his friend, sitting directly behind me. If my presence mattered for the men's interaction, it seems likely that his friend might have also signaled to him that I was present. Although I was unable to observe a possible nonverbal cue, the flow of their conversation suggests no such cue was conveyed. Second, the men might have been aware of my presence but chose to act with a sense of entitlement to Gotham's. In other words, they may have simply chosen to ignore the rules of common civility characteristic of urban nightlife and assumed that Gotham's was a space in which they were not expected to respectfully recognize the presence of African Americans. Yet on my previous visits to Gotham's I found civility to be the hallmark of the nightclub staff and other patrons, so these men's incivility or disregard for my presence rests with them and not the social atmosphere cultivated by nightclub staff. Third, perhaps the men may have been implicitly directing the comments toward me. They may have been attempting to insult me or to provoke me to engage in a verbal or physical confrontation. Yet given that they did not address me directly or provide additional racial comments, it is doubtful that they were attempting to engage in a confrontation. Thus, based on my assessment, I conclude that the men were simply using language they share with one another in more intimate settings, paying little regard to my presence. In this instance, I happened to be privy to this backstage behavior.

More troubling than the men's use of a pejorative term in this context is the imagery that the phrase "hotter than a nigger's balls" calls to mind. Although I did not question the men regarding the meaning of the phrase—an act itself that would have violated an implicit code of civility—I suggest that many nightlife participants hearing the phrase would have identified it as an unfavorable reference to African Americans. I found the phrase problematic because it brought to mind two references. First, "hot" symbolically references an image of hypersexualized African American men who are in persistent pursuit of women to meet their sexual desires.[9] Second, it calls to mind the imagery of African American men who were the victims of lynching at the hands of White vigilantes who commonly practiced torching them while they remained alive.[10] Both images are grounded in historical perceptions of

African Americans as beastlike, yet I suggest that the nightlife participants do not recognize the historical significance of their passing phrase. In fact, I argue that it is the participants' general inattentiveness to specific historical references that helps to support ongoing racial tension—a point that I expand upon in the next chapter. Indeed, nightlife participants understand that words like "nigger" are pejorative, but this understanding is superficial. Their general lack of knowledge regarding historical race relations supports contemporary racial tension that has become grounded in simple differences like skin color.

Passing comments like the one shared by the two men in Gotham's represent the most frequent kind of exchanges in which race talk is explicit. Since I had the opportunity to caravan with different groups ranging from those composed primarily of all White members to those composed of only African Americans, I also had the opportunity to observe how these groups managed passing comments explicitly about race. One evening I traveled the streets and nightclub with Keith and Brad, two White men and former BSU students whom I knew for several years from playing basketball at a local recreation center.[11] Our experience proved to be an interesting example of how nightlife participants might navigate explicit race talk on the downtown streets.

I met Keith and Brad at their apartment. They were drinking with three of their friends Chris, Stephen, and Sarah. . . . Keith rode with me and Brad rode with Chris. When we arrived at the parking garage on Farrell Street it was almost full and it was only about 11:50 p.m. The crowd was abuzz downtown. . . . Keith and I met Brad and the others at the parking deck stairwell and we all walked into downtown on the eastside of Reginald Street. We were nearing Stuckey Street where there were groups of folks all over the area.

As we walked closer to the corner there were three White men leaning against the wall of Kilpatrick's talking and watching people walk pass. The first one I could see was a tall thin guy, wearing a yellow polo shirt and blue jeans. The guy in the middle was shorter than the first guy and he was wearing a blue-and-white polo shirt, blue jeans, and a white baseball cap. The last guy was shorter and he wore a white shirt, but I didn't see what else he was wearing because I noticed that all three of the men were looking at Sarah who was walking a few steps in front of me and Keith. I was nearest to the curb and Keith walked on the inside next to the building. Brad was walking right behind me, and Stephen and Chris were next to him.

The men on the wall took glances back and forth between Sarah and us. Sarah was wearing a white sleeveless, low-cut blouse that accented her full chest with her blonde hair hanging down. She wore blue jeans and sandals. Although she was modestly dressed compared to the many other women downtown, she was clearly attractive to the three men. They seemed to be assessing her relationship to us. She walked passed them first and then as Keith and I walked passed, the man in the blue-and-white shirt said in an audible tone, "And they are even hanging out with niggers now."

When I heard the statement I played deaf, pretending as though I did not hear it. As Keith and I got about five steps away I glanced at him and he acknowledged awareness of the statement with his familiar smirk.

As Brad, Stephen, and Chris finished passing the three guys talking, Brad came up alongside of the curb and walked in front of Keith and me while we were still moving and said to Keith, "Did you hear what they said? That guy called Reuben a nigger."

Keith and I looked at one another in silence because we both knew what was coming next.

"Man, that's crazy," Brad added. "They can't say that shit. Let's go back there and kick their fucking asses."

"Calm down," Keith said.

"Man, it's not even worth it," I added.

"That's bullshit," Brad said. "They can't say that racist shit."

"We came to have fun. Fuck those guys," Keith said.

Brad turned to Stephen and Chris who signaled their agreement with us by saying nothing. Brad was frustrated but began to calm down as Keith said, "Where are we going?"

"We could go to Tranquility," I said.

"Yeah, they have good drinks there," Keith added.

We started for Tranquility on Stuckey Street. . . .

We got to Tranquility and purchased our drinks. Brad stood talking to Stephen, Chris, and Sarah as Keith stepped over to me. He started talking to me in a low voice so that Brad couldn't hear.

"Brad is crazy," Keith said. We both laughed.

"I know," I said. "He always wants to fight when he's been drinking."

"Yeah man," Keith acknowledged. "I didn't come down here for that. I came to look at the girls and drink." We both laughed.

"Yeah. I knew you had heard what that guy said when I saw the look on your face."

"I know. I just ignored that dude," Keith added.

"Brad wanted to fight," I said. "But if I fought every time I heard that word I wouldn't have time for anything else." Keith and I both laughed.

In downtown Northeast caravanning groups rarely consist of members from different racial backgrounds. When they do, the typical groups are predominantly White with just one or two African Americans. Perhaps this is due in part to the fact that racially mixed groups such as these might find it difficult to negotiate the underlying and sometimes explicit racial tension in urban nightlife. Given that caravanning groups are typically established through preexisting networks from other contexts like school, work, or recreational settings, it is likely that the Whites and African Americans caravanning together are well acquainted. Hence, one characteristic that I observed among those members of predominately White caravanning groups that include an African American is the other group members' sensitivity to racial issues when they arise.

For instance, both Keith and Brad demonstrate responses that acknowledge the potentially offensive nature of the other nightlife participant's comment. Keith conveyed sensitivity to the offensive statement through his facial expression. I easily apprehended Keith's expression since Keith and I had come to know one another well. Not only had we competed in basketball at the recreation center, but also we had participated as teammates at organized basketball tournaments and as camp counselors for sports camps. I had seen Keith's particular facial expression when we were together on other occasions. He usually kept quiet when people made comments that he found personally disturbing. When I asked him why he did not say anything on these occasions, he would simply say, "Like my mother always says, if you can't say anything nice, then don't say anything at all." Given my relationship with Keith, I read his smirk as disagreement with the statements made by the other nightlife participant.

Brad's response was more demonstrative than Keith's. His demand that we confront the other nightlife participant is based upon three factors grounded in group dynamics and his personal proclivities. First, as demonstrated in previous chapters, caravanning group members take as their responsibility the support and protection of other members irrespective of the gender or racial composition of the group. Hence there is little surprise that Brad responds to the comments made by the other nightlife participant. He is simply responding in the way that other members of his caravanning group would expect. Second, over the course of my study I found that few African Americans were willing to caravan with Whites as they drank alcohol, fearing that in their uninhibited state Whites would make racially insensitive comments. As one African American patron stated, "Man, White guys will get drunk and fuck around and call you a nigga or something like that. That's why I don't hang out with them." Those African

Americans who did caravan with Whites knew them well and were confident that they would at least recognize the offensive nature of such racial comments. Further still, some African Americans feel that Whites can become too preoccupied with confronting other Whites about racial comments that they themselves choose to ignore. Indeed, given the rarity of physical confrontations between Whites and Blacks around specific issues of race, it is likely that most nightlife participants simply ignore the passing comments in much the same way that Keith and I had.[12] Third, Brad's insistence that we confront the three patrons is based upon his tendency to become aggressive when intoxicated. Keith and I shared this understanding of Brad's typical "drunk behavior" and subverted it by refocusing our group's attention on "having fun." No doubt this is a strategy used among a number of caravanning groups who might have a member with the proclivity to seek out physical confrontations.

A final point about the interchange is that the White patron makes his comment in a very matter-of-fact way. It is this kind of casual statement that affirms for many African Americans that downtown is indeed a White space. According to Moore, these spaces are grounded in historical White racial exclusion of people of color and support racism in tacit and relatively invisible ways.[13] Within the context of downtown Northeast, patrons' passing comments support a space where Whites can feel comfortable and African Americans feel uncomfortable—undergirded by the sense that African Americans do not belong. This is a point easily apprehended by many African Americans who choose not to go downtown. Furthermore, comments like this also help to reinforce social boundaries between Whites and Blacks as they caravan through the streets, such that instead of stopping to engage individuals who have made a racially offensive remark, most nightlife participants simply continue moving in their segregated group to their desired location. This kind of movement undergirds integrated segregation in urban nightlife. Since patrons do not typically stop to provide challenges when racial comments are heard, this kind of behavior likely will endure as a characteristic of urban nightlife.

Race Talk among African Americans

The feeling among African Americans that downtown is a White space makes possible a sense of group solidarity or at least an acknowledgment of their collective otherness.[14] This feeling of otherness—a recognition of racial difference from the majority of nightlife participants and the social limitations stemming from that difference—may manifest in occasional interchanges in which African Americans acknowledge a social connectedness to one another with passing comments or jokes that reference race. Given this feeling of otherness, some African Americans, even strangers, take for granted that it is permissible for them to interact with one another in the nightlife about race. For instance, the following exchange occurred in Nap's, a nightclub with a reputation for attracting mostly frat boys.

I stood in line for the restroom. There had been a few White guys standing in front of me, each of whom had entered the restroom as another one came out. As I stood at the door next in line, a Black male standing behind me tapped me on the shoulder. He was brown skinned, a little taller than me, and was wearing a blue denim outfit. When I turned around he said in a high-pitched voice characteristic of Dave Chappelle—a Black comedian who frequently played the role of Whites on his sketch comedy show—"Hey buddy, you have to get to the end of the line."[15]

I looked at him and then laughed off his comment.

"You have to move," he continued, "us White folks gotta piss."

We both laughed as he stepped around me and went for the door adding in a tenor like voice, "I'm just kidding."

He proceeded to go through the restroom door as a White male left. I followed right behind him. When I went inside the restroom I was surprised to see that there were few patrons actually using the restroom and neither of us had to wait.

Beyond his obvious attempt to cut the restroom line, the Black male's initial comment acknowledges our otherness as African Americans. His "us White folks gotta piss" statement symbolically references the power of being White in the nightlife context. For me, the humorous twist in his statement is grounded in the fact that throughout my observations in downtown Northeast, it was clear to me that White patrons typically moved through the nightlife with a sense of comfort and entitlement that African Americans did not demonstrate—except for a few of the more prominent African American athletes to whom some White men and women deferred, and some of the Black college students who were well integrated into mainstream campus organizations. Although I had no further exchange with the patron inside the restroom or the nightclub, our interchange at least introduced us as African American coparticipants in urban nightlife.

Given his explicit racial reference and the fact that norms regarding common civility dictate interactions in nightlife, it is unlikely that the Black male would have used the same statement had I been White—unless of course he intended to initiate a verbal or physical confrontation. Furthermore, it is questionable that he would have even attempted to cut the line since many White nightclub owners, bouncers, and patrons regard African American men with suspicion and stand ready to take action against them for the slightest violation of implicit or explicit nightlife norms. Indeed, many African American men in urban nightlife are aware of this and thus act circumspectly so as to avoid trouble.

Although there is a burden on African American men to "disavow criminal intent," they acknowledge this burden as a necessary price to pay in order to participate in urban nightlife at all.[16] For instance, despite the fact that some of the African American men were frustrated by dress codes that they felt were enacted explicitly to thwart their participation in urban nightlife, they changed their clothing to gain access to the nightclubs. As shown previously no other nightlife participants had to consistently carry the burden of "proper" attire like African American men. Changing their dress was a strategy for demonstrating that they belonged in the urban nightlife.

It may be rare that strangers engage in race talk as in this example, but among African Americans who caravan together or spend time with one another on the streets of downtown Northeast, race talk is the norm. These nightlife participants use descriptors like "White dude," "White girl," or "White people" to make comments about perceived racial difference in behavior associated with having fun in the nightlife. Comments like "White people are annoying when they get drunk" exemplify the kind of race talk one might hear standing on the corners and streets where groups of African Americans have gathered. These collective exchanges among African Americans are cathartic and allow them the opportunity to affirm a positive racial self-identity while bonding with one another.[17]

Although African Americans may engage in race talk about Whites, they also discuss other African Americans, sometimes making negative comments about them as well. For instance, many African American women disapprove of African American men's pursuit of White women in urban nightlife. The women may convey their disapproval through jokes, quips, or biting commentary. Such commentary not only is shared in passing exchanges, but also may become a theme to be referenced again later that night. I experienced this kind of reoccurring theme one Thursday night when I saw Meeka with her friend Trina as they sat on the bench in front of Kilpatrick's. Meeka and Trina are both twenty-three-year-old African American women who graduated from BSU but continue to live in Northeast because, as Meeka points out, "It's cheaper than moving back to Atlanta to get my career started." Neither of the women are regulars to the nightlife, partly because they do not care for the social atmosphere created by the predominance of Whites. This becomes evident through their race talk. In this narrative I share their comments throughout the night to demonstrate the recurring theme that focuses on interactions between Blacks and Whites, particularly White women and African American men.

It was 10:45 p.m. and I spotted Meeka sitting on the bench talking to Trina. Meeka is brown-skinned, about five-foot-ten, and slender. She was dressed in a black tank top and fitted blue jeans with black flat slip-on shoes. Her hair was cut short. She introduced me to Trina, who is a little shorter than Meeka. Trina is also brown-skinned, but has long brown hair. She was wearing a fitted pink top with sequence in a circular design and blue jeans and black high heels. . . .

We watched the people passing the corner. Throughout the time we were on the corner Trina made comments about the women walking past. One woman was a tall, thin, White woman. She was wearing blue jeans and a white blouse with red high-heeled shoes. Her hair was blonde and came to her shoulders. She looked like a woman that most men that I encountered in the nightlife would have found attractive. As she walked past the bench going toward the Corral, Trina looked at her, then turned to Meeka and me and said, "I haven't seen so many ugly White girls." Meeka let out a hearty laugh of approval that caught the passing woman's attention for a moment. The woman glanced over but continued walking. I simply smiled shaking my head.

In urban nightlife women typically view other women as competitors seeking the attention of men, and hence it is not unusual for them to make negative comments about the appearance of another. Trina's comments reflect this idea and represent a verbal attack not only on the particular woman as unattractive, but also on White women more generally as the primary competitors for the attention of the men who participate in urban nightlife. Trina specifies White women since few other African American women are present, and many African American men seek interactions with White women in the nightlife. If only African American women had been present, Trina would have found another characteristic upon which to base her evaluation. For instance, I have observed in predominately Black nightlife contexts that women evaluate one another based on "proper" attire according to class sensibilities, frequently describing clothing associated with the Black urban poor as "ghetto" and the Black middle class as "bourgie."[18] These kinds of assessments are consistent with the kinds that women make about one another and about themselves in a number of contexts.[19]

Trina's comments might also be viewed as a legitimate evaluation of a specific type of White woman, rather than negative commentary about White women in general since she could in fact know other White women whom she views as more attractive. Yet, given the appearance of the passing White woman as the iconic representation of attractiveness seen in the nightlife, on television, and in print media, I take Trina's comments to be a verbal attack on the idea of White women as the standard of beauty more generally.[20] Later on that evening, Meeka shares similar negative evaluations of White women when commenting about Black men and White women.

As we were sitting on the bench Barry and Terp, both football players, were walking past. I stopped them for a moment to talk. Barry is about six-foot-four, 230 pounds with brown skin. He has a broad chest with muscles evenly distributed across his body. He was neatly dressed as usual. Tonight he was wearing an orange Ralph Lauren Polo shirt, and white-and-brown plaid shorts. Many of the women in nightlife find him to be attractive, citing his round facial features and bright smile. Terp is a few inches taller than Barry, and a little bit darker. He weighs about 220 pounds and is wearing a polo shirt and blue jeans. I know him from playing basketball in the gym.

As Meeka and Trina kept talking to one another, I shook Barry's hand and said, "What's up?"

"What's up, Reub," Barry replied.

"Nothing much," I said as I shook Terp's hand. Both the men acknowledged the presence of the women with a nod.

"Where are you headed?" I asked.

"We're going to the Labador's," Barry said. Right when he said this I could see Trina cut her eyes as if annoyed.

"All right," I said. "I'll let y'all get to enjoying yourselves."

"We'll catch you later," Barry said.

Barry and Terp turned and began walking across Reginald Street. As they walked away Meeka said, "Labador's is where all the football players go so they can pick up White girls. It's the tank to pick up White skanks."

Trina and I laughed.

Among most African American and White nightlife participants Labador's has the reputation as a frat bar that caters to the cultural tastes of fraternity and sorority participants, especially on Thursday nights when the
owner employs a guitarist to cover country music tunes. The attraction of
the nightclub for some of the more prominent African American athletes
like Barry and Terp is that the White patrons readily recognize them for
their status as athletes. Male groupies willingly purchase alcohol for the
athletes just for the opportunity to talk with them, while female groupies
eagerly approach the athletes seeking the opportunity to engage in flirtatious banter. African American athletes like Barry have talked about the
ease with which they meet White women in places like Labador's. This
point is not lost on Meeka, who pejoratively refers to the nightclub as a
tank, bringing to mind a physical space with a collection of women who
willingly engage in sexual activity with the athletes.

Both Meeka and Trina let their disdain for Barry and Terp's pursuit
of White women be known—Meeka through her statement and Trina
through her nonverbal gesture. Perhaps this disdain is rooted in unpleas-
ant feelings about interactions with Whites more generally, as indicated by
Trina's interaction later that night.

As we came to the bottom of the steps [inside Javelina Ranch, another frat bar], Trina
spotted two White women she knew. She walked over double time, leaving Meeka and me
standing a few feet way. As Trina got close to the women they all gave out loud shrieks in
excitement.

Meeka said to me, "Trina works at the mall and she knows everybody."

Trina embraced one of the women. The woman was large with long brown hair. She
was wearing red pants and a black top. The other woman was slender, with dark hair, and
she wore a black skirt and white blouse.

"She see some of her friends," Meeka said with a laugh.

"I see," I responded.

Meeka and I stood watching and waiting while Trina talked to the two women.

"Look at her," Meeka said. "Look how she's talking."

"I see her," I replied.

"She'll be back over here in a minute," Meeka said.

Sure enough Trina walked back to us in a matter of seconds and we started back up
the stairs. As we were leaving Meeka said, "I heard you change your voice, girl, when you
saw your White friends." We all laughed.

"Yeah, girl," Trina replied, "I have to give them a loud, high voice. But I can't keep it up too long. Laura wanted to hang out all night, but Laura is with Todd, and Trina can't be with Todd too long."

We laughed as she described herself in the third person.

Trina continued, "The White friend thing only last so long. So I told her that I would hang out tomorrow, but what Laura don't know is that Trina got something to do tomorrow." We all laughed again.

Trina's quick movement to address her "friends" is a nonverbal cue typically used by caravanning group members to convey to others in their group that the interchange in which the participant is about to enter is socially insignificant and will be brief in duration. The unspoken message to one's companions is that there is no need for introduction or interaction among all the members of the caravanning group and the encountered individual, because there is little social value in such a shared interaction for the goal of having fun in the nightlife. Although there may be a number of reasons why Trina wanted to avoid extended interaction with the two women, she makes explicit that race is one of her reasons. In particular, she feels that it is burdensome to "keep up" or perform a certain role in the presence of Whites, which she cannot or cares not to do for extended periods.

Despite her pleasant interaction with the women—an interaction characterized by the kind of common civility that one would expect to observe within a "cosmopolitan canopy"—Trina's race talk consistently illustrates disdain for Whites, particularly White women. She demonstrated her position again later in the evening as we were standing on the corner at Reginald and Stuckey Streets. Trina had observed me hug a White female as we said our good-byes, and when the White female walked away Trina and I had the following exchange:

"If you hug one more pink toe in front of me I'm going to kill you," Trina said as she pointed her finger at me in mock anger.

"Why? I'm down with pink toes or whoever," I said as we all laughed.

This was the first time that I had heard the term "pink toe." The phrase brought to my mind a visual image of White women wearing open toe shoes with visible "pink toes." Trina and Meeka revealed to me that they used the term as a generally pejorative descriptor for White women.[21] When I heard them make this reference in the nightlife I detected a sense of jealousy for the attention that White women received from African American men. This sense comes through as Trina uses the term once again that evening.

We went into the basement of Kilpatrick's where I saw Jordan and Jenny. Jordan is a tall, light-skinned, African American athlete, standing about six-foot-four. He has a thin face with accented cheekbones that women have admired. He stood in a blue polo shirt as he and Jenny finished a hug. Jenny is a White female, with short blonde hair. She likes to flirt when she's been drinking. She was wearing a light-colored halter top and a skirt. I made eye contact with Jordan and headed closer to shake his hand as Meeka and Trina followed behind me.

"What's up, Jordan?"

"What's up, Reub?" Jordan replied.

"Hey, Reuben," Jenny said with her flirty smile.

I turned to Jenny and hugged her. As I hugged Jenny, Trina poked me in the back with her fingers. When we finished hugging I turned away from Jenny to keep moving through the crowd. As we got a few feet away I turned back to Trina and said, "Why did you poke me in the back?"

"Because you hugged another pink toe," she said as she smirked.

African American women find it particularly difficult to have fun within the context of downtown Northeast since both White and African American men focus on pursuing interactions with White women. Hence the race talk occurring among African American women frequently focuses on both negative evaluations of White women as well as African American men who pursue these women. Given the gender dynamics in the nightlife wherein women wait for men to approach them, many African American women simply spend the evening interacting with one another as Trina and Meeka did.

Although race talk among African American women frequently includes negative comments regarding White women and African American men and generally references the prevailing gender dynamics in the nightlife, race talk among African American men focuses on what the men perceive as unfair treatment by nightclub bouncers or police. The men make their comments based on the belief that many Whites in the nightlife perceive them as a threat and hence regard them with apprehension. Thus, the men frequently talk about how they are treated or might be treated relative to Whites engaged in similar nightlife behavior. For instance, Skyler, a twenty-two-year-old African American male whom I knew from the gym, makes comments regarding a White male's interaction with a police officer as we stand on the corner.

The White officer then told the man, "Give me your hand." The White man, dressed in jeans, blue button-down shirt, and flip-flops complied. The officer forced the man's hand backward and took out his handcuffs and put it on the man's wrists.

The man, who appeared to have been drinking, moved his hand a little more in a defensive position to protest the illogical nature of what the officer was doing. All the people who were standing around observing seemed to be murmuring in agreement with the man that the officer's behavior was excessive. His friends that were with him as he was being handcuffed were telling him to calm down. They were all deferential toward the officer.

"Take out your wallet," the officer commanded.

The guy, with his hands cuffed, twisted with both hands and reached in his left back pocket and held out the wallet for the officer.

The officer grabbed the wallet and reviewed the man's ID. After a few moments of reviewing the identification cards in the wallet the officer closed the wallet and held onto it.

"Officer, can you give him his wallet back?" one of the guy's friends asked.

"Shut up," the officer said turning to the friend. "I have your friend's wallet and I'll give it back when I'm ready."

It was obvious to most people around that the cop was being a prick. I turned around to Skyler and said, "Man, look at that."

Skyler, who had been watching the interchange, said, "Man, I know. Just imagine if I were out there. Look at the way he is treating him. I probably would be eating concrete if he is treating that White boy like that and he ain't did nothing." We both laughed discreetly.

Skyler could envision himself being handled roughly and forced to lie down on the ground if he were in a similar encounter with the officer. His comments reflect the kinds of assessments that other African American men make about how they are treated in the nightlife and are consistent with my observations about the differences between how Whites and Blacks talk about race. For instance, unlike Whites' race talk wherein passing comments about race are mainly jokes using pejorative terms to describe other races, African American males' race talk typically arises out of situations in which the men are confronted by institutional authority in the form of bouncers or police in the nightlife. The men engage in race talk after being rejected from nightclubs for purported dress code violations, being stopped by police for purported cruising ban violations, or experiencing some other occurrence within which they feel their behavior, activities, or movements are constrained in a way that Whites' are not.

As a collective, African American men have a number of experiences that seem to support the idea that they are treated unfairly. One such event triggered a comment from an African American male who had been pepper-sprayed by a bouncer when he attempted to reenter a nightclub after leaving to look for a friend. I witnessed the man's attempt to reenter the club. Although he was intoxicated he did not seem particularly unruly, yet the bouncer sprayed him. There was noise and confusion by the entrance of the nightclub for a few minutes as the Black male, whom I knew, came out of the nightclub doorway and shouted to me, "My eyes are burning. Reuben, did you see him? He sprayed pepper spray in my eyes. Why did he do that shit? Man, they don't do that shit to White boys. They just push them away. He didn't have to pepper spray me." This kind of event, when retold, has a compounding effect such that it becomes part of a collective memory of racism and discrimination even for those African American men who do not experience the event personally.[22] It serves as a type of foundational experience that the men draw upon in their race talk.

Although race talk among African Americans varies by gender with African American women focusing their passing comments on gender dynamics and African American men focusing their comments on encounters with institutional authority, this talk consistently occurs among members of a caravanning group or with those individuals known to one another. Likewise, Whites also share their race talk within their caravanning groups or with individuals known to one another. Given the ways in which race talk occurs among members of caravanning groups a question arises: does race talk occur across racial boundaries? I turn to this question in the next section.

Interracial Race Talk

Many Whites attending Big South University and frequenting the downtown nightlife come from suburban areas surrounding Atlanta. They are the sons and daughters of parents who fled the central city of Atlanta as part of a nationwide trend of White flight occurring in cities throughout the United States during the latter part of the twentieth century.[23] These White families were ostensibly migrating to the suburbs from the city to take advantage of the growth in new homes and the amenities—such as schools and shopping centers—provided by suburban locations. Some scholars have suggested that these families migrated to the suburbs as a result of blockbusting wherein real estate agents helped Black families move into a White neighborhood, spread news of the impending incursion of Black residents to the area, and convinced White residents to sell their homes quickly, usually at a loss. For instance, Pattillo-McCoy, writing about the migration of the Black middle class into White communities on the South Side of Chicago, demonstrates the kinds of tactics used by real estate agents to increase the outmigration of Whites.[24] The real estate agents then sold these homes to Blacks for a profit.

Other scholars have suggested that White flight was in part a political resistance to change. For instance, the historian Kevin Kruse, in his analysis of White flight from Atlanta during the 1960s and 1970s, argues that rather than being a simple matter of Whites moving to take advantage of improved living conditions in the suburbs, White flight was a concerted political effort to resist desegregation stemming from the civil rights movement.[25] Kruse suggests that after the civil rights movement Whites had attempted a number of strategies to resist desegregation, but turned to White flight when those strategies proved ineffective in preventing Blacks from moving into predominantly White areas. He states, "Ultimately, the mass migration of Whites from cities to the suburbs proved to be the most successful segregationist response to the moral demands of the civil rights movement and the legal authority of the courts."[26]

Although White flight might have occurred for a number of reasons, one consequence of the outmigration of Whites to the suburbs has been that many Whites, including those who frequent nightlife in Northeast, come from communities wherein very few African Americans reside. Similarly, African Americans are also coming from racially segregated communities—although they are likely to have interacted with Whites in other contexts of everyday life. Since few Whites and Blacks in downtown Northeast share in close relationships, it is unlikely that they would engage one another in race talk across racial boundaries. On the rare occasion that I observed such talk, the patrons were members of the same caravanning group and made passing comments like "You a crazy

White boy," "Where are the Black men," or "Hook me up with a Black girl." These comments were lighthearted and humorous and fit within the overall revelry of friends drinking in the nightlife. Still, interracial race talk is rare.

Beyond the rare interactions within which I observed explicit race talk across racial boundaries, I had an opportunity to engage in such talk based upon my relationship with a number of White nightlife participants. For instance, in the following discussion I share in explicit conversation about race. Although our interchange does not represent the typical occurrence in the nightlife across racial boundaries, it provides insights into important personal characteristics that might influence how people engage one another in such race talk.

As I made my usual pass through the bars I ran into Charlotte and Stephen in Stillwaters. They had been dating a year. Stillwaters was having a drink special and both Charlotte and Stephen had had a few drinks. Charlotte seemed tipsier than Stephen, but both spoke coherently. I sat down and chatted with them since I hadn't seen them out in a while. . . .

After talking for a few minutes I went to the restroom. While I was in the restroom I saw a chalkboard sign where patrons could write their own graffiti. There were a number of random notes written about sex and other topics. One note stood out. Scrawled on the chalkboard in bold letters was the word, "Nigger." When I came out and sat back down at the table I said, "I love restroom graffiti because people write all kinds of stuff. They had a sign in the restroom that read 'Nigger.'"

"Did you write it?" Stephen asked jokingly. We all laughed.

"No," I said.

"I know why someone wrote it," Charlotte said.

"Why?" I asked.

Charlotte leaned close to the table and pointed discreetly to a corner booth with a group of four Blacks sitting and said, "Because of that over there." We started laughing. There were two men and two women sitting having a drink. They were the only other African Americans in Stillwater's at the time.

"I hope nobody wrote that because of my brothers," I said, as Stephen and Charlotte laughed.

"You know when I first got to Big South University I was excited," Charlotte said. "I had gone to an all-White Catholic school in Virginia. There were fifteen Blacks in the whole school. When I got accepted to BSU I thought, 'Great now I'm going to be around diversity.' But it's not diverse here."

Stephen added, "Growing up with Blacks in rural Georgia I took for granted that I would see a lot of them at BSU but it was just plain old White. I had never really thought that there were too many places where there weren't any Blacks."

This interchange presents key considerations that come into play as patrons negotiate race talk across racial boundaries in urban nightlife. First, those participants engaged in race talk must share a relationship of familiarity. This familiarity is developed in contexts outside of the nightlife and is the basis upon which participants interpret comments about race. Second, interactions across racial boundaries are part of an ongoing discourse about race among the participants, rather than passing statements about a variety of evolving issues. For instance, in this discussion Charlotte and Stephen returned to observations they made on previous occasions about the scarcity of African Americans as part of the university community and nightlife activities. Our sharing in this theme originated from our initial classroom discussions. This recurring theme is reflected in our joke discourse. Third, irrespective of the sense of familiarity, nightlife participants still recognize limits to their discussions about race. They practice common civility in accordance with the perceived relationships and the parameters for discussion they perhaps develop during more engaged conversations elsewhere. Again, race talk across racial boundaries is rare, but the aforementioned considerations seem to be important for the ways in which explicit discussions about race occur in the nightlife.

Conclusion

Nightlife participants rarely engage in race talk because discussions of sensitive topics like race interfere with the participants' goals of having fun in the nightlife. Given nightlife participants' general avoidance of such sensitive topics, one might expect there to exist what Anderson identifies as a cosmopolitan canopy wherein diverse groups come together and engage in common civility. Indeed, nightlife participants engage in common civility, yet as I have demonstrated this civility does little to improve relationships across social boundaries, especially racial boundaries since patrons are merely navigating these fleeting, superficial exchanges with strangers to advance their own enjoyment rather than attempting to develop substantive relationships with such strangers. Still race talk occurs, but usually among individuals who have preexisting relationships. These exchanges help to protect social boundaries and aid in the maintenance of integrated segregation. In the next chapter, I draw on observations made throughout this book to demonstrate conditions under which we would expect to observe integrated segregation in a number of contexts. I then discuss the implications of integrated segregation for race relations in America.

7

Having Fun in
Black and White

● ● ● ● ● ● ● ● ● ● ● ● ●

Downtown Northeast, like many other urban nightlife areas, is a public space where young men and women go to have fun. Accompanied by their friends and acquaintances in caravanning groups, the patrons move from nightclub to nightclub seeking to engage one another in games of alcohol consumption and flirtation with members of the opposite sex. One main attraction of a place like downtown is the density of participants in the nightlife. Frat boys, sorority girls, athletes, locals, college students, and alternative types crowd the streets in throngs with the possibility of meeting someone new with whom they might have fun.

Although downtown is frequented by mostly White college students, the fact that it is the only public space in Northeast where young men and women can interact with a significant number of other individuals means that people from varying backgrounds are drawn to the area. Given the diversity of individuals who might enter the public space of downtown Northeast, there is little surprise that patrons seeking to have fun spend time assessing one another as they move through downtown. In a matter of seconds, patrons evaluate class and cultural cues like clothing styles to determine whether another patron is worthy of approach or should be allowed to approach. This is easily seen when a young man dressed in frat boy attire approaches a young woman. His style of dress conveys to all that he possesses the kind of qualities that young women would find desirable. Since he has presented himself in a desirable manner, young women are more likely to give him the opportunity to approach. Yet if the young man is queried about his fraternity membership and it is found lacking, he is usually quickly dismissed. Hence, the opportunity to have fun in downtown Northeast is very much related to one's perceived or real social status.

There is no surprise in the finding that patrons are evaluating one another's class and cultural status using cues like clothing. People have consistently used such markers to place others into groups or to make distinctions between one another in implicit and explicit ways.[1] In fact, the character of urban living, with large, dense, and heterogeneous populations, is such that these assessments are part and parcel of navigating the city streets both day and night. What might be surprising to some, however, is the extent to which race continues to be a significant factor in these judgments given the popular notion that America is moving toward a postracial society, and evidence that there are heterogeneous public spaces wherein individuals might have positive interpersonal contact with others from diverse backgrounds.[2] Indeed, to the casual observer the nightlife in downtown Northeast might appear to be such a place.

What I have demonstrated throughout this book, however, is that rather than being a public space where diverse groups interact with one another with overall civility, downtown Northeast, like many other urban public spaces that I have observed with heterogeneous populations, is demonstrative of what I have called integrated segregation: that individuals in public space, rather than experiencing unfettered interaction with others on the downtown streets, are socially bound to interaction with those social types like themselves. Individuals who share similar characteristics are nestled together in social groupings through which they vie for use of downtown public space. In short, groups share physical space in close proximity with diverse others, but rarely engage one another in interpersonal interaction. Although I introduced "integrated segregation" as a general term to talk about how groups set themselves apart from one another along class and cultural boundaries, within the context of downtown Northeast this idea unfolds in a complicated way and is centered on race. Furthermore, local institutions that create policies or rules influence the nature of interaction among patrons and support integrated segregation. In this concluding chapter I briefly recap the idea of integrated segregation, examine how it is centered on race, and discuss the implications of this idea beyond the nightlife of Northeast.

Integrated Segregation and Race

Patrons entering downtown most frequently do so with friends and acquaintances they know from activities or places outside of the nightlife. They develop relationships through interaction at work, in school, at play, or through their frequent patronage of local coffee shops or restaurants, or even through illicit activities like underage drinking and drug use. As people get to know one another in these contexts, they establish both loose and close-knit ties that become the basis of the caravanning groups within which they travel through the nightlife. These caravanning groups of usually two to ten patrons are a key element of integrated segregation. Since the caravanning groups typically bond together around interests outside of merely having fun within the nightlife, patrons often establish an allegiance to the other members in their caravanning group. Hence, the caravanning group influences not only where individuals might go to have fun, but also the kinds of people they might find desirable. This influence cannot be overstated. It is through the internal boundary maintenance of caravanning groups that broader social boundaries are also enforced. Furthermore, I argue that irrespective of the size of the city or nightlife area, caravanning groups are the central unit of cohesion and influence in the nightlife.

One way that caravanning groups shape participation in the nightlife is through preparty or pregaming drinking activities wherein smaller groups or clusters of caravanning groups gather to drink and socialize before they go out. As indicated previously, individuals invited to participate in these pregaming activities are usually known to one another through some previous experience. Furthermore since individuals often seek out others with whom they might share some common points of interests, it is likely that people who share similar class and cultural sensibilities will attend the same pregaming gatherings. For instance, frat boys pregame with other frat boys, locals congregate with other locals, and alternative types gather with other alternative types. Since these gatherings are based on preexisting networks established in other contexts, and since I have demonstrated that these other contexts like fraternity and sorority organizations are highly stratified by race, then these pregaming gatherings also become stratified by race.

Thus, groups may not be coming together with the explicit goal of excluding others based on race, as in the past, but this outcome is a by-product of preexisting social relationships that become reflected in patrons' use patterns in the nightlife.

As patrons at these pregaming gatherings sort through the approximately forty nightclubs in downtown Northeast to determine the ones they will patronize, their selections are not made within a vacuum. The patrons, through knowledge gathered by word of mouth and personal observation, are well aware of which nightclubs are frat bars, freshman bars, dance clubs, and alternative bars and which are frequented by Blacks or locals. Hence, clusters of caravanning groups, made up of individual patrons who share common sensibilities, move through the public spaces in pursuit of fun at nightclubs they have deemed desirable. These clustered caravanning groups make up what I have termed "social capsules," consisting of individuals who share similar characteristics taken as important to that particular group. These characteristics may include social, cultural, or physical markers that are recognized by individuals who are internal or external to the group.

For instance, patrons I talked to and observed easily identified styles of dress expected of frat boys, sorority girls, athletes, alternative types, and individuals with an affinity for hip-hop. These styles of dress serve as indicators of an individual's status and place within the nightlife. Patrons sharing this status frequent the same places and are likely to engage one another socially. Yet as they pass other kinds of caravanning groups on the streets or in some cases within nightclubs, they are not likely to engage those groups socially. Thus diverse groups occupy the same physical space, but are socially encapsulated from one another giving rise to the idea of integrated segregation. Interestingly, despite the fact that there are many groups seeking to have fun in the nightlife, and many ways that individuals might draw distinctions from others, patrons gravitate toward race as an important primary distinction.

Given the complex array of individuals who might gather in the nightlife, assessing their identities takes a great deal of effort. Some patrons are quite adept at this task, while others are not. For instance, many African Americans are able to recognize subtle class and cultural status differences among Whites. On the other hand, many Whites fail to recognize such differences among African Americans, often viewing them as a monolithic group. Still, middle-class African Americans work to escape from being identified with their lower-class kindred by perhaps choosing to adopt certain styles of dress like buttoned-down shirts and khaki shorts. They do this not out of some disdain for lower-class African Americans who are generally associated with hip-hop clothing, but as a basic strategy for attempting to have fun in the nightlife. They are well aware that there are consequences that impinge upon the goal of having fun for persons identified as interlopers, especially African Americans. Yet despite their efforts middle-class African Americans find it difficult to create this distance since White patrons, bar owners, bouncers, and police habitually fail to recognize distinctions among African Americans even when a segment of that population shares similar styles of dress as their White middle-class counterparts. It is as if the educational and social class achievements of middle-class African Americans are nullified by the taken-for-granted idea that race, in the case of African Americans, equals lower class status—a status associated with criminal and violent behavior. Hence, social boundaries among groups become entrenched around racial difference, creating spaces within which most African Americans, irrespective of their class and cultural sensibilities, are physically integrated within a space, but remain socially segregated.

Despite integrated segregation there are instances in which boundaries among groups are challenged. Most notable among these instances is African American men's pursuit of interaction with White women. African American men, like other men, seek to have fun by engaging members of the opposite sex. These men attempt to engage the caravanning groups of sorority girls or college girls on the streets and in the nightclubs. Although they meet with general disapproval from White men and African American women, and White women frequently rebuff their advances, African American men continue to pursue interactions in much the same way as their White male counterparts. Their racial status within a predominately White context, however, heightens perceptions of their activities. For instance, White women generally characterize African American men as more aggressive in their approach than other men. Indeed, some African American men are more aggressive than typical male patrons, just as are some White men. Yet it is because of Whites' general inability, or unwillingness, to decipher nuanced class and cultural differences among African Americans that many African American men are wrongly categorized as having aggressive approaches to women.

Patrons feel a sense of underlying racial tension especially resulting from African American men's pursuit of White women, but it is rare that such tension results in patrons' explicit dialogue or action regarding race and racial boundaries. Rather, policing of these boundaries is left to women's caravanning groups, which are adept at terminating advances from undesirable men irrespective of race. Women employ a number of strategies including aggressively intervening for one another when an undesirable man approaches, giving false information, or simply locking arms and ignoring the pleas for interaction. Bouncers, police, and other patrons generally support women's resistance to overtures from undesirable men, thereby making their strategies particularly effective. Thus, caravanning groups do the work of maintaining social boundaries without having to ever explicitly acknowledge race as a factor. The fact that race is rarely engaged explicitly has profound implications that I take up in later discussion.

Despite little explicit acknowledgment of underlying racial tension in downtown Northeast, there are occasions in which this tension rises to the surface. On such occasions Black and White patrons, usually male, engage in verbal or physical confrontations. These confrontations may stem from individuals' responses to incidental contact, conflict over a man's approach to a woman, or the purported or actual use of a racial epithet. Irrespective of the initial source of conflict, these confrontations take on greater significance than simply two men arguing or fighting. When confrontations occur across racial boundaries, Black and White patrons figuratively "take sides" with their racial representative. As I have demonstrated elsewhere, this is readily observed in patrons' retelling of incidents within their own racially segregated groups.[3] They typically retell the events with a sympathetic bent toward members of their racial group. Whether these incidents are shared in this manner as a means of bonding with one's racial group or an actual reflection of one's own perspective, these retellings work to sharpen the social boundaries between racial groups in the nightlife. In effect, they help to bolster a social climate wherein integrated segregation continues to flourish as the norm where diverse groups share public space with one another.

Integrated Segregation Beyond Northeast Georgia

Based upon the findings from this in-depth study of downtown Northeast, a question arises: does integrated segregation also exist in other urban nightlife contexts? In order to answer this question I suggest three conditions under which one might expect to find integrated segregation in other nightlife contexts.

One such condition is in locations that are easily accessible and open to a number of patrons. In places like downtown Northeast there are clearly designated nightlife districts or areas with clusters of nightclubs, bearing neon lights and iconic images of beer and liquor, suggesting to most passersby an accessible space for relaxation and enjoyment. Accessibility includes not only the extent to which an area is perceived as open to the public, but also the extent to which transportation to that nightlife district is readily available. Irrespective of the size of an area, a dense population of nightlife revelers in a particular nightlife area is one condition under which we would expect to find integrated segregation.

A second and related condition under which we would expect to find integrated segregation is in locations that attract sizable diverse populations. Here diverse might be thought of as difference by class, culture, race, sexual orientation, religion, or other categories that are typically manifest in physical markers that patrons can use for making distinctions among one another. Although individuals from diverse groups might be found in virtually any nightlife setting, it is in contexts in which these groups are represented by sizable populations capable of leaving a collective imprint on the social landscape of the nightlife that we might observe integrated segregation.

What constitutes a sizable diverse population? In some respects, the answer to this question turns on matters of interpretation and perspective. For instance, if we think of African Americans as a diverse group within a predominately White nightlife area, we might ask this: what percentage of a nightclub's clientele would have to be African American before patrons began designating that club as a "Black nightclub"? In other words, is there a "tipping point"—a point at which Blacks' participation in a nightclub shifts the composition of that club from White to Black? The "tipping point" concept is frequently applied to residential housing patterns and typically estimates that when minorities' share of a neighborhood reaches between 5 percent and 20 percent, Whites will begin moving from the neighborhood rapidly, thereby producing a predominately minority neighborhood within ten years.[4] One could envision a similar process occurring in the transformation of nightclubs. Although I have no actual percentages regarding the "tipping point" at which a nightclub may be identified as a "Black club," it is clear that once there is a critical mass of Blacks Whites begin to opt for alternative nightclubs. The perception of a critical mass, however, depends significantly on the collective comfort level of individual White patrons. Hence, a nightclub may simply be designated as a "Black club" when it "feels" like one to those patrons opting to patronize other nightclubs.

Irrespective of the exact "tipping point" for nightclubs, it is clear that the presence of a sizable and diverse population—in this example African Americans—influences patrons' use patterns and contributes to integrated segregation. As patrons pursue having fun, they seek out venues wherein this can be achieved in the company of others like themselves. When a variety of drinking establishments that cater to sizable and diverse groups of patrons are located within the same area, patrons must expend energy to distinguish themselves from one another. At the same time, since nightclubs are generally accessible to the public, nightclub owners must also implement strategies to indicate which groups they desire as clientele—for example through dress codes. Thus, patrons gravitate toward places and spaces where nightclub owners and other patrons welcome them. The presence of sizable and diverse populations vying for use of the nightclubs and public space sharpens boundaries among groups and intensifies integrated segregation in nightclubs and on the streets.

If there is little or no diversity of clientele in an area, then patrons are less likely to spend time drawing distinctions between one another along broad categorical lines, and more likely to spend time focused on individual differences. This observation supports the condition that the existence of a sizable diverse population within the same public space facilitates integrated segregation.

An additional condition under which we would expect to find integrated segregation is in locations where many patrons have preexisting relationships. In such areas, patrons who know one another from other contexts come together to take advantage of the social atmosphere provided by the nightlife. Patrons in such nightlife contexts may seek interaction with anonymous others, but they are also likely to interact with broader groups of friends or acquaintances based upon their preexisting relationships. This is observed in the case of patrons from downtown Northeast who engage in pregaming activities with others and then seek out those others later that night. Hence, preexisting relations dictate patrons' use patterns and support integrated segregation. These preexisting relationships are often structured by and reflective of broader institutions and racial dynamics as in the case of downtown Northeast.

In this section, I have suggested three conditions under which we might expect to observe integrated segregation. Based upon these observations we would expect to observe integrated segregation in nightlife areas that are open and accessible to a number of patrons, attract sizable diverse populations, and are frequented by patrons who share preexisting relationships. Although I have suggested these conditions as important for the occurrence of integrated segregation, I do not wish to suggest that one or more of these conditions are necessary for integrated segregation to occur. Rather, my goal has been to introduce ways in which to think about how individuals within nightlife districts may become socially bound to interaction with those social types like themselves. Whether these conditions necessarily occur within the context of nightlife is an empirical question best left to more in-depth investigation in nightlife areas in large and small cities. What is clear from my observations is that nightlife activity typically has consequences for interaction in broader contexts. In the next section I discuss the implications derived from my study of nightlife in downtown Northeast.

Race and Historical Context Beyond Having Fun in Urban Nightlife

When I initially began this study of downtown Northeast, I took the observation of people from diverse backgrounds sharing the same public space and interacting with one another as an indication that times had changed considerably from my own experience of growing up and having fun in primarily racially segregated contexts in Chicago.[5] Indeed downtown Northeast had the feel of a utopian place to me. Not only were economically and racially diverse groups sharing in the same public space, but this diversity seemed welcomed. I found this particularly interesting given all that I had learned about the South and its history of segregation. There was something inspirational about my initial observations.

Yet, the more I watched, listened to, and talked with patrons the more the utopian image of a place welcoming diversity gave way to a complicated picture of the ways in which culture, class, and race placed constraints on interaction. I soon realized that the nightlife in Northeast reflected the same kinds of tensions I had observed in other contexts.[6] Hence, it was not surprising to observe patrons evaluating one another's cultural sensibilities or class backgrounds based on styles of dress. It was not surprising to learn that patrons use physical indicators such as skin color as a means of racially identifying one another. Nor was it surprising to feel an underlying tension lying just beneath the surface of passing interactions between groups of Blacks and Whites. Furthermore, given the history of racial hostility and violence in America, I was not surprised to note that the occasional verbal and physical confrontation among White and Black patrons took on racial significance beyond the precipitating event.

What I did find surprising, however, was the extent to which the racial tension among Whites and Blacks seemed to be devoid of historical context. Patrons seemed to give little consideration to the ways in which historical understandings of race might influence their current attitudes and behavior toward one another. Hence, although patrons associated certain attitudes or behaviors with specific groups, they usually talked about their negative racial encounters as individual conflicts, as if these conflicts took place within a vacuum isolated from not only similar events within the context of downtown, but also broader historical events that bear on current race relations. This shift in thinking about negative racial encounters as individual occurrences might be perceived as a positive change in race relations given Americans' general preoccupation with individualism, but I find it troubling for two reasons.

First, when patrons think of their negative racial encounters as isolated incidents, they fail to acknowledge the historical role of broader institutions in creating the conditions for these encounters, and this has consequences. For instance, one source of conflict between Blacks and Whites in the nightlife is Whites' feelings that Blacks are encroaching upon their social space, and Blacks' feelings that they are entitled to be in that space. Historical factors undergirding these feelings include the fact that social institutions like schools and public accommodations supported segregated spaces for Whites and Blacks even long after it was illegal to do so. An example of this phenomenon is seen clearly in school desegregation.

Although *Brown v. Board of Education of Topeka* declared state laws establishing separate public schools for Black and White students unconstitutional in 1954, many school districts struggled to desegregate schools through the 1970s.[7] Furthermore, many students and administrators at public universities and colleges were slow to desegregate. Within the immediate context of Northeast, Georgia, Big South University had its own history of resistance to desegregation. Like at other colleges and universities throughout the South, White students met the first African

Americans to enroll in Big South University with hostility. I would submit that most current Big South students remain largely uninformed about the historical events related to desegregation, and this lack of historical knowledge has consequences for interaction in the nightlife.

Since nightlife participants do not take into account this kind of historical understanding, their view of negative racial encounters focuses on singular racial adversaries. The shortcoming in this kind of thinking is that as long as individuals are viewed as the sole culprits in racial hostilities, the reoccurrence of such hostilities will be viewed without the proper depth of understanding about the role of institutions in these hostilities. Without considering the significance of historical context on current interaction, collective change in nightlife participants' thinking about shared public space remains limited.

Second, when patrons view issues of race devoid of historical context, they likely will also fail to apprehend how contemporary institutions may be manipulated to produce racially discriminatory outcomes. Interestingly, although both White and Black patrons demonstrate limited knowledge of historical context, many African American patrons seem to think contemporary institutions might be used for discriminatory purposes. For instance, although nightclub owners implemented dress codes for the explicit purpose of creating "a certain atmosphere" and local government implemented a cruising ban for the explicit purpose of addressing "safety concerns," many African Americans took such policies to be racially discriminatory given the disproportionate impact of these policies on African Americans. These patrons envisioned local business owners and politicians covertly manipulating such regulations to create racially discriminatory outcomes, while many White patrons were unaware that such policies even existed. Perhaps African Americans considered covert manipulation a possibility given their general collective sense that institutions had been manipulated in the past. Still, this general collective sense is ineffective in helping African Americans sort through the pervasive and complicated ways in which race operates in their everyday lives.

The fact that both Black and White nightlife participants are generally disconnected from an historical understanding regarding race relations, coupled with a contemporary emphasis on color blindness—that is, the ideology that individuals should be treated fairly irrespective of racial background—makes complicated the question of how one even engages in conversations about the role of race in everyday life. Many people simply avoid discussions of race to escape being labeled racist, while others who do talk about race use coded language—for example, descriptors like "ghetto" to indicate those things associated with poor, urban African Americans and "trailer park" to indicate those things associated with poor, rural Whites. Furthermore, the ways in which individuals talk about race have been complicated by the election of America's first Black president, Barack Obama, in 2008. His presence on the public stage has brought issues of racial identity to the fore. Political opponents, pundits, news commentators, and President Obama himself have had to carefully negotiate how his racial identity is debated across a wide array of discussion topics in the media. At the same time President Obama's presence has also put to rest for many people the need for explicit discussion about race—particularly those discussions regarding the persistent structural inequalities faced by many African Americans. Indeed, some commentators suggest that we have moved to a postracial society wherein race and racial identity are nominal considerations. All of these factors, taken together, work to limit the perceived need or desire to discuss the persistent role of race in everyday life.

Conclusion

The findings from this study demonstrate that although there are class and cultural differences within, and across, racial groups that make for a complicated picture about race, and although America is becoming more racially and culturally diverse, the dichotomy of Black and White remains a central influence over how people engage one another on many city streets. Yet perhaps more troubling is that many people fail to draw a connection between contemporary racial issues and the historical and institutional forces that support these ongoing issues. It is as if there is a generation of racial antagonists who do not know why they are antagonistic. I speculate that as we become further removed from historical and institutional explanations for our racial antagonisms, the further removed we will become from rational and reasoned discussions about these antagonisms.

Appendix A
A Brief History
of Northeast

Northeast and Big South University have histories similar to those of many colleges and universities and their respective towns in the South.[1] Northeast began as a trading settlement. After the early 1800s when the state set aside land for the university, wealthy private citizens secured additional portions of land and donated it to the university. Plantation owners, farmers, and southern aristocrats were drawn to the area. There was a growth in textile manufacturers and cotton mill production, and this increased the size of Northeast and the wealth of those residing there.

Through the 1850s Northeast attracted not only businessmen in agriculture, but also professors who came to educate the sons of those wealthy men. Throughout this time there were several antebellum homes built for the wealthy families in the area. These homes remain standing near campus today and are home to local chapters of some of the oldest fraternities in the nation. As the aristocrat population grew in Northeast, so did its slave population: by 1860 slaves composed nearly half of the population.

Once the Civil War began in 1861, growth of the town and university slowed considerably. Some of the manufacturing plants were converted into wartime supply centers, as many of the city's male residents volunteered for military service. Many young men and boys lost their lives in battle.[2] Slave masters, who were off to war, permitted their slaves to "hire out" in town to earn a wage, increasing the number of slaves in Northeast. During the Civil War, Big South University diminished in enrollment due to a demand for servicemen. Despite the draw on human and material resources for the war, Northeast avoided the physical damage experienced by other southern towns because no major battles took place within the city.

After the Civil War, Northeast was able to return to its prewar productivity, and Big South University enrollments grew beyond those seen prior to the war. Northeast had become not only a place to educate White men returning from war, but also a center of education for freedmen. As in many of the southern towns, Union troops occupied Northeast, and freed slaves celebrated their emancipation. The Freedman's Bureau provided funds used to open a private school for educating freed Blacks, and two additional schools opened later and provided primary, intermediate, and industrial education and nurses' training for the freedman.[3] In addition to the educational training being provided, African American newspapers provided the news to the Black population in the area.

In the 1870s, Northeast was chartered as a city and added phone lines and streetcar public transit. By the early 1900s, Northeast was home to slightly more Black residents than Whites. Although confined to segregated locations in Northeast, the Black population was diverse and included laborers, skilled tradesmen, and professionals. Also during this time the corners of Farrell and Oak Streets in downtown Northeast became known as the Spot, the cultural center for the Black community. Black lawyers, dentists, doctors, and other professionals established offices in this segregated area.

During World War II thousands of young men who were stationed at a nearby military training facility flooded the city. Although Big South University had admitted women in the early 1900s, it remained racially segregated well after World War II. Like the situation at other colleges and universities in the South, desegregation of the university was met with racial hostility. Southerners, set on maintaining Jim Crow segregation through the 1950s and 1960s, resisted the presence of African Americans on southern campuses with actions ranging from political leaders' demonstrations of power to mob violence on campuses.

By the late 1970s Northeast again saw significant growth and manufacturers built plants in the area. With this construction significant numbers of executives moved into Northeast and the surrounding suburbs. Through the 1980s and 1990s Northeast's population continued to grow and the city itself developed a reputation as a place to have fun and enjoy nightlife entertainment. Aspiring artists from a number of areas were drawn to Northeast, giving it a reputation for its burgeoning art scene.

Although legal segregation no longer exists, de facto segregation of Northeast's residents remains significant, with over half the local African American population residing in predominately Black neighborhoods throughout the city. In addition, persistent poverty troubles the area, with Northeast's poverty levels among the highest among cities of a similar size within the United States. African Americans and Hispanics disproportionately represent those living in poverty. Many commentators have described Northeast as a place where African Americans and Whites have very different living experiences, like other cities and towns in the South. These experiences are reflected in the ways in which African Americans and Whites think about the downtown nightlife.

Appendix B
Methodology

Crowds of people gathering in places like streets, parks, and malls have always intrigued me. I find the interactions occurring among friends and strangers to be stimulating because these capture both the simplicity and complexity of communication among people. Perhaps this is why I was drawn to the work of Goffman soon after I began my graduate training. Goffman and others who articulated the patterns, taken-for-granted rules, and social consequences of face-to-face interaction provided me with the tools to articulate the multiplicity of activities I had been observing.[1] My everyday activities became mini-sociological excursions wherein I, armed with their ideas, looked for meaning in the simplest of interactions. My inclination toward observing interaction, especially within densely populated settings, drew me to the nightlife in Northeast, Georgia, in 1996. Although I had not developed a formal question for the study of nightlife, I spent the next several years observing the throngs of participants as they engaged in the revelry of a party scene that rivaled nightlife areas that I had seen in larger cities.

After completing work on two projects—*Talking at Trena's* and *Living Through the Hoop*—I became specifically curious about how people "got along" in their interactions in the nightlife.[2] In 2002, I began systematic visits to the nightlife on Thursday, Friday, and Saturday evenings and nights, taking notes after each visit with the purpose of understanding how people go about having fun. I typically stood in front of Kilpatrick's by the yellow parking box on the northeastern corner of Reginald and Stuckey Streets, the busiest area in the nightlife. I observed interactions among men and women, police and patrons, and various groups of nightlife participants.

After spending time on that corner I would walk the streets of downtown, visiting the nightclubs and streets in other areas of downtown. I varied the times when I visited the corner and other locations in the nightlife. Using this approach I was able to determine significant crowd flow, differences in interaction among nightlife participants in different areas, and alternative styles of dress associated with particular areas in the nightlife. As I collected data, I read through my notes looking for emergent themes. The most significant themes became the subject of this book.

I maintained this pattern of data collection until 2005, when I accepted a position at Texas A&M University. At that time I was confident that I had collected significant data and had noted observable patterns occurring in the nightlife. Still, I made one return visit to the nightlife in Northeast in each of the following years: 2006, 2007, and 2008. I spent each visit observing the nightlife and looking for significant changes or inconsistencies from the observations I had made during my previous fieldwork.

One noted change in the nightlife was the transformations of a number of nightclubs over the years. Some had closed and not reopened. The founding and closing of various nightclubs indicated a constant shift on the part of bar owners to maximize their profits by identifying a niche. It is telling that the clubs that enjoy longevity, and seem the most financially successful, cater to the BSU student population, particularly the fraternity and sorority participants. Nightclubs attempting to create social spaces that attract diverse crowds appeared to have very limited success. I viewed this observation as significant because it suggested that nightclub owners were responding to a market that selected for White, middle-class clientele. This observation buttressed the idea that nightclubs, as social institutions, were supporting integrated segregation. Beyond the observations of club openings and closing over the years of my return visits to Northeast, my subsequent observations about the nightlife generally confirmed what I had observed during my previous extended fieldwork.

Although the insights of this book are primarily derived from observation and on-the-street conversations with participants, bouncers, and bartenders, I conducted tape-recorded interviews on my return visit in 2006 with ten Northeast nightlife participants (four White men, three White women, two Black men, and one Black woman). These interviews were conducted with nightlife participants whom I located through students whom I had known during my previous time in the field. They were selected based on their willingness and ability to be interviewed by me during my short return visit. Missing from this list of interviewees are bouncers and nightclub owners. Although interviews with bouncers and nightclub owners would have been telling, none of those I approached were willing to be interviewed. Perhaps this is not surprising given that nightclubs in Northeast consistently receive criticism from various parties for allowing underage drinking and enforcing dress codes. Hence, it is reasonable to conclude that owners and bouncers had little interest in participating in an interview that might bring greater scrutiny to them personally or to nightclubs generally.

Despite the limitations on sampling for interview subjects, I surmised that these interviews would easily meet my goal of reflecting with participants on the observations that I had made during previous data collection, and perhaps provide additional insights. After having potential interviewees telephoned by our mutual acquaintance, I telephoned them and set a time to meet. I met with the participants on campus during the day, and each completed an informed consent form.

During the interviews the participants shared interesting stories that were by and large consistent with the previous observations I had made. In some instances, their observations were inconsistent with mine. In most cases, these inconsistencies were not matters of fact but rather matters of perspective. Sorting out matters of perspective is a challenge that most researchers face when conducting social research. Interestingly, and perhaps not surprising, it was the White nightlife participants who were more likely to share observations that varied from those I had made previously, particularly with respect to issues of race. I explore these occurrences in my broader discussion of challenges in the field.

Challenges in the Field

Like other social scientists, ethnographers experience challenges to their research based upon the methodological approaches they use to collect data. For this study, many of the challenges I faced were based on three factors: my age, race, and status as a professor. Here I briefly describe each of these challenges as they relate to collecting data so that the reader might contextualize the overall insights shared throughout the book.

My Age

Since urban nightlife is typically associated with twentysomethings, the first challenge I confronted in collecting data was my age. I was thirty-seven years old when I began the study in earnest. Many nightlife participants perceived me to be older than they were, but few would have guessed me to be over thirty. This was evident from their responses after learning my age. Perhaps their impressions of my age were due to the fact that I consistently dressed the part of a college nightlife participant, wearing button-down shirts, khaki shorts, flip-flops, and other attire typically associated with the frat boy style of dress. The effect of wearing this clothing was that I appeared to be someone who could appropriately participate in nightlife activities. In fact, I received scrutiny from a number of bouncers who reviewed my driver's license and asked, "Is that you? 1965?"

Despite the fact that some participants viewed me as being an appropriate age, some used cues like my wedding band to assess my age. One female patron looked at my wedding band, turned to me, and in a drunken state said, "Hey, old man, you should be at home with your wife." Still, many nightlife participants treated me as an acceptable participant, in part because I treated their activities as normative as well. Overall, my age seemed to be a minor consideration for patrons, due in part to the fact that at least a few other thirtysomethings could be seen taking part in the nightlife each week.

My Race

My racial identity proved to be a more complex challenge to data collection. As an African American male, I had become familiar with the level of scrutiny accorded to my movement and actions in public spaces.[3] As Anderson demonstrates, police and community members frequently perceive African American males as criminal threats.[4] Similarly, nightlife participants and police seemed to use the same kind of scrutiny to assess my presence in the nightlife. Given the consistency of these kinds of assessments, I was purposeful in my efforts to reduce others' apprehensions. For instance, I rarely caravanned with groups of African American males—whose collective presence was often perceived as intimidating—and I consistently wore frat boy attire in an effort to fit in. Based upon my observations, those African Americans who easily navigated the nightlife had engaged in these behaviors. Despite this approach, my race was particularly significant for the kinds of interactions that I could have with both Black and White nightlife participants. For example, as demonstrated in chapter 6, it was rare that I had explicit conversations about race with White participants, whereas these conversations did occur with African Americans.

Interestingly, the complications associated directly with my racial identity most readily surfaced in my interviews with White interviewees. At the crux of these complications was the central question of whether an African American researcher could be a racial "insider" in conversations with White interviewees. In other words, would White subjects be forthright in sharing their thoughts, particularly on matters of race? Some scholars, engaging in what is now regarded as the "insider/outsider" debate, have argued that the pairing of researcher and subjects based on racial similarity—that is, "race matching"—is the most effective means by which to conduct qualitative research.[5] A key assumption undergirding this argument is that subjects are more willing to share intimate details with a researcher whom they consider an insider, or one whom they believe can relate to their worldview. Despite this apparent insider advantage, some scholars have argued that there are significant advantages to having outsiders conduct qualitative research.[6] A key assumption supporting this argument is that outsiders take less for granted and hence ask more probing questions about the subjects' lives than would an insider.

Based on my interview experiences, I suggest elsewhere that rather than experiencing a solely insider or outsider status, researchers and subjects experience what I call "insider moments" wherein their interests converge and they are able to share in the kinds of interactions that yield important insights.[7] I conclude that these "insider moments" can occur despite researchers' differing racial backgrounds, and hence insider research and outsider research mutually serve to meet our goal of gaining knowledge and understanding of social phenomena.

In an effort to reveal some of the complex issues that arose in my interviews with White nightlife participants, I find it useful to share portions of my interview with Danny, a twenty-two-year-old White male who grew up in a northwestern suburb of Atlanta. During our conversation I learned that Danny's parents had been part of the massive exodus of Whites from central Atlanta to surrounding suburban areas in the 1970s and 1980s. At the time that Danny was considering colleges to attend, he wanted to attend a prominent private university in the Midwest, but when his application was rejected he settled on BSU, noting that his "scholarship was too good to pass up." When I interviewed him he was starting his "fifth year," a celebrated time for some students because it is typically accompanied by a reduced course load and greater opportunity to enjoy the party scene.

In this first interview segment Danny and I discuss the public area around Club Sleepless, a nightclub that has a reputation as a place where local African Americans gather. White college students who frequented downtown labeled Club Sleepless "the Black club." As indicated in chapter 2, this moniker took on greater significance when William Ernest Moore, a twenty-year-old White male and out-of-town visitor to Northeast, was shot and killed shortly before three o'clock in the morning on the northeastern corner of Chesterwood and Maxine Streets, near Club Sleepless. In talking with Danny I had the opportunity to ask him about specific perceptions in the nightlife regarding Club Sleepless and race.

MAY: Do you ever walk passed there [Club Sleepless] or . . . ?

DANNY: Yeah, every once in a while.

MAY: Someone [another White interviewee] said to me that they, you risk your life or something [in passing Club Sleepless]. . . .

DANNY: Well, I heard like somebody got stabbed like, I think like last year or a year or two ago. [We both laugh.]

MAY: Naw. Well somebody actually got shot in front of there.

DANNY: Oh really?

MAY: This is, I think, Melissa [our mutual acquaintance] said it was her freshman year. I don't know what year that would have been for you.

DANNY: It would have been my sophomore year.

MAY: Actually I have a newspaper article about the guy. He was from another town and he bumped into a guy and the guy came outside. They were on the street. They weren't even in the club. You know so people, you know they [Club Sleepless] had a reputation that's funny.

DANNY: Oh yeah, it definitely has a negative connotation.

MAY: I wonder if actually, if somebody actually did get stabbed or is that like kind of the thing that's like. . . .

DANNY: Yeah, like word of mouth gets blown out of proportion, some guy pushed him and all of a sudden it's like, I don't know. . . .

MAY: All of a sudden [mock newscaster voice] "Somebody got stabbed." Yeah, okay.

DANNY: But I think it definitely does have like a slightly negative connotation, people are just, I think. . . .

MAY: Why does it have the connotation, you think?

DANNY: I think the shooting and the . . . and everyone who's always out there, there's always a ton of people and they're always like you know uh, pretty loud—I mean everybody's loud—I don't know, I walk by there and I don't think anything of it all.

MAY: Yeah. So do you think the race of the people that go there has anything to do with that perception at all?

DANNY: I don't know. I'd like to think it doesn't but, you know, who knows.

MAY: Right. You're not just saying that because I'm Black, are you?

DANNY: No, No [intently]. [I laugh.] Of course not, I'm the farthest thing from a racist.

MAY: Right. Well yeah, like I would like to know, 'cause it makes me curious about, you know, because I know that's one of the places that they [Blacks] go.

DANNY: Right, yeah.

Danny and I were both insiders to the nightlife—each of us knew the location of Club Sleepless, that incidents of violence had occurred in the area, and that local African Americans frequented the club—thus there was no need for what the sociologist Amy Best calls narrative "bracketing or translating" like that which may occur regularly between an insider and an outsider.[8] Although our knowledge and information about the violence occurring near Club Sleepless varied, our exchange indicated, at the least, a mutual understanding of the common thinking that one "risks their life" at a place where "somebody got stabbed" and "got shot," or that had a "reputation that's funny" with "slightly negative connotations." As long as Danny and I were engaged in a general discourse that did not move beyond our tacit understandings of Club Sleepless, we were able to maintain a relationship of insiderness—one that even permits us to share a laugh about serious violence in the area.

As we continued our collective insider experience, Danny and I questioned whether people actually got stabbed in Club Sleepless or if this idea was rumor, conjecture, or stereotyping. Despite the fact that we were talking about a nightclub establishment that was frequented by African Americans, we had yet to discuss race explicitly in the interview. I intentionally questioned the origin of reference to stabbings with the hope of stimulating discussion about race, but Danny seemed to strategically avoid making such a response. It was as if he understood that our shared insider status as nightlife participants was predicated upon the condition that we avoid explicit talk about race. Still, it was possible that Danny might also be avoiding race talk in this instance because, as Best suggests, Whites "rarely see themselves as racial meaning makers."[9] In other words, Danny may have viewed race as unimportant, while others, like myself, may have emphasized it in conversation. Irrespective of his specific reason for not talking about race, our conversation remained a comfortable abstraction from the tensions typical of interracial conversations with race as a topic.

During our interview, it was clear that tension existed around who had power to direct the interview. Although research subjects are informed that they can terminate an interview at anytime and demand the tape recording, Institutional Review Boards, researchers, and subjects alike tend to assume that researchers maintain the explicit power to determine the direction of the interview.[10] Indeed, as Danny and I were discussing the "slightly negative connotation" of Club Sleepless, my question "Why does it have the connotation you think?" was an exercise in the researcher's power to change the dynamic of the interview. Not only does this question assert my power in the interview context, but it also positions me away from Danny and insider status. It is as if I had become a racial outsider seeking to know about the thoughts of (White) insiders, and Danny had become the insider guarding these thoughts. An indication of what I perceived to be Danny's effort to manage a neutral stance toward the unnamed African Americans occurred when he told me that the "people are loud," but in an almost intuitive recognition that I might interpret his statements as negative toward African Americans he quickly offered the corrective that "everybody's loud" and he "thinks nothing of it at all." Danny's statement seemed to be a move to avoid a discussion of race.

Since I wanted to know if race mattered, I asked a direct question: "So you think the race of the people that go there has anything to do with that perception at all?" With this question the boundaries between (racial) insider/ outsider and researcher/respondent were made clear. By making race an explicit consideration, I seemed to have pressed Danny into a defensive position in our conversation—a position from which he may have felt socially safer saying "I don't know" than making an assertion and appearing racist.

In fact, Danny's subsequent matter-of-fact response, "Of course not, I'm the farthest thing from a racist," suggests that he was well aware of the importance of managing our interaction so that he does not appear racist. His response was consistent with what Bonilla-Silva identifies as a shift from Whites' explicit negative commentary about African Americans that was characteristic of the Jim Crow era to race-neutral commentary cloaking new racism, that is, "color-blind racism," wherein Whites espouse political and economic liberalism in an abstract way to explain racial matters.[11]

Interestingly, as our conversation progressed, I wondered whether my presumed insider status as a nightlife participant was in fact secondary to my race. Despite the explicit exchange regarding race that positioned me squarely as a racial outsider and researcher, Danny and I again had an insider moment based upon our shared knowledge of the nightlife when we talked about whether different racial groups interact with one another.

> MAY: Do you think that in downtown Northeast—like they have all of these places that people go to and that some people, I mean similar places they will go to, but do you think that people from different places, uh you know—I've seen Whites, Blacks, Hispanics, Asians. Do you think that those people interact together in downtown Northeast?
>
> DANNY: Um, I'd say the Hideaway [nightclub]. I've seen people of all races in the Hideaway. That's a big melting pot so to speak.
>
> MAY: You just have to kind of like music.
>
> DANNY: Yeah if you like dancing and you like music, everybody kind of like congregates, there's always like huge lines out the door to get in. So I think that's one of the biggest ones, people from all different cultures and races go to.
>
> MAY: What about on the streets?
>
> DANNY: Um, no. I mean I feel like, you know when I walk on the streets I feel like I see mostly White people. And, uh, I don't walk by Club Sleepless too much 'cause most of the bars we go to are on the other side of downtown.
>
> MAY: Do you think—so that's probably not that much interaction?
>
> DANNY: No. I mean like I said it depends on where you go, like, I don't think I've ever seen a Black person in Mutineer's. I know one Black guy who's like super fratty, he's like "frat guy" so nobody . . . I don't know, he's not really. . . .
>
> MAY: Questions that. It's like oh. . . .
>
> DANNY: Exactly. He would be in there but other than that. 'Cause it's very southern, they have like Confederate flags up and stuff like that.

Danny and I shared an insider moment as we talked about the places where different groups might be seen interacting. Even when discussing Mutineer's—an establishment whose Confederate flag and "Old South" atmosphere had drawn antiracist protests—we shared an understanding of who goes where and why.

Although Danny and I shared an insider moment in our discussion, it was clear that he and I were negotiating the meaning of race as we interacted as interviewer and interviewee. For instance, Danny's references to "super fratty" and "frat guy" in the context of downtown nightlife were taken to mean that the individual was wealthy relative to other male nightlife participants; but more important, both Black and White nightlife participants used the term "frat boy" to reference White fraternity members despite there being Black fraternities. Hence, Danny's reference to a Black male as a "frat guy" immediately conjured up a contradictory image for me. Having been to Mutineer's, as well as recognizing that some individuals use the stereotype that African Americans of the middle and upper classes are culturally "White," I surmised Danny's meaning. Given our implicitly negotiated definition of race, I took the "frat guy's" behavior to be such that few White nightlife participants would take him to be "really" Black and thus a real threat to the social setting.

During the interview, Danny and I experienced insider moments as nightlife participants, yet a key interpretive challenge that remained evident throughout our conversation, and in other interviews as well, was how to assess both my own and the interviewees' motives for talking about race in a particular way. Although I was privileged to know my own motives—primarily to probe interviewees in order to understand their perspectives on race in the nightlife—I was not privy to insights regarding my respondents' motives. This raises questions related to the advantages and disadvantages of insider/outsider status in research. For instance, would Danny or the other interviewees have talked about race the same way with their White counterparts or a White researcher? Were the interviewees avoiding more explicit negative commentary about race because I am African American? Knowing answers to these questions is the challenge. Yet I believe that although these challenges were particularly difficult for me as an outsider, the interviews proved useful for exposing the complexity of everyday conversations about race. Furthermore, I believe that my analyses of interviews were conducted in good faith and have produced representations of at least some nightlife participants' "realities." Certainly throughout this research I have learned, if nothing else, that interracial interactions continue to be challenging for researchers engaged in qualitative investigation.

My Status

Although my race provided a challenge to gaining access to the perspectives of White nightlife participants, my status as a professor created opportunities for access to those perspectives. My frequent presence in the nightlife meant that I often encountered current and former students, mostly White. Many of my students were surprised to see me in the nightlife. Some students told me that they thought my presence was odd, but most of them responded with excitement when they encountered me. I felt that students grew comfortable seeing me out, especially when they realized that I was not evaluating their nightlife participation specifically, but rather generally observing the nightlife. Some students, caravanning with friends, would look for me on the corner. They took our corner meeting as an opportunity to introduce their friends to a "cool" professor. These introductions and conversations proved to be valuable sources of information. Some students confided in me about their personal difficulties like situations with boyfriends or girlfriends, while other students talked explicitly about their negative nightlife experiences. In a sense, I felt that these participants treated the corner as an extension of my office. Perhaps this thinking is nothing more than a belief in my own self-worth.

My interaction with students and former students frequently led to invitations to pregaming parties. I typically "stopped by" these parties, met friends or acquaintances of the students, and departed. Most students were excited to have had me pass through their gathering. It was through these passing interactions that I was able to chart the ways in which nightlife participants were socially connected to one another prior to arriving to the nightlife. I would later observe these participants caravanning with one another or with a subgroup from the pregaming location, thereby garnering evidence of the importance of caravanning groups for social interactions in the nightlife.

As a professor interacting with current and former students within the context of urban nightlife, I was presented with potential ethical issues. I used two simple strategies for navigating these issues. First, I avoided using as research data direct observations or stories garnered from students who were currently enrolled in my classes at the time that I conducted the research. These particular stories and events became part of a broader way to think about behavior and activities of other nightlife participants, but the actual events themselves have not been specifically cited in this book. Furthermore, I rarely engaged current students in specific conversations about observations I had made in the nightlife when we were outside of the nightlife. Many students approached me to reflect upon these nightlife events when we were on campus, in the gym, passing between classes, or around town, but I generally indicated that those events had no bearing on my interactions outside of the nightlife.

The second strategy I used for navigating potential ethical issues was to make certain to speak explicitly with former students indicating that I was wearing the "hat of a researcher." This strategy gave former students the opportunity to opt out of conversations about their experiences. In general, the students made me feel as though they trusted me. Whether this was in fact the case can be confirmed only by the subjects themselves. As Duneier discovered in his research on homeless book sellers, there are times when subjects act as though they accept the researcher, but in her or his absence they may indicate to others that they do not.[12] Despite the possibility that students may have feigned their trust or acceptance of me, I felt trusted and accepted. This is because many former students—who understood that I kept things in confidence based upon the ways I had interacted with them regarding personal matters that might have arisen during their time in class—sought me out when they wanted to explicitly share observations with me for my research. If they were former students, I welcomed such insights. Using these two strategies I was generally able to manage my role as a professor, researcher, nightlife participant, gym regular, collegiate athlete fan, observer of everyday life, community basketball coach, and so on without much conflict.

The fact that many students approached me meant that I garnered attention from other nightlife participants as I stood on the corner or moved through the nightclubs. These onlookers seemed to be trying to assess my identity. I later discovered that some of these assessments included being identified by others as a university athlete, a drug dealer, or a police officer. Despite the variety of impressions that others had of me, one that seemed to resonate with several nightlife participants who did not know me was that of a police officer. This was because of my apparent striking resemblance to an officer of similar build, complexion, and appearance. On at least three different occasions passing nightlife participants said, "What's up, Rod?" Fortunately, I was able to clarify my identity by looking at the patrons closely and proclaiming, "I'm not Rod." One patron responded, "Sorry, man. I thought you were Rod. He's a police officer that hangs out down here."

Perhaps nightlife participants' perceptions of my identity were fostered by the fact that I rarely drank alcoholic beverages when I was conducting fieldwork. On the occasions that I did have a drink, I would simply sip on a bottle of beer through the night as a means of supporting my identity as a participant in the nightlife. There were several times students offered to buy me a drink, even as I stood on the corner. I simply refused these offers given the potential complications that might arise from accepting such offers. I typically stated something like, "I have to keep my mind clear because I'm working." Most nightlife participants accepted this as a viable explanation for my refusal of their offer. These occurrences were kept to a minimum by simply caravanning from nightclub to nightclub and spending considerable amounts of time on the corner. Hence, I rarely became fully engaged in the activities of nightlife participants who were seeking to have fun.

Writing about the Nightlife

In ethnography, the experiences of the researcher become the most significant sources of data. Whether these experiences include direct interaction with other participants, hearing participants' conversations about their experiences, or observing participants' interactions with one another, the ethnographic endeavor is contingent upon how the researcher perceives the activities. Furthermore, the ethnographer's perceptions of activities are viewed through the lens of her or his own background. Hence, how ethnographers write about their observations is decidedly personal. This fact limits the generalizability of the observations of any ethnographic project, yet there is much to be gained by an in-depth understanding of particular social contexts. My approach to this limitation has been to write a narrative that includes my personal experiences, and then to extract explicit concepts that readers or other researchers might employ in their observations of other contexts. The success of this effort must be measured by the utility of my concepts for explaining social life beyond the observations that I have made about the nightlife in Northeast. Ultimately, this is a matter for the reader to determine.

Notes

Chapter 1   Integrated Segregation in Urban Nightlife

1. The names of people and places have been changed so that their identities might remain anonymous.
2. Some of the scholars associated with this school include Robert E. Park, Ernest Burgess, Louis Wirth, Everett C. Hughes, Florian Znaniecki and W. I. Thomas, among others. For a discussion of the Chicago School, see Martin Bulmer, *The Chicago School of Sociology: Institutionalization, Diversity, and the Rise of Sociological Research* (Chicago: University of Chicago Press, 1984); Andrew Abbott, *Department and Discipline: Chicago Sociology at One Hundred* (Chicago: University of Chicago Press, 1999); and for a discussion of researchers associated with subsequent waves of the Chicago School, see Gary Alan Fine, ed., *A Second Chicago School? The Development of a Postwar American Sociology* (Chicago: University of Chicago Press, 1995).
3. For instance, see Robert E. Park and Ernest W. Burgess, *Introduction to the Science of Sociology* (Chicago: University of Chicago Press, 1924); Robert E. Park, Ernest W. Burgess, and Roderick D. McKenzie, *The City* (Chicago: University of Chicago Press, 1925); Frederic M. Thrasher, *The Gang: A Study of 1,313 Gangs in Chicago*, 2nd rev. ed. (Chicago: University of Chicago Press, 1936); and St. Clair Drake and Horace R. Cayton, *Black Metropolis: A Study of Negro Life in a Northern City* (New York: Harcourt, Brace, 1945).
4. Elijah Anderson, "Folk Ethnography and the Cosmopolitan Canopy," *Annals of the American Academy of Political and Social Science* 595, no. 1 (2004): 14–31, 22.
5. For a collection of readings addressing the topic, see, for example, Norman K. Denzin and Yvonna S. Lincoln, eds., *The Sage Handbook of Qualitative Research*, 3rd ed. (Thousand Oaks, CA: Sage, 2005).
6. For discussion of the idea of "place" over "space," see Thomas F. Gieryn, "A Space for Place in Sociology," *Annual Review of Sociology* 26 (2000): 463–496.
7. Lyn H. Lofland, *The Public Realm: Exploring the City's Quintessential Social Territory* (Hawthorne, NY: Aldine de Gruyter, 1998), 8.
8. Henri Lefebvre, *The Social Production of Space*, trans. Donald Nicholson-Smith (1974; repr., Malden, MA: Blackwell, 2000).

9. See John Dixon, Mark Levine, and Rob McCauley, "Locating Impropriety: Street Drinking, Moral Order, and the Ideological Dilemma of Public Space," *Political Psychology* 27, no. 2 (2006): 187–206, 190.

10. Lofland, *Public Realm*, 8.

11. Elijah Anderson, *Streetwise: Race, Class, and Change in an Urban Community* (Chicago: University of Chicago Press, 1990).

12. Ibid., 5–6.

13. Ibid., 6.

14. Lyn H. Lofland, *A World of Strangers: Order and Action in Urban Public Space* (New York: Basic Books, 1973); Lofland, *Public Realm*; Elijah Anderson, *Code of the Street: Decency, Violence, and the Moral Life of the Inner City* (New York: Norton, 1999); and Mitchell Duneier, *Slim's Table: Race, Respectability, and Masculinity* (Chicago: University of Chicago Press, 1992).

15. Mitchell Duneier, *Sidewalk* (New York: Farrar, Straus and Giroux, 1999), 190.

16. Ibid., 213.

17. Ibid., 214.

18. Lofland refers to this process of assessment as appearential and spatial ordering. For a discussion, see *World of Strangers*.

19. Elijah Anderson, *Cosmopolitan Canopy: Race and Civility in Everyday Life* (New York: Norton, 2011).

20. Ibid., xiv.

21. Anderson acknowledges that there is continued racism and discrimination in public places. For instance, he talks extensively about tension between African Americans and Whites on the city streets. See ibid., chaps. 5, 7, and 8. Although Anderson acknowledges these tensions, he remains optimistic about the transformative power of cosmopolitan canopies that make people aware of the humanity of strangers whom they might have simply dismissed if it were not for consistent interaction under the canopy. Anderson suggests that because strangers are given the opportunity to meet and get to know not only individuals, but also "types" of strangers, cosmopolitan canopies can be a "profoundly humanizing experience." Ibid., 275.

22. Big South University is ranked each year as one of the top party schools in the country by several listings including PubClub, *Princeton Review*, and Redeye.

23. See Appendix A for a brief discussion of the history of Northeast and Big South University.

24. See "Population & Demographics 2000," Northeast County information, http://factfinder.census.gov (retrieved May 20, 2005).

25. *Big South University 2004 Statistics* (retrieved May 24, 2005).

26. These data were garnered through a detailed physical mapping of the area on foot. I especially thank my research assistant Kenneth Sean Chaplin for compiling this information.

27. See Gerald Suttles, *The Social Order of the Slum: Ethnicity and Territory in the Inner City* (Chicago: University of Chicago Press, 1970).

28. Ibid., 10.

29. Ibid., 52–54.

30. See Marcus A. Hunter, "The Nightly Round: Space, Social Capital, and Urban Black Nightlife," *City & Community* 9, no. 2 (2010): 165–186.

31. For a discussion of symbolic and social boundaries, see Michèle Lamont, *Money, Morals, and Manners: The Culture of the French and the American Upper-Middle*

Class (Chicago: University of Chicago Press, 1992); and Michèle Lamont and Virag Molnar, "The Study of Boundaries in the Social Science," *Annual Review of Sociology* 28 (2002): 167–195.

32. Lamont, *Money, Morals, and Manners,* 9.

33. Lamont and Molnar, "Study of Boundaries," 168.

34. For a detailed discussion of pregaming rituals for college students in Philadelphia, see David Grazian, *On the Make: The Hustle of Urban Nightlife* (Chicago: University of Chicago Press, 2007).

35. According to some sociologists "scenes" draw particular kinds of individuals who wish to consume particular kinds of amenities, for example, arts, music, or foods. Although the concept of "scenes" is useful for explaining why particular individuals are drawn to particular amenities, the concept of integrated segregation enhances our understanding of scenes by demonstrating ways in which patterns of consumption might also be determined by the collective action of groups, for instance, caravanning groups, outside of the scenes. For a discussion of scenes, see Daniel Silver, Terry Nichols Clark, and Clemente Jesus Navarro Yanez, "Scenes: Social Context in an Age of Contingency," *Social Forces* 88, no. 5 (2010): 2293–2324.

36. See Beverly D. Tatum, *Why Are All the Black Kids Sitting Together in the Cafeteria: And Other Conversations about Race* (1997; repr., New York: Basic Books, 2003). Similarly Amanda Lewis demonstrates the ways in which racial signification structures the kinds of interactions that minority youth have in the schoolyard, thereby producing segregated play spaces as the youth choose to gravitate toward those who have a shared racial identification. See Amanda E. Lewis, *Race in the Schoolyard: Negotiating the Color Line in Classrooms and Communities* (New Brunswick, NJ: Rutgers University Press, 2003).

37. For a discussion of status, status honor, and status group, see Max Weber, *From Max Weber: Essays in Sociology,* ed. H. H. Gerth and C. Wright Mills (New York: Oxford University Press, 1946).

38. According to Lofland, the "parochial realm" is characterized "by a sense of commonality among acquaintances and neighbors who are involved in interpersonal networks that are located within "communities." See Lofland, *Public Realm,* 9. Unlike the "public realm" characterized by contact between strangers and the "private realm" characterized by kin networks, the parochial realm suggests familiarity among participants.

39. Sociologists have argued that there is no biological basis for race, yet physical characteristics, like skin color, continue to be given social significance. For an analysis and overview of some of the social consequences of race in America, see Neil J. Smelser, William Julius Wilson, and Faith Mitchell, eds., *America Becoming: Racial Trends and Their Consequences,* vol. 1 (Washington, DC: National Academies Press, 2001).

40. Eduardo Bonilla-Silva, *Racism Without Racists: Colorblind Racism and the Persistence of Racial Inequality in the United States,* 2nd ed. (Lanham, MD: Rowman & Littlefield, 2006).

41. Joe R. Feagin, *Systemic Racism: A Theory of Oppression* (New York: Routledge, 2006).

42. Scholars like Bonilla-Silva and Feagin have argued that anti-Black racism is rooted in the structure of American society. For a discussion of these issues, see Bonilla-Silva, *Racism Without Racists* and Feagin, *Systemic Racism.*

43. For a discussion of how physical characteristics are used as a proxy for race, see Anderson, *Streetwise*; Duneier, *Sidewalk*; Edward W. Morris, "Researching Race: Identifying a Social Construction through Qualitative Methods and an Interactionist Perspective," *Symbolic Interaction* 30, no. 3 (2007): 409–425; and Patricia Hill Collins, *Black Sexual Politics: African Americans, Gender, and the New Racism* (New York: Routledge, 2004).

44. The listing of these categories is not to suggest that the groups are mutually exclusive. For example, there are White and Black students who are also both athletes and fraternity members. Indeed, the nuanced analysis in subsequent chapters reveals that it is the intersecting of these group memberships that may become the basis for conflict in the patrons' use of urban public space.

45. For example, see Herminia Ibarra, "Paving an Alternative Route: Gender Differences in Managerial Networks," *Social Psychology Quarterly* 60 (1997): 91–102, for a discussion of gender and networks; Herminia Ibarra, "Race, Opportunity, and Diversity of Social Circles in Managerial Networks," *Academy of Management Journal* 38 (1995): 673–703, for a discussion of race and social networks; and Edward Laumann, *Networks of Collective Action* (New York: Academic Press, 1976) and Claude S. Fischer, *To Dwell among Friends: Personal Networks in Town and City* (Chicago: University of Chicago Press, 1982) for a discussion of social class and networks.

46. Although members of the same category—White students in this instance—will be brought into contact with one another based on population density, there are a number of factors that impact the strength and nature of the social ties they establish within the subpopulations. For instance, the organizational context might structure the level of interaction between individuals within the same group. See Peter M. Blau, *Inequality and Heterogeneity: A Primitive Theory of Social Structure* (New York: Free Press, 1977). The strength of these ties might also be influenced by interpersonal interaction, positive identification, competition for resources, and the statuses of one's friends. For example, see Ray E. Reagans, "Preferences, Identity, and Competition: Predicting Tie Strength from Demographic Data," *Management Science* 51 (2005): 1374–1383; and Kazuo Yamaguchi, "Homophily and Social Distance in the Choice of Multiple Friends: An Analysis Based on Conditionally Symmetric Log-Bilinear Association Models," *Journal of the American Statistical Association* 85 (1990): 356–366.

47. In general, individuals seeking to form social ties to others may self-select based upon status. For example, see Laumann, *Networks of Collective Action*; J. Miller McPherson and Lynn Smith-Lovin, "Homophily in Voluntary Organizations: Status Distance and the Composition of Face-to-Face Groups," *American Sociological Review* 52 (1987): 370–379; and Michael A. Hogg and Sarah C. Hains, "Intergroup Relations and Group Solidarity: Effects of Group Identification and Social Beliefs on Depersonalized Attraction," *Journal of Personality and Social Psychology* 70, no. 2 (1996): 295–309.

48. For a discussion, see Michael Hogg, *The Social Psychology of Group Cohesiveness: From Attraction to Social Identity* (Hemel Hempstead, UK: Harvester Wheatsheaf, 1992); Michael Hogg, "Group Cohesiveness: A Critical Review and Some New Directions," *European Review of Social Psychology* 4 (1993): 85–111; and Reagans, "Preferences, Identity, and Competition."

49. Social scientists have long recognized how unfavorable feelings toward out-groups have drawn racial and ethnic groups together. For instance, see Gordon W. Allport,

The Nature of Prejudice (Reading, MA: Addison-Wesley, 1954); Herbert Blumer, "Race Prejudice as a Sense of Group Position," *Pacific Sociological Review* 1, no. 1 (1958): 3–7; Mary R. Jackman and Mary Scheuer Senter, "Different Therefore Unequal: Beliefs about Groups of Unequal Status," *Research in Social Stratification and Mobility* 2 (1983): 309–335; Hurbert M. Blalock, *Toward a Theory of Minority-Group Relations* (New York: John Wiley, 1967); Lawrence Bobo and Vincent L. Hutchings, "Perceptions of Racial Group Competition: Extending Blumer's Theory of Group Position to a Multiracial Social Context," *American Sociological Review* 61, no. 6 (1996): 951–972; and Tatum, *Why Are.*

50. Although there has been a recent decline in the levels of residential segregation throughout the United States, according to Iceland, Weinberg, and Steinmetz residential segregation in the country remains significant. See John Iceland, Daniel H. Weinberg, and Erica Steinmetz, *U.S. Census Bureau, Series CENSR-3, Racial and Ethnic Residential Segregation in the United States: 1980–2000* (Washington, DC: Government Printing Office, 2002). For a discussion of the persistence of residential segregation in America's urban areas, see Douglass Massey and Nancy A. Denton, *American Apartheid: Segregation and the Making of the Underclass* (Cambridge, MA: Harvard University Press, 1993); Reynolds Farley and William H. Frey, "Changes in the Segregation of Whites from Blacks during the 1980s: Small Steps toward a More Integrated Society," *American Sociological Review* 59 (1994): 23–45; Lawrence Bobo, Howard Schuman, and Charlotte Steeh, "Changing Attitudes toward Residential Integration," in *Housing Desegregation and Federal Policy*, ed. John M. Goering (Chapel Hill: University of North Carolina Press, 1986), 152–169; Iceland, Weinberg, and Steinmetz, *U.S. Census Bureau*; David Card, Alexandre Mas, and Jesse Rothstein, "Tipping and the Dynamics of Segregation," *Quarterly Journal of Economics* 123, no. 1 (February 2008): 177–218; and John Farley, "Even Whiter Than We Thought: What Median Residential Exposure Indices Reveal about White Neighborhood Contact with African Americans in U.S. Metropolitan Areas," *Social Science Research* 37 (2008): 604–623.

51. The concept of class is indicated in the classical works of Karl Marx and Max Weber, both of whom viewed class status as a basis of one's location within the context of the economy. For a discussion, see Karl Marx, "Communist Manifesto [1848]," in *The Marx-Engels Reader*, ed. Robert C. Tucker (New York: Norton, 1978) and Weber, *From Max Weber.* One measure of participation within the economic structure and hence one's social class is occupational attainment. This perspective was elaborated in the work of Blau and Duncan, who focused on the occupational structure and patterns of mobility. For a discussion, see Peter Blau and Otis Dudley Duncan, *The American Occupational Structure* (New York: John Wiley, 1967). In general, stratification theorists link categories of educational attainment, income, and schooling to talk about social class. Recent discussions of class have also considered the malleability of class status. I am particularly concerned with the symbols patrons use and the meanings they give those symbols as markers of class.

52. For a discussion, see Reuben A. Buford May, *Talking at Trena's: Everyday Conversations at an African American Tavern* (New York: New York University Press, 2001), chap. 2. In addition, literature on the Black middle class examines the ongoing tensions between racial identity and social class status. In general, these studies posit the image work that middle-class Blacks must undertake to navigate class and

race within various social contexts. For a discussion about this tension for Blacks in Harlem, see John L. Jackson, *Harlemworld: Doing Race and Class in Contemporary America* (Chicago: University of Chicago Press, 2001); for Blacks in Washington, D.C., see Karyn Lacy, *Blue Chip Black: Race, Class, Status in the New Black Middle Class* (Berkeley: University of California Press, 2007); and for Blacks in Chicago, see Mary E. Pattillo, *Black on the Block: The Politics of Race and Class in the City* (Chicago: University of Chicago Press, 2007).

53. Pattillo, *Black on the Block*, 13.

54. William J. Wilson, *More Than Just Race: Being Black and Poor in the Inner City* (New York: Norton, 2009), 14–15. For an excellent discussion expounding upon the idea of culture as values, norms, behaviors, and beliefs, see Wendy Griswold, *Cultures and Societies in a Changing World* (Thousand Oaks, CA: Pine Forge Press, 1994). The literature also focuses on the interpretive function of culture as a "tool kit" for understanding one's social world. For an interesting discussion, see Ann Swidler, "Culture in Action: Symbols and Strategies," *American Sociological Review* 51, no. 2 (1986): 273–286.

55. For an elaboration of the notions of "cultural capital" and habitus, see Pierre Bourdieu, *Distinction: A Social Critique of the Judgment of Taste*, trans. Richard Nice (Cambridge, MA: Harvard University Press, 1984). Bourdieu's theoretical ideas have been readily utilized, yet his work on cultural capital has also received substantial criticism. For instance, see Michèle Lamont and Annette Lareau, "Culture Capital: Allusions, Gaps, and Glissandos in Recent Theoretical Developments," *Sociological Theory* 6 (1988): 153–168; John R. Hall, "The Capital(s) of Cultures: A Nonholistic Approach to Status Situations, Class, Gender, and Ethnicity," in *Cultivating Differences: Symbolic Boundaries and the Making of Inequality*, ed. Michèle Lamont and Marcel Fournier (Chicago: University of Chicago Press, 1992), 257–285; Lamont, *Money, Morals, and Manners*; Alan Warde, "Dimensions of a Social Theory of Taste," *Journal of Cultural Economy* 1, no. 3 (2008): 322–336; and Prudence Carter, "Black Cultural Capital, Status Positioning, and Schooling Conflicts for Low-Income African American Youth," *Social Problems* 50 (2003): 136–155. For Bourdieu's response to some of these critiques, see Pierre Bourdieu, "Social Space and Symbolic Power," *Sociological Theory* 7, no. 1 (1989): 14–25.

56. Mary T. Douglas and Baron Isherwood, *The World of Goods* (New York: Basic Books, 1979).

57. For example, see Georg Simmel, "The Stranger [1903]," in *On Individuality and Social Forms*, ed. D. Levine (Chicago: University of Chicago Press, 1971), 143–149; Georg Simmel, "The Metropolis and Mental Life [1903]," in Levine, *On Individuality and Social Forms*, 324–339; William Foote Whyte, *Street Corner Society: The Social Structure of an Italian Slum* (Chicago: University of Chicago Press, 1943); Herbert J. Gans, *The Urban Villagers: Group and Class in the Life of Italian-Americans* (New York: Free Press, 1962); and Lofland, *World of Strangers*.

58. For instance, see classic studies like Suttles, *Social Order of the Slum*, and Jonathan Rieder, *Canarsie: The Jews and Italians of Brooklyn Against Liberalism* (Cambridge, MA: Harvard University Press, 1985).

59. See, for instance, Anderson, *Streetwise* and Anderson, *Code of the Street*.

60. Sociologists concerned with interaction on the city streets often draw upon the work of Erving Goffman, who has written extensively about the nature of face-to-face interaction. For example, see Erving Goffman, *The Presentation of Self in*

Everyday Life (New York: Doubleday, 1959) for an analysis of face-to-face interaction as a dramaturgical event; Erving Goffman, *Encounters: Two Studies in the Sociology of Interaction* (Indianapolis: Bobbs Merrill, 1961) for the analysis of interaction using the metaphor of games; Erving Goffman, *Behavior in Public Places: Notes on the Social Organization of Gatherings* (New York: Free Press, 1963) for analysis of face-to-face interaction as an effort to maintain the social order; and Erving Goffman, *Forms of Talk* (1981; repr., Philadelphia: University of Pennsylvania Press, 1983) for the contextual nature of face-to-face interaction. I draw on Goffman's work variously throughout my analysis of interaction on the city streets and in the nightclubs.

Chapter 2   What Is Having Fun and Who Has It

1. Amanda Coffey, *The Ethnographic Self: Fieldwork and the Representation of Identity* (Thousand Oaks, CA: Sage, 1999), 78.
2. For a discussion, see Paul Chatterton and Robert Hollands, *Urban Nightscapes: Youth Cultures, Pleasure Spaces, and Corporate Power* (New York: Routledge, 2003).
3. For a discussion of ideal types, see Max Weber, "Basic Sociological Terms," in *Economy and Society*, ed. G. Roth and C. Wittich (Berkeley: University of California Press, 1978), 3–62.
4. Segregation and alienation from White social life pressed a group of young Black men at Cornell University to form the first Black national Greek-letter organization in 1906. For a discussion, see Charles H. Wesley, *The History of Alpha Phi Alpha: A Development in College Life, 1906–1969*, 11th ed. (Chicago: Foundation, 1969).
5. Lawrence C. Ross, *The Divine Nine: The History of African American Fraternities and Sororities* (New York: Kensington, 2000).
6. For a discussion of the usefulness of loose network ties for gaining access to opportunities and resources, see Mark S. Granovetter, "The Strength of Weak Ties," *American Journal of Sociology* 78, no. 6 (1973): 1360–1380. For an interesting counterargument suggesting the ineffectiveness of network ties in the case of jobs among the urban poor, see Sandra Susan Smith, *Lone Pursuit: Distrust and Defensive Individualism among the Black Poor* (New York: Russell Sage Foundation, 2007).
7. See Northeast County, Municipal Code of Ordinances.
8. For an interesting discussion of White spaces, see Wendy L. Moore, *Reproducing Racism: White Space, Elite Law Schools, and Racial Inequality* (Lanham, MD: Rowman & Littlefield, 2007).
9. See Northeast County, Municipal Code of Ordinances.

Chapter 3   Gendered Interaction, Caravanning Groups, and Social Boundaries

1. Elijah Anderson, *Cosmopolitan Canopy: Race and Civility in Everyday Life* (New York: Norton, 2011), xiv.
2. Following Lorber, I use the designations of male and female to represent the biological designations assigned to the sexes, while gender is the social meaning given to those biological designations. According to Lorber, gender "is a human invention; like language, kinship, religion, and technology; like them, gender organizes human social life in culturally patterned ways" (6). For a discussion of the contradictions

in the concepts of gender, see Judith Lorber, *Paradoxes of Gender* (New Haven, CT: Yale University Press, 1994).

3. See Lorber, *Paradoxes*; Candace West and Don Zimmerman, "Doing Gender," *Gender and Society* 1, no. 2 (1987): 125–151; R. W. Connell, *Masculinities* (Berkeley: University of California Press, 1995); R. W. Connell, *The Men and the Boys* (Berkeley: University of California Press, 2000); G. Canada, "Learning to Fight," in *Men's Lives*, ed. M. Kimmel and M. Messner (Boston: Allyn and Bacon, 2001), 100–103; Judith Butler, *Gender Trouble: Feminism and the Subversion of Identity* (New York: Routledge, 1999); Michael Kimmel, *The Gendered Society* (New York: Oxford University Press, 2000); Michael Messner, *Power at Play: Sports and the Problem of Masculinity* (Boston: Beacon, 1999); and Patricia Hill Collins, *Black Feminist Thought: Knowledge, Consciousness, and the Politics of Empowerment* (New York: Routledge, 2000).

4. Lorber, *Paradoxes*, 6.

5. For a discussion of regional differences, see Rebecca S. Powers, Jill J. Suitor, Susana Guerra, Monisa Shackelford, Dorothy Mecom, and Kim Gusman, "Regional Differences in Gender-Role Attitudes: Variations by Gender and Race," *Gender Issues* 21, no. 2 (2003): 40–54.

6. David Grazian, *On the Make: The Hustle of Urban Nightlife* (Chicago: University of Chicago Press, 2007), 135.

7. Annette Markham, "'Go Ugly Early': Fragmented Narrative and Bricolage as Interpretive Method," *Qualitative Inquiry* 11, no. 6 (2005): 813–839, 814.

8. Grazian, *On the Make*, 139.

9. For a discussion of women's attempts to balance casual relationships with the ideal of long-term relationships, see Norval Glenn, *Hooking Up, Hanging Out, and Hoping for Mr. Right: College Women on Dating and Mating Today* (New York: Institute for American Values, 2001).

10. For an examination of first marriage trend data, see Tavia Simmons and Jane Lawler D.ye, "What Has Happened to Median Age at First Marriage Data?" (paper, American Sociological Association, San Francisco, August 14–17, 2004).

11. Carol Brooks Gardner, *Passing By: Gender and Public Harassment* (Berkeley: University of California Press, 1995). For additional perspectives, see Ross MacMillan, Annette Nierobisz, and Sandy Welsh, "Experiencing the Streets: Harassment and Perceptions of Safety among Women," *Journal of Research in Crime and Delinquency* 37 (2000): 306–322; Emanuela Guano, "Respectable Ladies and Uncouth Men: The Performative Politics of Class and Gender in the Public Realm of an Italian City," *Journal of American Folklore* 120 (2007): 48–72; and Hille Koskela and Sirpa Tani, "Sold Out! Women's Practices of Resistance against Prostitution-Related Sexual Harassment," *Women's Studies International Forum* 28, no. 5 (2005): 418–429.

12. For an interesting discussion, see Kathleen Bogle, *Hooking Up: Sex, Dating, and Relationships on Campus* (New York: New York University Press, 2008).

13. For instance, David Grazian cites a study by Edward O. Laumann, John H. Gagnon, Robert T. Michael, and Stuart Michaels, *The Social Organization of Sexuality: Sexual Practices in the United States* (Chicago: University of Chicago Press, 1994), in which only 16.7 percent of men and 5.5 percent of women reported engaging in sexual activity with a member of the opposite sex within two days of meeting them. An additional study found that one-fifth of heterosexual adults aged eighteen to fifty-nine report having met their most recent sexual partner in a bar, nightclub,

or dance club. See Jenna Mahay and Edward O. Laumann, "Neighborhoods as Sex Markets," in the *Sexual Organization of the City*, ed. Edward O. Laumann, Stephen Ellingson, Jenna Mahay, Anthony Paik, and Yoosik Youm (Chicago: University of Chicago Press, 2004), 74. Irrespective of these statistics, the idea of immediate sexual conquests looms large for patrons of the urban nightlife.

14. For discussions of how general physical descriptors and other factors influence mate selection, see Raymond Fisman, Sheena Iyengar, Emik Kamenica, and Itamar Simonson, "Gender Differences in Mate Selection: Evidence from a Speed Dating Experiment," *Quarterly Journal of Economics* 121, no. 2 (2006): 673–697; Claire A. Conway, Benedict C. Jones, Lisa M. DeBruine, and Anthony C. Little, "Sexual Dimorphism of Male Face Shape, Partnership Status, and the Temporal Context of Relationship Sought Modulate Women's Preferences for Direct Gaze," *British Journal of Psychology* 101 (2010): 109–121; Nicolas Guéguen, "Brief Report: The Effects of Women's Cosmetics on Men's Approach: An Evaluation in a Bar," *North American Journal of Psychology* 10, no. 1 (2008): 221–227; Piers L. Cornelissen, Peter J. B. Hancock, Vesa Kiviniemi, Hannah George, and Martin J. Tovée, "Patterns of Eye Movements When Male and Female Observers Judge Female Attractiveness, Body Fat, and Waist-to-Hip Ratio," *Evolution and Human Behavior* 30, no. 6 (2009): 417–428; Thomas E. Currie and Anthony C. Little, "The Relative Importance of the Face and Body in Judgments of Human Physical Attractiveness," *Evolution and Human Behavior* 30, no. 6 (2009): 409–416. These kinds of studies, taken collectively, suggest that male and female evaluation of potential mate attractiveness is influenced by a number of conditions, including, as I argue, the social context within which these judgments are being made.

15. David Grazian suggests that the female patrons in his study use strategies of *combat, engagement, avoidance,* and *deceit.* He groups these strategies according to whether they are confrontational or evasive and whether they require forthrightness or deception. For a discussion of these categories and examples, see Grazian, *On the Make*, 181–190.

16. Markham, "'Go Ugly Early,'" 813–839.

17. Ibid., 824.

18. For a discussion of public streets as the domain of men, see Gardner, *Passing By*; Laura Beth Nielsen, "Situating Legal Consciousness: Experiences and Attitudes of Ordinary Citizens about Law and Street Harassment," *Law & Society Review* 34, no. 4 (2000): 1055–1090; and Deirdre E. Davis, "The Harm That Has No Name: Street Harassment, Embodiment, and African American Women," in *Critical Race Feminism: A Reader*, ed. Adrien Katherine Wing (New York: New York University Press, 1997).

19. Mitchell Duneier, *Sidewalk* (New York: Farrar, Straus and Giroux, 1999), 210.

20. For a discussion, see Laura Rivera, "Status Distinctions in Interaction: Social Selection and Exclusion at an Elite Nightclub," *Qualitative Sociology* 33 (2010): 229–255.

21. Sociologists have long used social types as abstract concepts to describe human life and behavior. For an early formulation of such types, see Max Weber, *The Methodology of the Social Sciences*, trans. and ed. Edward A. Shils and Henry A. Finch (1903–1917; repr., New York: Free Press, 1997), 88.

22. Many scholars have focused on the social significance of styles of dress as a key means for assigning others to social groupings. For a discussion, see Diana Crane, *Fashion and Its Social Agendas: Class, Gender, and Identity in Clothing* (Chicago:

University of Chicago Press, 2000); Ruth P. Rubinstein, *Dress Codes: Meanings and Messages in American Culture*, 2nd ed. (Boulder, CO: Westview, 2001); Thorstein Veblen, *The Theory of the Leisure Class: An Economic Study of Institutions* (1899; repr., New York: Dover, 1994); and Georg Simmel, "Fashion [1904]," *American Journal of Sociology* 62 (May 1957): 541–558.

23. Rivera, "Status Distinctions," 229–255.

24. Despite wearing popular brands like Abercrombie & Fitch and Hollister, many college students attempt to carve out their own individual fashion identity. For a discussion of the process by which consumers assert their individualism despite wearing brands made popular through advertisement campaigns, see Terry Newholm and Gillian C. Hopkinson, "I Just Tend to Wear What I Like: Contemporary Consumption and the Paradoxical Construction of Individuality," *Marketing Theory* 9, no. 4 (2009): 439–462.

25. For a detailed description of the process of categorizing strangers based on appearance and spatial location in the public space, see Lyn H. Lofland, *A World of Strangers: Order and Action in Urban Public Space* (New York: Basic Books, 1973).

26. For a discussion of the fluid definitions of social class, see Karl Marx, "Communist Manifesto [1848]," in *The Marx-Engels Reader*, ed. Robert C. Tucker (New York: Norton, 1978); Max Weber, *From Max Weber: Essays in Sociology*, ed. H. H. Gerth and C. Wright Mills (New York: Oxford University Press, 1946); Peter Blau and Otis Dudley Duncan, *The American Occupational Structure* (New York: John Wiley, 1967). The issue of class status is especially complicated for African Americans, who also negotiate racial status within the context of America. For a discussion of the added complexity of social class distinctions when race is a consideration, see John L. Jackson, *Harlemworld: Doing Race and Class in Contemporary America* (Chicago: University of Chicago Press, 2001); Karyn Lacy, *Blue Chip Black: Race, Class, Status in the New Black Middle Class* (Berkeley: University of California Press, 2007); and Mary E. Pattillo, *Black on the Block: The Politics of Race and Class in the City* (Chicago: University of Chicago Press, 2007).

27. Grazian, *On the Make*, 103–109.

28. For further discussion of African American males negotiation of city streets, see Duneier, *Side Walk*; Elijah Anderson, *Code of the Street: Decency, Violence, and the Moral Life of the Inner City* (New York: Norton, 1999); and Reuben A. Buford May, "The Sid Cartwright Incident and More: An African American Male's Interpretive Narrative of Interracial Encounters at the University of Chicago," *Studies in Symbolic Interaction* 24 (2001): 75–100. Joe Feagin and colleagues have argued that African Americans endure mental costs from having to negotiate racism like that undergirding presumptions of criminality in everyday life. For instance, see Joe R. Feagin and Melvin P. Sikes, *Living with Racism: The Black Middle-Class Experience* (Boston: Beacon, 1994); and Joe R. Feagin and Karyn McKinney, *The Many Costs of Racism* (Lanham, MD: Rowman & Littlefield, 2003). These studies demonstrate how African Americans navigate public space given their perception of the influence of race on interactions in public contexts.

29. Elijah Anderson, *Streetwise: Race, Class, and Change in an Urban Community* (Chicago: University of Chicago Press, 1990).

30. Robin Engel and Jennifer Calnon, "Examining the Influence of Driver's Characteristics during Traffic Stops with Police: Results from a National Survey," *Justice Quarterly* 21, no. 1 (2004): 49–91.

31. For a discussion of the ways in which media perpetuate stereotypes about African American males in the role of athletes, see Linda Tucker, "Blackballed: Basketball and the Representation of the Black Male Athlete," *American Behavioral Scientist* 47, no. 3 (2003): 306–328; and Todd Boyd, "The Day the Niggaz Took Over: Basketball, Commodity Culture, and Black Masculinity," in *Out of Bounds: Sports, Media, and The Politics of Identity*, ed. Aaron Baker and Todd Boyd (Bloomington: Indiana University Press, 1997), 123–141.

32. Lyn H. Lofland, *The Public Realm: Exploring the City's Quintessential Social Territory* (Hawthorne, NY: Aldine de Gruyter, 1998).

33. See Patricia Hill Collins, *Black Sexual Politics: African Americans, Gender, and the New Racism* (New York: Routledge, 2004).

34. Ibid., 27.

35. Ibid., 34.

36. Grazian, *On the Make*, 135.

37. Gardner, *Passing By*.

38. It is important to reiterate that the students who attend Big South University generally come from areas in Georgia that are highly segregated by class and race, hence their home community experiences do not necessarily allow for substantial interaction between individuals from different racial and ethnic backgrounds. For a groundbreaking study on the degree of residential segregation throughout the United States, see Douglass Massey and Nancy A. Denton, *American Apartheid: Segregation and the Making of the Underclass* (Cambridge, MA: Harvard University Press, 1993).

39. According to the Urban Dictionary, a "booty call" is "a person with whom one has sex at random times outside of a relationship." See http://www.urbandictionary. com/define.php?term=Booty-Call (retrieved October 29, 2010).

Chapter 4   Is It a Blackout? Dress Codes in Urban Nightlife

1. For a discussion, see Reuben A. Buford May, *Talking at Trena's: Everyday Conversations at an African American Tavern* (New York: New York University Press, 2001).

2. For a discussion of a variety of formal and informal rules for access to bars, see Elijah Anderson, *A Place on the Corner* (Chicago: University of Chicago Press, 1978); May, *Talking at Trena's*; Michael J. Bell, *The World from Brown's Lounge: An Ethnography of Black Middle-Class Play* (Urbana: University of Illinois Press, 1983); and Ray Oldenburg, *The Great Good Place: Cafes, Coffee Shops, Bookstores, Bars, Hair Salons, and Other Hangouts at the Heart of a Community* (New York: Marlowe, 1997).

3. For discussion of dress codes at work, schools, and restaurants, see Owen Edwards, "Informal Wear," *Forbes* 159, no. 7 (1997): S98–S99; Dave Zielinski and Daniel Guidera, "Cracking the Dress Code," *Presentations* no. 2. (February 19, 2005): 26–27; Nathan L. Essex, "Student Dress Codes Using Zero Tolerance?," *Education Digest* 70, no. 2 (October 2004): 32; Theodore Dalrymple, "Wrong from Head to Toe," *National Review* 57, no. 5 (March 28, 2005): 30; Milford Prewitt, "Ties No Longer Binding: '21' Club Eases Dress Code Permanently," *Nation's Restaurant News* 31, no. 6 (February 10, 1997): 6; and Paul O'Donnell, Michelle Memran, and Victoria S. Stefanakos, "No-Jean Scene," *Newsweek* 134, no. 16 (October 18, 1999): 6.

4. Georg Simmel, "Fashion [1904]," *American Journal of Sociology* 62 (1957): 541–558.

5. Diana Crane, *Fashion and Its Social Agendas: Class, Gender, and Identity in Clothing* (Chicago: University of Chicago Press, 2000).

6. Ibid., 15.

7. Pierre Bourdieu, *Distinction: A Social Critique of the Judgment of Taste*, trans. Richard Nice (Cambridge, MA: Harvard University Press, 1984).

8. Ibid., 2.

9. Bourdieu, exploring the ways in which individuals learn their judgment of taste, suggests that cultural cues are passed on explicitly and implicitly through institutions like the family and education. He uses the concept of habitus to express the ways in which practices structure individuals' cultural sensibilities. For a discussion of habitus, see Bourdieu, *Distinction*, 170.

10. For a discussion, see Michèle Lamont and Virag Molnar, "The Study of Boundaries in the Social Science," *Annual Review of Sociology* 28 (2002): 167–195.

11. Tricia Rose, *Black Noise: Rap Music and Black Culture in Contemporary America* (Hanover, NH: Wesleyan University Press, 1994).

12. For discussion of punk rocker subculture, see Dick Hebdige, *Subculture: The Meaning of Style* (1979; repr., New York: Routledge, 1994); for a discussion of the working-class subculture in Britain, see Paul Willis, *Learning to Labor: How Working Class Kids Get Working Class Jobs* (New York: Columbia University Press, 1981); and for a discussion of subculture as it relates to Puerto Rican drug dealers, see Phillipe Bourgois, *In Search of Respect: Selling Crack in El Barrio* (1996; repr., New York: Cambridge University Press, 2003).

13. Michèle Lamont and Virag Molnar, "How Blacks Use Consumption to Shape Their Collective Identity: Evidence from Marketing Specialists," *Journal of Consumer Culture* 1 (2001): 31–45.

14. See Mary E. Pattillo-McCoy, *Black Picket Fences: Privilege and Peril among the Black Middle Class* (Chicago: University of Chicago Press, 1999), 118.

15. Ibid., 119.

16. Elijah Anderson, *Streetwise: Race, Class, and Change in an Urban Community* (Chicago: University of Chicago Press, 1990); Mitchell Duneier, *Sidewalk* (New York: Farrar, Straus and Giroux, 1999); and Rachel Pain, "Gender, Race, Age, and Fear in the City," *Urban Studies* 38, nos. 5–6 (2001): 899–913.

17. Elijah Anderson, *Code of the Street: Decency, Violence, and the Moral Life of the Inner City* (New York: Norton, 1999).

18. Laura Rivera, "Status Distinctions in Interaction: Social Selection and Exclusion at an Elite Nightclub," *Qualitative Sociology* 33 (2010): 229–255.

19. Although it might seem that this generation of partygoers might be unfamiliar with Mr. T, their knowledge of such entertainers and television programs from the 1980s is based on the constant replay of television programs, music, and videos from this time. In fact, the popularity of such programs can be affirmed by the fact that the Hollywood film industry continues to remake movies based on them. For instance, in 2010, Twentieth Century Fox released the feature length film *The A-Team* starring Liam Neeson, Bradley Cooper, Jessica Biel, and Quinton "Rampage" Jackson and directed by Joe Carnahan. The Northeast partygoers also participate in several eighties music theme parties. I observed at these parties that college students collectively sang the lyrics to songs that were popular before they were born.

20. For example, see Joe Feagin, "The Continuing Significance of Race: Antiblack Discrimination in Public Places," *American Sociological Review* 56 (1991): 101–116;

Joe R. Feagin and Melvin P. Sikes, *Living with Racism: The Black Middle-Class Experience* (Boston: Beacon, 1994); and May, *Talking at Trena's*.

21. Reuben A. B. May and Kenneth Sean Chaplin, "Cracking the Code: Race, Class, and Access to Nightclubs in Urban America," *Qualitative Sociology* 31 (2008): 57–72.

22. For a discussion see Bourdieu, *Distinction*.

23. Peterson and Kern suggest that geographical migration and social mobility have brought mixes of people together who hold different tastes. See Richard A. Peterson and Roger M. Kern, "Changing Highbrow Taste: From Snob to Omnivore," *American Sociological Review* 61, no. 5 (1996): 900–907.

24. For a discussion of this tension see Pattillo-McCoy, *Black Picket Fences*.

25. Ibid., 120.

26. Peterson and Kern, "Changing Highbrow Taste," 905.

27. For a discussion of the implications of a misreading of cultural cues, see Anderson, *Code of the Street*; Pattillo-McCoy, *Black Picket Fences*; and Sudhir Venkatesh, *American Project: The Rise and Fall of a Modern Ghetto* (Cambridge, MA: Harvard University Press, 2000).

28. For further discussion of the ways in which African Americans' negative interracial encounters have a compounding effect in everyday life, see May, *Talking at Trena's*.

29. Girbaud is a shortened reference to Marithé François Girbaud, a French clothing company established by husband and wife François and Marithé Girbaud in 1964. They initially specialized in casual clothing and emphasized creative styling in jeans. Among their styles is the Brand X line of jeans that are cut to give a "baggy" look. Although these jeans were not directly marketed to African Americans, they became an important part of urban fashion adopted by fans of hip-hop culture. For a discussion of Girbaud, see Aitana Lleonart, "Marithé & Françios Girbaud," in *Ultimate Paris Design*, ed. Aitana Lleonart, trans. Jay Noden (New York: teNeues, 2007).

30. For an interesting analysis of the limits of urban nightlife in bridging social capital across diverse groups, see David Grazian, "Urban Nightlife, Social Capital, and the Public Life of Cities," *Sociological Forum* 24, no. 4 (2009): 908–917.

31. Ibid., 912.

32. Gary A. Fine, "The Sociology of the Local: Action and Its Publics," *Sociological Theory* 28 (2010): 367.

33. For a brief discussion of the history of Northeast, see Appendix A.

34. See Joe R. Feagin, *Systemic Racism: A Theory of Oppression* (New York: Routledge, 2006); Joe R. Feagin, *Racist America: Roots, Current Realities, and Future Reparations* (New York: Routledge, 2000); and Leslie Houts Picca and Joe R. Feagin, *Two-Faced Racism: Whites in the Backstage and Frontstage* (New York: Routledge, 2007).

35. Wendy L. Moore, *Reproducing Racism: White Space, Elite Law Schools, and Racial Inequality* (Lanham, MD: Rowman & Littlefield, 2007).

36. For a discussion of "colorblind" racism, see Leslie G. Carr, *"Color-Blind" Racism* (Thousand Oaks, CA: Sage, 1997); Eduardo Bonilla-Silva, *Racism Without Racists: Colorblind Racism and the Persistence of Racial Inequality in the United States*, 2nd ed. (Lanham, MD: Rowman & Littlefield, 2006); Michael K. Brown, Matrin Carnoy, Elliott Currie, Troy Duster, David B. Oppenheimer, Marjorie M. Sulz, and David Wellman, *White-Washing Race: The Myth of a Color-Blind Society* (Berkeley: University of California Press, 2005).

37. Some scholars would argue further that Whites are able to participate in an economic system largely built on the slave labor of African Americans, in addition that slavery, segregation, and discrimination created oppressive conditions for African Americans, who have until recently not been able to reap economic benefits. For example, see Feagin, *Systemic Racism*; and Brown et al., *White-Washing Race*.

Chapter 5   Knockout: Verbal and Physical Confrontations

1. For an elaborate discussion of interaction rituals between individuals, see Erving Goffman, *Interaction Ritual: Essays in Face-to-Face Behavior* (Chicago: Aldine, 1967); and Erving Goffman, *Behavior in Public Places: Notes on the Social Organization of Gatherings* (New York: Free Press, 1963).
2. For a discussion of the influence of varied contexts on perceptions of masculinity, see E. Anthony Rotundo, *American Manhood: Transformations in Masculinity from the Revolution to the Modern Era* (New York: Basic Books, 1993); Ann Lombard, *Making Manhood: Growing Up Male in Colonial New England* (Cambridge, MA: Harvard University Press, 2003); Ian Harris, Jose B. Torres, and Dale Allender, "The Responses of African American Men to Dominant Norms of Masculinity within the United States," *Sex Roles* 31 (1994): 703–719; Andrea G. Hunter and James E. Davis, "Constructing Gender: An Exploration of Afro-American Men's Conceptualization of Manhood," *Gender and Society* 6 (1992): 464–479; R. W. Connell, *Masculinities* (Berkeley: University of California Press, 1995); R. W. Connell, *The Men and the Boys* (Berkeley: University of California Press, 2000); and Candace West and Don Zimmerman, "Doing Gender," *Gender and Society* 1, no. 2 (1987): 125–151.
3. Connell, *Men*, 215.
4. "Pimped out" is a popular term in urban culture that refers to the process by which vehicle owners add nonfactory accessories including custom rims, acrylic paint, enhanced stereo systems, and television screens to their cars. This process is very expensive. Following the popularity of custom car design among urban car owners, MTV created a television program in 2005, hosted by rapper Xzibit, called *Pimp My Ride*. Each week a viewer was selected to have her or his car "pimped out" at no expense. For a description of the program, see http://www.mtv.com/shows/pimp_my_ride/season_5/series.jhtml (retrieved December 11, 2011).
5. See Northeast County, Municipal Code of Ordinance.
6. Elijah Anderson, *Code of the Street: Decency, Violence, and the Moral Life of the Inner City* (New York: Norton, 1999).
7. Violent response to eye contact is a popular theme within the gangsta rap genre of hip-hop music. For a contemporary example, see Soulja Boy and 50 Cent, "Mean Mug," on *DeAndre Way* (ColliPark Music/Interscope Records, 2010).
8. For instance, see Stephen L. Buka, Theresa L. Stichick, Isolde Birdthistle, and Felton J. Earls, "Youth Exposure to Violence: Prevalence, Risks, and Consequences," *American Journal of Orthopsychiatry* 71, no. 3 (2001): 298–310; and Kevin M. Fitzpatrick, "Violent Victimization among America's School Children," *Journal of Interpersonal Violence* 14, no. 10 (1999): 1055–1069. This exposure to violence has profound effects on youth, including PTSD (posttraumatic stress disorder) and depression. For a discussion, see Kevin M. Fitzpatrick, "Aggression and Environmental Risk among Low-Income African-American Youth," *Journal of Adolescent Health* 21, no. 3 (1997):

172–178; and Kevin M. Fitzpatrick, Darlene R. Wright, Bettina F. Piko, and Mark LaGory, "Depressive Symptomatology, Exposure to Violence, and the Role of Social Capital among African American Adolescents," *American Journal of Orthopsychiatry* 75, no. 2 (2005): 262–274.

9. Anderson, *Code of the Street*, 72.

10. Mary E. Pattillo-McCoy, *Black Picket Fences: Privilege and Peril among the Black Middle Class* (Chicago: University of Chicago Press, 1999).

11. See Fitzpatrick, "Violent Victimization," 1066.

12. Hunter and Davis, "Constructing Gender," 464–479.

13. Ibid., 477.

14. For interesting analyses of stereotypical displays of African Americans in mass media, see Travis L. Dixon and Keith B. Maddox, "Skin Tone, Crime News, and Social Reality Judgments: Priming the Stereotypes of the Dark and Dangerous Black Criminal," *Journal of Applied Social Psychology* 35, no. 8 (2006): 1555–1570; Dennis Rome, *Black Demons: Media's Depiction of the African American Male Criminal Stereotype* (Westport, CT: Praeger, 2004); and Patricia Hill Collins, *Black Sexual Politics: African Americans, Gender, and the New Racism* (New York: Routledge, 2004). For an interesting alternative perspective of the presentation of African Americans as violent criminals in the mass media, see Anthony Walsh, "African Americans and Serial Killing in the Media: The Myth and the Reality," *Homicides Studies* 9, no. 4 (2005): 271–291. Walsh suggests that although African Americans are overrepresented in the ranks of serial killers from 1945 to mid-2004, they receive significantly less media attention than their White serial killer counterparts. He suggests that one explanation for this is that mass media simply ignored the existence of Black serial killers for fear of being labeled racists.

15. For a discussion, see Connell, *Men*; Mark Pope, "Fathers and Sons: The Relationship between Violence and Masculinity," *Family Journal* 9, no. 4 (2001): 367–374; Debby A. Phillips, "Punking and Bullying: Strategies in Middle School, High School, and Beyond," *Journal of Interpersonal Violence* 22, no. 2 (2007): 158–178; Lawson V. Bush, "Am I a Man? A Literature Review Engaging the Sociohistorical Dynamics of Black Manhood in the United States," *Western Journal of Black Studies* 23 (1999): 49–57; G. Canada, "Learning to Fight," in *Men's Lives*, ed. M. Kimmel and M. Messner (Boston: Allyn and Bacon, 2001), 100–103; Brian Doss and J. Roy Hopkins, "The Multicultural Masculinity Ideology Scale: Validation from Three Cultural Perspectives," *Sex Roles* 38 (1998): 719–741; and Michelle Mitchell, "The Black Man's Burden: African Americans, Imperialism, and Notions of Racial Manhood 1890–1910," *International Review of Social History* 44, no. 7 (1999): 77–99.

16. This song, written and produced by Sir Mix-a-Lot for the Def American label in 1992, remains a nightclub anthem for many partygoers.

17. Anderson observes a similar kind of collective bonding among doormen within the Rottenburg Square area in Philadelphia. The doormen develop a collective sense of purpose through their efforts to help tenants who live in the upscale apartments in downtown Philadelphia. For a discussion, see Elijah Anderson, *Cosmopolitan Canopy: Race and Civility in Everyday Life* (New York: Norton, 2011), 142–148.

18. Reuben A. Buford May, *Talking at Trena's: Everyday Conversations at an African American Tavern* (New York: New York University Press, 2001).

19. Anderson, *Code of the Street*.

20. For a discussion, see Bonnie Berry and Earl Smith, "Race, Sport, and Crime: The Misrepresentation of African Americans in Team Sports and Crime," *Sociology of Sport* 17 (2000): 171–197.

21. Some sport commentators have argued that athletes who compete in violent sports like football, boxing, and hockey are predisposed to loosing control in off-the-field confrontations. In other words, their sporting violence is said to "spill over" from the playing field. Yet there is very little empirical evidence to support such asserrtions. In fact, some scholars argue that competition in sport serves a cathartic function within which athletes are able to relieve pent-up aggression. For a discussion of these issues, see Gordon A. Bloom, "Hockey Violence: A Test of Cultural Spillover Theory," *Sociology of Sport Journal* 13, no. 1 (March 1997): 65–77; and Craig Greenlee, "Out-of-Bounds," *Black Issues in Higher Education* 12 (November 1995): 24–26. Given the paucity of research in this area, it is difficult to know the extent to which football players' participation in sport might predispose them to violent responses in confrontations like that discussed here.

22. For a discussion of the complex issues surrounding the use of the word "nigga" and its meaningful variant "nigger," see Michel Marriott, "Rap's Embrace of 'Nigger' Fires Bitter Debate," *New York Times*, January 24, 1993, http://www.nytimes.com/1993/01/24/nyregion/rap-s-embrace-of-nigger-fires-bitter-debate.html; Randall Kennedy, *Nigger: The Strange Career of a Troublesome Word* (Toronto: Pantheon, 2002); and Jabari Asim, *The N Word: Who Can Say It, Who Shouldn't, and Why* (New York: Houghton Mifflin, 2007).

23. For a discussion of the concept of "nigger moment," see Anderson, *Cosmopolitan Canopy*, 154, 249–273.

Chapter 6   When Race Is Explicit

1. Michael Omi and Howard Winant, *Racial Formation in the United States from 1960s to the 1980s* (New York: Routledge, 1986), 62.

2. Elijah Anderson, *Cosmopolitan Canopy: Race and Civility in Everyday Life* (New York: Norton, 2011).

3. Ibid.

4. Georg Simmel, "Sociability [1910]," in *On Individuality and Social Forms*, ed. Donald N. Levine (Chicago: University of Chicago Press, 1971), 133.

5. Many feminists argue that the objectification of women's bodies supports the status quo oppression of women within broader institutions. For example, see Catherine MacKinnon, *Toward a Feminist Theory of the State* (Cambridge, MA: Harvard University Press, 1989); Laura Kipnis, *The Female Thing: Dirt, Envy, Sex, Vulnerability* (New York: Vintage, 2007); Joane Nagel, *Race, Ethnicity, and Sexuality: Intimate Intersections, Forbidden Frontiers* (New York: Oxford University Press, 2003); and Rose Weitz, ed., *The Politics of Women's Bodies: Sexuality, Appearance, and Behavior* (Oxford: Oxford University Press, 2009). For an interesting discussion of how women take control of "sexual scripts" and empower themselves through their objectified bodies, see Shayne Lee, *Erotic Revolutionaries: Black Women, Sexuality, and Popular Culture* (Blue Ridge Summit, PA: Rowman & Littlefield, 2010).

6. For further discussion, see Leslie Houts Picca and Joe R. Feagin, *Two-Faced Racism: Whites in the Backstage and Frontstage* (New York: Routledge, 2007).

7. Reuben A. Buford May, *Talking at Trena's: Everyday Conversations at an African American Tavern* (New York: New York University Press, 2001).

8. For a thorough consideration of the ways in which racial identity influences participants' expectations, see ibid., chap. 4 and the appendix. For a discussion of how racial and gender differences influence participants' willingness to talk about particular topics in the presence of researchers, see Reuben A. Buford May and Mary E. Pattillo-McCoy, "Do You See What I See? Examining a Collaborative Ethnography," *Qualitative Inquiry* 6, no. 1 (2000): 65–87.

9. Patricia Hill Collins, *Black Sexual Politics: African Americans, Gender, and the New Racism* (New York: Routledge, 2004), chap. 5.

10. The atrocities of lynch mob vigilantism committed by Whites against African Americans are well documented. These atrocities included mutilation of the body while the victim was alive, hanging, burning, castrating, and severing other body parts to be kept and traded as souvenirs from the lynching. For both a description of these documented atrocities and powerful visual images, see James Allen, *Without Sanctuary: Lynching Photography in America* (Santa Fe, NM: Twin Palms, 2000). For additional perspectives on lynching, see Steward E. Tolnay and E. M. Beck, *A Festival of Violence: An Analysis of Southern Lynchings, 1882–1930* (Urbana: University of Illinois Press, 1995); Oliver Cromwell Cox, *Race: A Study in Social Dynamics*, Reprint ed. (New York: Monthly Review Press, 2000); and Reuben A. Buford May, "Review of *Without Sanctuary: Lynching Photography in America*," *Human Rights Review* 2, no. 4 (2001): 88–92.

11. Keith and Brad were like many of the young men whom I knew who remained in Northeast after completing school. They had service jobs in the area and took part in the revelry of downtown almost each weekend. For many of the young men, the affordable cost of living, high density of young women, and inexpensive alcoholic beverages indeed made Northeast a desirable place to live. Most of the men leave Northeast within a few years to continue their professional careers. Both Keith and Brad remained in the area until their late twenties.

12. Researchers have explored the mental health consequences for African Americans managing stress resulting from these kinds of encounters. For a discussion, see Elizabeth A. Klonoff, Hope Landrin, and Jodie B. Ullman, "Racial Discrimination and Psychiatric Symptoms among Blacks," *Cultural Diversity and Ethnic Minority Psychology* 5 (1999): 329–339; Shelly P. Harrell, "A Multidimensional Conceptualization of Racism-Related Stress: Implications for the Well-Being of People of Color," *American Journal of Orthopsychiatry* 70 (2000): 42–57; Shawn O. Utsey, Joseph G. Ponterotto, Amy L. Reynolds, and Anthony A. Cancelli, "Racial Discrimination, Coping, Life Satisfaction, and Self-Esteem among African Americans," *Journal of Counseling & Development* 78, no. 1 (2000): 72–80; Margaret O'Brien Caughy, Patricia J. O'Camp, and Carles Muntaner, "Experiences of Racism among African American Parents and the Mental Health of Their Preschool-Aged Children," *American Journal of Public Health* 94, no. 12 (2004): 2118–2124; Tawanda M. Greer, "Coping Strategies as Moderators of the Relation between Individual Race-Related Stress and Mental Health Symptoms for African American Women," *Psychology of Women Quarterly* 35, no. 2 (2011): 215–226.

13. Wendy L. Moore, *Reproducing Racism: White Space, Elite Law Schools, and Racial Inequality* (Lanham, MD: Rowman & Littlefield, 2007).

14. African Americans, like other racial or ethnic groups, derive a sense of collective identity drawn from their perceived threats from outside groups. For interesting early treatments of in-group/out-group formation and maintenance with respect to race, see Gordon W. Allport, *The Nature of Prejudice* (Reading, MA: Addison-Wesley, 1954); Milton Gordon, *Assimilation in American Life* (New York: Oxford University Press, 1964); Stanley Lieberson, "A Societal Theory of Race and Ethnic Relations," *American Sociological Review* 26, no. 6 (1961): 902–910; Joseph S. Himes, "The Functions of Racial Conflict," *Social Forces* 45, no. 1 (1966): 1–10; Donald L. Noel, "A Theory of the Origin of Ethnic Stratification," *Social Problems* 16, no. 2 (1968): 157–172; and Henri Tajfel and John C. Turner, "An Integrative Theory of Intergroup Conflict," in *The Social Psychology of Intergroup Relations*, ed. W. G. Austin and S. Worchel (Monterey, CA: Brooks/Cole, 1979), 33–47.

15. Dave Chappelle is an African American stand-up comedian known primarily for the success of his *Chappelle's Show*, a sketch comedy television program that aired on the Comedy Central cable network from 2003 to 2006. Chappelle became famous for parodying American culture including racial stereotypes. He unexpectedly walked away from the show's third season and a contract for $50 million, citing stress related to the grueling schedule and his displeasure at the direction of the show. For a discussion, see "Dave Chappelle: I Wasn't Crazy," February 11, 2009, http://www.cbsnews.com/stories/2006/02/03/entertainment/main1281321.shtml (retrieved September 10, 2011).

16. For a discussion of strategies to disavowal criminal intent, see Elijah Anderson, *Streetwise: Race, Class, and Change in an Urban Community* (Chicago: University of Chicago Press, 1990), chaps. 6 and 7.

17. See Reuben A. Buford May, "Race Talk and Local Collective Memory among African American Men in a Neighborhood Tavern," *Qualitative Sociology* 23, no. 2 (2000): 201–214.

18. "Bourgie" is a colloquialism for "bourgeois" frequently used among African Americans to set oneself or others apart as middle or upper class with no desire to interact with members of the lower class. It can often be heard used among African Americans in phrases like "You are so bourgie" and "Look at my bourgie self."

19. For a discussion of how women evaluate appearance of themselves and others, see Naomi Wolfe, *The Beauty Myth: How Images of Beauty Are Used Against Women* (New York: HarperCollins, 2002).

20. For a discussion of these typical standards of beauty in mass media, see Sara Halprin, *Look at My Ugly Face: Myths and Musings on Beauty and Other Perilous Obsessions with Women's Appearance* (New York: Penguin, 1995); and Amy R. Malkin, Kimberlie Wornian, and Joan C. Chrisler, "Women and Weight: Gendered Messages on Magazine Covers," *Sex Roles* 40, nos. 7–8 (1999): 647–655.

21. The Urban Dictionary provides the following definitions of "pink toe": "Young White Female, esp. with jungle fever" and "A code word for White girls used by African American men when they are in the presence of the opposite gender or ethnic group." See http://www.urbandictionary.com/define.php?term=pink+toe (retrieved November 8, 2011).

22. For a discussion of the compounding effects of racism and discrimination, see May, *Talking at Trena's*, chap. 7.

23. For a detailed discussion of the trends of residential segregation over time, see Douglass Massey and Nancy A. Denton, *American Apartheid: Segregation and the Making of the Underclass* (Cambridge, MA: Harvard University Press, 1993).

24. For a discussion of this tactic used in Chicago, see Mary E. Pattillo-McCoy, *Black Picket Fences: Privilege and Peril among the Black Middle Class* (Chicago: University of Chicago Press, 1999), 33–34.

25. For a detailed discussion of White flight in Atlanta and its impact on surrounding areas as well as its connections to modern conservatism, see Kevin M. Kruse, *White Flight: Atlanta and the Making of Modern Conservatism* (Princeton, NJ: Princeton University Press, 2005).

26. Ibid., 8.

Chapter 7   Having Fun in Black and White

1. Georg Simmel, "Fashion [1904]," *American Journal of Sociology* 62 (May 1957): 541–558.

2. Elijah Anderson, *Cosmopolitan Canopy: Race and Civility in Everyday Life* (New York: Norton, 2011).

3. Reuben A. Buford May, *Talking at Trena's: Everyday Conversations at an African American Tavern* (New York: New York University Press, 2001).

4. David Card, Alexandre Mas, and Jesse Rothstein, "Tipping and the Dynamics of Segregation," *Quarterly Journal of Economics* 123, no. 1 (February 2008): 177–218.

5. For an examination of the ways in which my experiences not only shape my perspective regarding race and racialized encounters, but also suggest ways in which African Americans generally might manage these encounters, see Reuben A. Buford May, "The Sid Cartwright Incident and More: An African American Male's Interpretive Narrative of Interracial Encounters at the University of Chicago," *Studies in Symbolic Interaction* 24 (2001): 75–100.

6. For a discussion, see May, *Talking at Trena's*, chap. 4; and Reuben A. Buford May, *Living Through the Hoop: High School Basketball, Race, and the American Dream* (New York: New York University Press, 2008), chap. 4.

7. For a discussion of the *Brown v. Board of Education of Topeka*, 347 U.S. 483 (1954) case, see Richard Kluger, *Simple Justice: The History of Brown v. Board of Education and Black America's Struggle for Equality* (New York: Vintage, 2004); and Derrick Bell, *Silent Covenants: Brown v. Board of Education and the Unfulfilled Hopes for Racial Reform* (New York: Oxford University Press, 2005).

Appendix A   A Brief History of Northeast

1. For instance, see J. Douglas Smith, *Managing White Supremacy: Race, Politics, and Citizenship in Jim Crow Virginia* (Chapel Hill: University of North Carolina Press, 2002); Scott R. Baker, *Paradoxes of Desegregation: African American Struggles for Educational Equity in Charleston, South Carolina, 1926–1972* (Columbia: University of South Carolina Press, 2006); James Meredith (with William Doyle), *A Mission from God: A Memoir and Challenge for America* (New York: Atria Books, 2012); and Frye Gaillard, *Cradle of Freedom: Alabama and the Movement That Changed America* (Tuscaloosa: University of Alabama Press, 2004).

2. Like the residents of Northeast, many southerners fought for the Confederacy during the Civil War. For instance, see Stuart Salling, *Louisianians in the Western Confederacy: The Adams-Gibson Brigade in the Civil War* (Jefferson, NC: McFarland, 2010); and Larry M. Logue, "Who Joined the Confederate Army? Soldiers, Civilians, and Communities in Mississippi," *Journal of Social History* 26, no. 3 (1993): 611–623.

3. For an eloquent description of the contributions and failings of the Freedmen's Bureau, see W.E.B. Du Bois, *The Souls of Black Folk* (1903; repr., New York: Penguin, 1989).

Appendix B   Methodology

1. For instance, see Erving Goffman, *The Presentation of Self in Everyday Life* (New York: Doubleday, 1959); Erving Goffman, *Encounters: Two Studies in the Sociology of Interaction* (Indianapolis: Bobbs Merrill, 1961); Erving Goffman, *Behavior in Public Places: Notes on the Social Organization of Gatherings* (New York: Free Press, 1963); and Erving Goffman, *Forms of Talk* (1981; repr., Philadelphia: University of Pennsylvania, 1983).

2. Reuben A. Buford May, *Talking at Trena's: Everyday Conversations at an African American Tavern* (New York: New York University Press, 2001); and Reuben A. Buford May, *Living Through the Hoop: High School Basketball, Race, and the American Dream* (New York: New York University Press, 2008).

3. For a discussion of the ways in which my racial identity attracted scrutiny as I moved to and fro on the streets of Chicago, see Reuben A. Buford May, "The Sid Cartwright Incident and More: An African American Male's Interpretive Narrative of Interracial Encounters at the University of Chicago," *Studies in Symbolic Interaction* 24 (2001): 75–100.

4. Elijah Anderson, *Code of the Street: Decency, Violence, and the Moral Life of the Inner City* (New York: Norton, 1999); and Elijah Anderson, *Cosmopolitan Canopy: Race and Civility in Everyday Life* (New York: Norton, 2011).

5. For instance, see Butler B. Wilson, "Results of the Investigation," in *Social and Physical Condition of Negroes in Cities*, ed. T. N. Chase, Atlanta University Publications No. 2 (Atlanta: Atlanta University Press, 1897); and Joyce A. Ladner, ed., *The Death of White Sociology* (New York: Random House, 1973).

6. For instance, see Robert K. Merton, "Insiders and Outsiders: A Chapter in the Sociology of Knowledge," *American Journal of Sociology* 77 (1972): 8–47; and William J. Wilson, "The New Black Sociology: Reflections on the 'Insiders' and the 'Outsiders' Controversy," in *Black Sociologists: Historical and Contemporary Perspectives*, ed. J. E. Blackwell and M. Janowitz (Chicago: University of Chicago Press, 1974), 322–338.

7. See Reuben A. Buford May, "When the Methodological Shoe Is on the Other Foot: African American Interviewer and White Interviewees," *Qualitative Sociology* (forthcoming).

8. Amy L. Best, "Doing Race in the Context of Feminist Interviewing: Constructing Whiteness through Talk," *Qualitative Inquiry* 9 (2003): 895–914.

9. Ibid., 909.

10. For instance, see Susan Boser, "Power, Ethics, and the IRB: Dissonance over Human Participant Review of Participatory Research," *Qualitative Inquiry* 13

(2007): 1060–1074; Marcia Marx, "Invisibility, Interviewing, and Power: A Researcher's Dilemma," *Resources for Feminist Research* 28 (2001): 131–152; and Ursula Plesner, "Studying Sideways: Displacing the Problem of Power in Research Interviews with Sociologists and Journalists," *Qualitative Inquiry* 17 (2011): 471–482.

11. Eduardo Bonilla-Silva, *Racism Without Racists: Colorblind Racism and the Persistence of Racial Inequality in the United States*, 2nd ed. (Lanham, MD: Rowman & Littlefield, 2006).

12. For a discussion, see Mitchell Duneier, *Sidewalk* (New York: Farrar, Straus and Giroux, 1999), appendix.

Bibliography

Abbott, Andrew. *Department and Discipline: Chicago Sociology at One Hundred*. Chicago: University of Chicago Press, 1999.

Allen, James. *Without Sanctuary: Lynching Photography in America*. Santa Fe, NM: Twin Palms, 2000.

Allport, Gordon W. *The Nature of Prejudice*. Reading, MA: Addison-Wesley, 1954.

Anderson, Elijah. *Code of the Street: Decency, Violence, and the Moral Life of the Inner City*. New York: Norton, 1999.

———. *Cosmopolitan Canopy: Race and Civility in Everyday Life*. New York: Norton, 2011.

———. "Folk Ethnography and the Cosmopolitan Canopy." *Annals of the American Academy of Political and Social Science* 595, no. 1 (2004): 14–31.

———. *A Place on the Corner*. Chicago: University of Chicago Press, 1978.

———. *Streetwise: Race, Class, and Change in an Urban Community*. Chicago: University of Chicago Press, 1990.

Asim, Jabari. *The N Word: Who Can Say It, Who Shouldn't, and Why*. New York: Houghton Mifflin, 2007.

Baker, Scott R. *Paradoxes of Desegregation: African American Struggles for Educational Equity in Charleston, South Carolina, 1926–1972*. Columbia: University of South Carolina Press, 2006.

Beattie, Irenee, Karen Christopher, Dina Okamoto, and Sandra Way. "Momentary Pleasures: Social Encounters and Fleeting Relationships at a Singles Dance." In *Together Alone: Personal Relationships in Public Places*, edited by C. Morrill, D. Snow, and C. H. White, 46–65. Berkeley: University of California Press, 2005.

Bell, Derrick. *Silent Covenants: Brown v. Board of Education and the Unfulfilled Hopes for Racial Reform*. New York: Oxford University Press, 2005.

Bell, Michael J. *The World from Brown's Lounge: An Ethnography of Black Middle-Class Play*. Urbana: University of Illinois Press, 1983.

Berry, Bonnie, and Earl Smith. "Race, Sport, and Crime: The Misrepresentation of African Americans in Team Sports and Crime." *Sociology of Sport* 17 (2000): 171–197.

Best, Amy L. "Doing Race in the Context of Feminist Interviewing: Constructing Whiteness through Talk." *Qualitative Inquiry* 9 (2003): 895–914.

Blalock, Hurbert M. *Toward a Theory of Minority-Group Relations*. New York: John Wiley, 1967.

Blau, Peter M. *Inequality and Heterogeneity: A Primitive Theory of Social Structure*. New York: Free Press, 1977.

Blau, Peter, and Otis Dudley Duncan. *The American Occupational Structure*. New York: John Wiley, 1967.

Bloom, Gordon A. "Hockey Violence: A Test of Cultural Spillover Theory." *Sociology of Sport Journal* 13, no. 1 (March 1997): 65–77.

Blumer, Herbert. "Race Prejudice as a Sense of Group Position." *Pacific Sociological Review* 1, no. 1 (1958): 3–7.

Bobo, Lawrence, and Vincent L. Hutchings. "Perceptions of Racial Group Competition: Extending Blumer's Theory of Group Position to a Multiracial Social Context." *American Sociological Review* 61, no. 6 (1996): 951–972.

Bobo, Lawrence, Howard Schuman, and Charlotte Steeh. "Changing Attitudes toward Residential Integration." In *Housing Desegregation and Federal Policy*, edited by John M. Goering, 152–169. Chapel Hill: University of North Carolina Press, 1986.

Bogle, Kathleen. *Hooking Up: Sex, Dating, and Relationships on Campus*. New York: New York University Press, 2008.

Bonilla-Silva, Eduardo. *Racism Without Racists: Colorblind Racism and the Persistence of Racial Inequality in the United States*. 2nd ed. Lanham, MD: Rowman & Littlefield, 2006.

Boser, Susan. "Power, Ethics, and the IRB: Dissonance over Human Participant Review of Participatory Research." *Qualitative Inquiry* 13 (2007): 1060–1074.

Bourdieu, Pierre. *Distinction: A Social Critique of the Judgment of Taste*. Translated by Richard Nice. Cambridge, MA: Harvard University Press, 1984.

———. "Social Space and Symbolic Power." *Sociological Theory* 7, no. 1 (1989): 14–25.

Bourgois, Phillipe. *In Search of Respect: Selling Crack in El Barrio*. 1996. Reprint, New York: Cambridge University Press, 2003.

Boyd, Todd. "The Day the Niggaz Took Over: Basketball, Commodity Culture, and Black Masculinity." In *Out of Bounds: Sports, Media, and the Politics of Identity*, edited by Aaron Baker and Todd Boyd, 123–141. Bloomington: Indiana University Press, 1997.

Brown, Michael K., Matrin Carnoy, Elliott Currie, Troy Duster, David B. Oppenheimer, Marjorie M. Sulz, and David Wellman. *White-Washing Race: The Myth of a Color-Blind Society*. Berkeley: University of California Press, 2005.

Buka, Stephen L., Theresa L. Stichick, Isolde Birdthistle, and Felton J. Earls. "Youth Exposure to Violence: Prevalence, Risks, and Consequences." *American Journal of Orthopsychiatry* 71, no. 3 (2001): 298–310.

Bulmer, Martin. *The Chicago School of Sociology: Institutionalization, Diversity, and the Rise of Sociological Research*. Chicago: University of Chicago Press, 1984.

Bush, Lawson V. "Am I a Man? A Literature Review Engaging the Sociohistorical Dynamics of Black Manhood in the United States." *Western Journal of Black Studies* 23 (1999): 49–57.

Butler, Judith. *Gender Trouble: Feminism and the Subversion of Identity*. New York: Routledge, 1999.

Canada, G. "Learning to Fight." In *Men's Lives*, edited by M. Kimmel and M. Messner, 100–103. Boston: Allyn and Bacon, 2001.

Card, David, Alexandre Mas, and Jesse Rothstein. "Tipping and the Dynamics of Segregation." *Quarterly Journal of Economics* 123, no. 1 (February 2008): 177–218.

Carr, Leslie G. *"Color-Blind" Racism*. Thousand Oaks, CA: Sage, 1997.

Carter, Prudence. "Black Cultural Capital, Status Positioning, and Schooling Conflicts for Low-Income African American Youth." *Social Problems* 50 (2003): 136–155.

Caughy, Margaret O'Brien, Patricia J. O'Camp, and Carles Muntaner. "Experiences of Racism among African American Parents and the Mental Health of Their Preschool-Aged Children." *American Journal of Public Health* 94, no. 12 (2004): 2118–2124.

Chatterton, Paul, and Robert Hollands. *Urban Nightscapes: Youth Cultures, Pleasure Spaces, and Corporate Power.* New York: Routledge, 2003.

Coffey, Amanda. *The Ethnographic Self: Fieldwork and the Representation of Identity.* Thousand Oaks, CA: Sage, 1999.

Collins, Patricia Hill. *Black Feminist Thought: Knowledge, Consciousness, and the Politics of Empowerment.* New York: Routledge, 2000.

———. *Black Sexual Politics: African Americans, Gender, and the New Racism.* New York: Routledge, 2004.

Connell, R. W. *Masculinities.* Berkeley: University of California Press, 1995.

———. *The Men and the Boys.* Berkeley: University of California Press, 2000.

Conway, Claire A., Benedict C. Jones, Lisa M. DeBruine, and Anthony C. Little. "Sexual Dimorphism of Male Face Shape, Partnership Status, and the Temporal Context of Relationship Sought Modulate Women's Preferences for Direct Gaze." *British Journal of Psychology* 101 (2010): 109–121.

Corbin, Juliet, and Anslem Strauss. "Grounded Theory Research: Procedures, Canons, and Evaluative Criteria." *Qualitative Sociology* 13 (1990): 4–21.

Cornelissen, Piers L., Peter J. B. Hancock, Vesa Kiviniemi, Hannah George, and Martin J. Tovée. "Patterns of Eye Movements When Male and Female Observers Judge Female Attractiveness, Body Fat, and Waist-to-Hip Ratio." *Evolution and Human Behavior* 30, no. 6 (2009): 417–428.

Cox, Oliver Cromwell. *Race: A Study in Social Dynamics.* Reprint ed. New York: Monthly Review Press, 2000.

Crane, Diana. *Fashion and Its Social Agendas: Class, Gender, and Identity in Clothing.* Chicago: University of Chicago Press, 2000.

Currie, Thomas E., and Anthony C. Little. "The Relative Importance of the Face and Body in Judgments of Human Physical Attractiveness." *Evolution and Human Behavior* 30, no. 6 (2009): 409–416.

Dalrymple, Theodore. "Wrong from Head to Toe." *National Review* 57, no. 5 (March 28, 2005): 30.

Davis, Deirdre E. "The Harm That Has No Name: Street Harassment, Embodiment, and African American Women." In *Critical Race Feminism: A Reader*, edited by Adrien Katherine Wing, 192–202. New York: New York University Press, 1997.

Deliobsky, Kathy. "Normative White Femininity: Race, Gender, and the Politics of Beauty." *Atlantis* 33, no. 1 (2008): 48–58.

Denzin, Norman K., and Yvonna S. Lincoln, eds. *The Sage Handbook of Qualitative Research.* 3rd ed. Thousand Oaks, CA: Sage, 2005.

DiMaggio, Paul. "Culture and Cognition." *Annual Review of Sociology* 23 (1997): 263–287.

Dixon, John, Mark Levine, and Rob McCauley. "Locating Impropriety: Street Drinking, Moral Order, and the Ideological Dilemma of Public Space." *Political Psychology* 27, no. 2 (2006): 187–206.

Dixon, Travis L., and Keith B. Maddox. "Skin Tone, Crime News, and Social Reality Judgments: Priming the Stereotypes of the Dark and Dangerous Black Criminal." *Journal of Applied Social Psychology* 35, no. 8 (2006): 1555–1570.

Doss, Brian, and J. Roy Hopkins. "The Multicultural Masculinity Ideology Scale: Validation from Three Cultural Perspectives." *Sex Roles* 38 (1998): 719–741.

Douglas, Mary T., and Baron Isherwood. *The World of Goods.* New York: Basic Books, 1979.

Drake, St. Clair, and Horace R. Cayton. *Black Metropolis: A Study of Negro Life in a Northern City.* New York: Harcourt, Brace, 1945.

Du Bois, W.E.B. *The Souls of Black Folk*. 1903. Reprint, New York: Penguin, 1989.

Duneier, Mitchell. *Sidewalk*. New York: Farrar, Straus and Giroux, 1999.

———. *Slim's Table: Race, Respectability, and Masculinity*. Chicago: University of Chicago Press, 1992.

Eagly, Alice H., and Amanda B. Diekman. "Examining Gender Gaps in Sociopolitical Attitudes: It's Not Mars and Venus." *Feminism & Psychology* 16, no. 1 (2006): 26–34.

Edwards, Owen. "Informal Wear." *Forbes* 159, no. 7 (1997): S98–S99.

Eitle, Tamela M., and David J. Eitle. "Race, Cultural Capital, and the Education Effects of Participation in Sports." *Sociology of Education* 75, no. 2 (2002): 123–146.

Engel, Robin, and Jennifer Calnon. "Examining the Influence of Driver's Characteristics during Traffic Stops with Police: Results from a National Survey." *Justice Quarterly* 21, no. 1 (2004): 49–91.

Entine, Jon. *Taboo: Why Black Athletes Dominate Sports and Why We're Afraid to Talk about It*. New York: Public Affairs, 1997.

Essex, Nathan L. "Student Dress Codes Using Zero Tolerance?" *Education Digest* 70, no. 2 (October 2004): 32.

Farley, John. "Even Whiter Than We Thought: What Median Residential Exposure Indices Reveal about White Neighborhood Contact with African Americans in U.S. Metropolitan Areas." *Social Science Research* 37 (2008): 604–623.

Farley, Reynolds, and William H. Frey. "Changes in the Segregation of Whites from Blacks during the 1980s: Small Steps toward a More Integrated Society." *American Sociological Review* 59 (1994): 23–45.

Feagin, Joe R. "The Continuing Significance of Race: Antiblack Discrimination in Public Places." *American Sociological Review* 56 (1991): 101–116.

———. *Racist America: Roots, Current Realities, and Future Reparations*. New York: Routledge, 2000.

———. *Systemic Racism: A Theory of Oppression*. New York: Routledge, 2006.

Feagin, Joe R., and Karyn McKinney. *The Many Costs of Racism*. Lanham, MD: Rowman & Littlefield, 2003.

Feagin, Joe R., and Melvin P. Sikes. *Living with Racism: The Black Middle-Class Experience*. Boston: Beacon, 1994.

Fine, Gary A., ed. *A Second Chicago School? The Development of a Postwar American Sociology*. Chicago: University of Chicago Press, 1995.

———. "The Sociology of the Local: Action and Its Publics." *Sociological Theory* 28 (2010): 355–376.

Fischer, Claude S. *To Dwell among Friends: Personal Networks in Town and City*. Chicago: University of Chicago Press, 1982.

Fisman, Raymond, Sheena Iyengar, Emik Kamenica, and Itamar Simonson. "Gender Differences in Mate Selection: Evidence from a Speed Dating Experiment." *Quarterly Journal of Economics* 121, no. 2 (2006): 673–697.

Fitzpatrick, Kevin M. "Aggression and Environmental Risk among Low-Income African-American Youth." *Journal of Adolescent Health* 21, no. 3 (1997): 172–178.

———. "Violent Victimization among America's School Children." *Journal of Interpersonal Violence* 14, no. 10 (1999): 1055–1069.

Fitzpatrick, Kevin M., Darlene R. Wright, Bettina F. Piko, and Mark LaGory. "Depressive Symptomatology, Exposure to Violence, and the Role of Social Capital among African American Adolescents." *American Journal of Orthopsychiatry* 75, no. 2 (2005): 262–274.

Flynn, Mary K. "Success Codes." *U.S. News & World Report* 137, no. 16 (November 8, 2004): EE14.

Frith, Katherine, Ping Shaw, and Hong Cheng. "The Construction of Beauty: A Cross-Cultural Analysis of Women's Magazine Advertising." *Journal of Communication* 55 (2005): 56–70.

Gaillard, Frye. *Cradle of Freedom: Alabama and the Movement That Changed America.* Tuscaloosa: University of Alabama Press, 2004.

Gans, Herbert J. *The Urban Villagers: Group and Class in the Life of Italian-Americans.* New York: Free Press, 1962.

Gardner, Carol Brooks. *Passing By: Gender and Public Harassment.* Berkeley: University of California Press, 1995.

Gieryn, Thomas F. "A Space for Place in Sociology." *Annual Review of Sociology* 26 (2000): 463–496.

Glaser, Barney, and Anslem Strauss. *The Discovery of Grounded Theory: Strategies for Qualitative Research.* Chicago: Aldine, 1967.

Glenn, Norval. *Hooking Up, Hanging Out, and Hoping for Mr. Right: College Women on Dating and Mating Today.* New York: Institute for American Values, 2001.

Goffman, Erving. *Behavior in Public Places: Notes on the Social Organization of Gatherings.* New York: Free Press, 1963.

———. *Encounters: Two Studies in the Sociology of Interaction.* Indianapolis: Bobbs Merrill, 1961.

———. *Forms of Talk.* 1981. Reprint, Philadelphia: University of Pennsylvania Press, 1983.

———. *Interaction Ritual: Essays in Face-to-Face Behavior.* Chicago: Aldine, 1967.

———. *The Presentation of Self in Everyday Life.* New York: Doubleday, 1959.

———. *Relations in Public: Micro Studies of the Public Order.* New York: Basic Books, 1971.

Gold, S. "Big Easy Is Uneasy after Death of Black Clubgoer." *Los Angeles Times.* http://articles.latimes.com/2005/may/30/nation/na-orleans30.

Gordon, Milton. *Assimilation in American Life.* New York: Oxford University Press, 1964.

Gordon, Susan M. *Heroin: Challenge for the 21st.* Wernersville, PA: Century Caron Foundation, 2001.

Gosselink, Carol A., Deborah L. Cox, Sarissa J. McClure, and Mary L. G. De Jong. "Ravishing or Ravaged: Women's Relationships with Women in the Context of Aging and Western Beauty Culture." *International Journal of Aging and Human Development* 66, no. 4 (2008): 307–327.

Gottdiener, Mark. *The Social Production of Urban Space.* 2nd ed. Austin: University of Texas Press, 1994.

Granovetter, Mark S. "The Strength of Weak Ties." *American Journal of Sociology* 78, no. 6 (1973): 1360–1380.

Grazian, David. *Blue Chicago: The Search for Authenticity in Urban Blues Clubs.* Chicago: University of Chicago Press, 2003.

———. *On the Make: The Hustle of Urban Nightlife.* Chicago: University of Chicago Press, 2007.

———. "Urban Nightlife, Social Capital, and the Public Life of Cities." *Sociological Forum* 24, no. 4 (2009): 908–917.

Greenlee, Craig. "Out-of-Bounds." *Black Issues in Higher Education* 12 (November 1995): 24–26.

Greer, Tawanda M. "Coping Strategies as Moderators of the Relation between Individual Race-Related Stress and Mental Health Symptoms for African American Women." *Psychology of Women Quarterly* 35, no. 2 (2011): 215–226.

Griswold, Wendy. *Cultures and Societies in a Changing World.* Thousand Oaks, CA: Pine Forge Press, 1994.

Guano, Emanuela. "Respectable Ladies and Uncouth Men: The Performative Politics of Class and Gender in the Public Realm of an Italian City." *Journal of American Folklore* 120 (2007): 48–72.

Guéguen, Nicolas. "Brief Report: The Effects of Women's Cosmetics on Men's Approach: An Evaluation in a Bar." *North American Journal of Psychology* 10, no. 1 (2008): 221–227.

Gwaltney, John L. *Drylongso: A Self-Portrait of Black America.* New York: Random House, 1980.

Hall, John R. "The Capital(s) of Cultures: A Nonholistic Approach to Status Situations, Class, Gender, and Ethnicity." In *Cultivating Differences: Symbolic Boundaries and the Making of Inequality*, edited by Michèle Lamont and Marcel Fournier, 257–285. Chicago: University of Chicago Press, 1992.

Halprin, Sara. *Look at My Ugly Face: Myths and Musings on Beauty and Other Perilous Obsessions with Women's Appearance.* New York: Penguin, 1995.

Harrell, Shelly P. "A Multidimensional Conceptualization of Racism-Related Stress: Implications for the Well-Being of People of Color." *American Journal of Orthopsychiatry* 70 (2000): 42–57.

Harris, Ian, Jose B. Torres, and Dale Allender. "The Responses of African American Men to Dominant Norms of Masculinity within the United States." *Sex Roles* 31 (1994): 703–719.

Harris, John, and Ben Clayton. "The First Metrosexual Rugby Star: Rugby Union, Masculinity, and Celebrity in Contemporary Wales." *Sociology of Sport Journal* 24, no. 2 (2007): 145–164.

Hebdige, Dick. *Subculture: The Meaning of Style.* 1979. Reprint, New York: Routledge, 1994.

Higgins, George, Melissa Ricketts, and Deborah Vegh. "The Role of Self-Control in College Student's Perceived Risk and Fear of Online Victimization." *American Journal of Criminal Justice* 33 (2008): 223–233.

Himes, Joseph S. "The Functions of Racial Conflict." *Social Forces* 45, no. 1 (1966): 1–10.

Hoberman, John. *Darwin's Athletes: How Sports Has Damaged Black America and Preserved the Myth of Race.* New York: Houghton Mifflin, 1997.

Hoek, Hans W. "Review of the Epidemiological Studies of Eating Disorders." *International Journal of Psychiatry* 5 (1993): 61–74.

Hogg, Michael. "Group Cohesiveness: A Critical Review and Some New Directions." *European Review of Social Psychology* 4 (1993): 85–111.

———. *The Social Psychology of Group Cohesiveness: From Attraction to Social Identity.* Hemel Hempstead, UK: Harvester Wheatsheaf, 1992.

Hogg, Michael, and Sarah C. Hains. "Intergroup Relations and Group Solidarity: Effects of Group Identification and Social Beliefs on Depersonalized Attraction." *Journal of Personality and Social Psychology* 70, no. 2 (1996): 295–309.

Hunter, Albert. "Private, Parochial and Public Social Orders: The Problem of Crime and Incivility in Urban Communities." In *The Challenge of Social Control: Citizenship and Institution Building in Modern Society*, edited by G. D. Suttles and M. N. Zald, 230–242. Norwood, NJ: Ablex, 1985.

Hunter, Andrea G., and James E. Davis. "Constructing Gender: An Exploration of Afro-American Men's Conceptualization of Manhood." *Gender and Society* 6 (1992): 464–479.

Hunter, Marcus A. "The Nightly Round: Space, Social Capital, and Urban Black Nightlife." *City & Community* 9, no. 2 (2010): 165–186.

Ibarra, Herminia. "Paving an Alternative Route: Gender Differences in Managerial Networks." *Social Psychology Quarterly* 60 (1997): 91–102.

———. "Race, Opportunity, and Diversity of Social Circles in Managerial Networks." *Academy of Management Journal* 38 (1995): 673–703.

Iceland, John, Daniel H. Weinberg, and Erica Steinmetz. *U.S. Census Bureau, Series CENSR-3, Racial and Ethnic Residential Segregation in the United States: 1980–2000.* Washington, DC: Government Printing Office, 2002.

Jackman, Mary R., and Mary Scheuer Senter. "Different Therefore Unequal: Beliefs about Groups of Unequal Status." *Research in Social Stratification and Mobility* 2 (1983): 309–335.

Jackson, John L. *Harlemworld: Doing Race and Class in Contemporary America.* Chicago: University of Chicago Press, 2001.

Judge, Timothy A., and Beth A. Livingston. "Is the Gap More Than Gender? A Longitudinal Analysis of Gender, Gender Role Orientation, and Earnings." *Journal of Applied Psychology* 93, no. 5 (2008): 994–1012.

Kennedy, Randall. *Nigger: The Strange Career of a Troublesome Word.* Toronto: Pantheon, 2002.

Kimmel, Michael. *The Gendered Society.* New York: Oxford University Press, 2000.

Kipnis, Laura. *The Female Thing: Dirt, Envy, Sex, Vulnerability.* New York: Vintage, 2007.

Klonoff, Elizabeth A., Hope Landrin, and Jodie B. Ullman. "Racial Discrimination and Psychiatric Symptoms among Blacks." *Cultural Diversity and Ethnic Minority Psychology* 5 (1999): 329–339.

Kluger, Richard. *Simple Justice: The History of Brown v. Board of Education and Black America's Struggle for Equality.* New York: Vintage, 2004.

Koskela, Hille, and Sirpa Tani. "Sold Out! Women's Practices of Resistance against Prostitution-Related Sexual Harassment." *Women's Studies International Forum* 28, no. 5 (2005): 418–429.

Kruse, Kevin M. *White Flight: Atlanta and the Making of Modern Conservatism.* Princeton, NJ: Princeton University Press, 2005.

Lacy, Karyn. *Blue Chip Black: Race, Class, Status in the New Black Middle Class.* Berkeley: University of California Press, 2007.

Ladner, Joyce A., ed. *The Death of White Sociology.* New York: Random House, 1973.

Lamont, Michèle, and Annette Lareau. "Culture Capital: Allusions, Gaps, and Glissandos in Recent Theoretical Developments." *Sociological Theory* 6 (1988): 153–168.

———. *Money, Morals, and Manners: The Culture of the French and the American Upper-Middle Class.* Chicago: University of Chicago Press, 1992.

Lamont, Michèle, and Virag Molnar. "How Blacks Use Consumption to Shape Their Collective Identity: Evidence from Marketing Specialists." *Journal of Consumer Culture* 1 (2001): 31–45.

———. "The Study of Boundaries in the Social Science." *Annual Review of Sociology* 28 (2002): 167–195.

Lamont, Michèle, and Mario Luis Small. "How Culture Matters: Enriching Our Understanding of Poverty." In *The Colors of Poverty: Why Racial and Ethnic Disparities Exist,* edited by D. Harris and A. Lin, 76–102. New York: Russell Sage Foundation, 2009.

Laumann, Edward. *Networks of Collective Action.* New York: Academic Press, 1976.

Laumann, Edward, John H. Gagnon, Robert T. Michael, and Stuart Michaels. *The Social Organization of Sexuality: Sexual Practices in the United States.* Chicago: University of Chicago Press, 1994.

Lee, Shayne. *Erotic Revolutionaries: Black Women, Sexuality, and Popular Culture.* Blue Ridge Summit, PA: Rowman & Littlefield, 2010.

Lefebvre, Henri. *The Social Production of Space.* Translated by Donald Nicholson-Smith. 1974. Reprint, Malden, MA: Blackwell, 2000.

LeMasters, E. E. *Blue-Collar Aristocrats: Life-Styles at a Working-Class Tavern.* Madison: University of Wisconsin Press, 1975.

Lewis, Amanda E. *Race in the Schoolyard: Negotiating the Color Line in Classrooms and Communities.* New Brunswick, NJ: Rutgers University Press, 2003.

Lieberson, Stanley. *Matter of Taste: How Names, Fashions, and Culture Change.* New Haven, CT: Yale University Press, 2000.

———. "A Societal Theory of Race and Ethnic Relations." *American Sociological Review* 26, no. 6 (1961): 902–910.

Liebow, Elliot. *Tally's Corner: A Study of Negro Streetcorner Men.* Boston: Little, Brown, 1967.

Lleonart, Aitana. "Marithé & François Girbaud." In *Ultimate Paris Design,* edited by Aitana Lleonart, translated by Jay Noden, 440–455. New York: teNeues, 2007.

Lloyd, Richard. "The Neighborhood in Cultural Production: Material and Symbolic Resources in the New Bohemia." *City and Community* 3, no. 4 (2004): 343–372.

———. *Neo-Bohemia: Culture and Capital in Postindustrial Chicago.* New York: Routledge, 2005.

Lofland, Lyn H. *The Public Realm: Exploring the City's Quintessential Social Territory.* Hawthorne, NY: Aldine de Gruyter, 1998.

———. *A World of Strangers: Order and Action in Urban Public Space.* New York: Basic Books, 1973.

Logue, Larry M. "Who Joined the Confederate Army? Soldiers, Civilians, and Communities in Mississippi." *Journal of Social History* 26, no. 3 (1993): 611–623.

Lombard, Ann. *Making Manhood: Growing Up Male in Colonial New England.* Cambridge, MA: Harvard University Press, 2003.

Lorber, Judith. *Paradoxes of Gender.* New Haven, CT: Yale University Press, 1994.

MacKinnon, Catherine. *Toward a Feminist Theory of the State.* Cambridge, MA: Harvard University Press, 1989.

MacMillan, Ross, Annette Nierobisz, and Sandy Welsh. "Experiencing the Streets: Harassment and Perceptions of Safety among Women." *Journal of Research in Crime and Delinquency* 37 (2000): 306–322.

Mahay, Jenna, and Edward O. Laumann. "Neighborhoods as Sex Markets." In *The Sexual Organization of the City,* edited by Edward O. Laumann, Stephen Ellingson, Jenna Mahay, Anthony Paik, and Yoosik Youm, 69–92. Chicago: University of Chicago Press, 2004.

Malkin, Amy R., Kimberlie Wornian, and Joan C. Chrisler. "Women and Weight: Gendered Messages on Magazine Covers." *Sex Roles* 40, nos. 7–8 (1999): 647–655.

Markham, Annette. "'Go Ugly Early': Fragmented Narrative and Bricolage as Interpretive Method." *Qualitative Inquiry* 11, no. 6 (2005): 813–839.

Marriott, Michel. "Rap's Embrace of 'Nigger' Fires Bitter Debate." *New York Times,* January 24, 1993. http://www.nytimes.com/1993/01/24/nyregion/rap-s-embrace-of-nigger-fires-bitter-debate.html.

Marx, Karl. "Communist Manifesto [1848]." In *The Marx-Engels Reader,* edited by Robert C. Tucker. New York: Norton, 1978.

Marx, Marcia. "Invisibility, Interviewing, and Power: A Researcher's Dilemma." *Resources for Feminist Research* 28 (2001): 131–152.

Massey, Douglas, and Nancy A. Denton. *American Apartheid: Segregation and the Making of the Underclass.* Cambridge, MA: Harvard University Press, 1993.

May, Reuben A. B. "'Flirting with Boundaries': A Professor's Narrative Tale Contemplating Research of the Wild Side." *Qualitative Inquiry* 9, no. 3 (2003): 442–465.

———. *Living Through the Hoop: High School Basketball, Race, and the American Dream.* New York: New York University Press, 2008.

———. "Race Talk and Local Collective Memory among African American Men in a Neighborhood Tavern." *Qualitative Sociology* 23, no. 2 (2000): 201–214.

———. "Review of *Without Sanctuary: Lynching Photography in America.*" *Human Rights Review* 2, no. 4 (2001): 88–92.

———. "The Sid Cartwright Incident and More: An African American Male's Interpretive Narrative of Interracial Encounters at the University of Chicago." *Studies in Symbolic Interaction* 24 (2001): 75–100.

———. *Talking at Trena's: Everyday Conversation at an African American Tavern.* New York: New York University Press, 2001.

———. "When the Methodological Shoe Is on the Other Foot: African American Interviewer and White Interviewees." *Qualitative Sociology* (forthcoming).

May, Reuben A. B., and Kenneth Sean Chaplin. "Cracking the Code: Race, Class, and Access to Nightclubs in Urban America." *Qualitative Sociology* 31 (2008): 57–72.

May, Reuben A. B., and Mary Pattillo-McCoy. "Do You See What I See? Examining a Collaborative Ethnography." *Qualitative Inquiry* 6, no. 1 (2000): 65–87.

McPherson, J. Miller, and Lynn Smith-Lovin. "Homophily in Voluntary Organizations: Status Distance and the Composition of Face-to-Face Groups." *American Sociological Review* 52 (1987): 370–379.

Meredith, James, with William Doyle. *A Mission from God: A Memoir and Challenge for America.* New York: Atria Books, 2012.

Merton, Robert K. "Insiders and Outsiders: A Chapter in the Sociology of Knowledge." *American Journal of Sociology* 77 (1972): 8–47.

Messner, Michael. *Power at Play: Sports and the Problem of Masculinity.* Boston: Beacon, 1999.

Mitchell, Michelle. "The Black Man's Burden: African Americans, Imperialism, and Notions of Racial Manhood 1890–1910." *International Review of Social History* 44, no. 7 (1999): 77–99.

Moore, Wendy L. *Reproducing Racism: White Space, Elite Law Schools, and Racial Inequality.* Lanham, MD: Rowman & Littlefield, 2007.

Morris, Edward W. "Researching Race: Identifying a Social Construction through Qualitative Methods and an Interactionist Perspective." *Symbolic Interaction* 30, no. 3 (2007): 409–425.

Nagel, Joane. *Race, Ethnicity, and Sexuality: Intimate Intersections, Forbidden Frontiers.* New York: Oxford University Press, 2003.

Newholm, Terry, and Gillian C. Hopkinson. "I Just Tend to Wear What I Like: Contemporary Consumption and the Paradoxical Construction of Individuality." *Marketing Theory* 9, no. 4 (2009): 439–462.

Nielsen, Laura Beth. "Situating Legal Consciousness: Experiences and Attitudes of Ordinary Citizens about Law and Street Harassment." *Law & Society Review* 34, no. 4 (2000): 1055–1090.

Noel, Donald L. "A Theory of the Origin of Ethnic Stratification." *Social Problems* 16, no. 2 (1968): 157–172.

O'Donnell, Paul, Michelle Memran, and Victoria S. Stefanakos. "No-Jean Scene." *Newsweek* 134, no. 16 (October 18, 1999): 6.

Oldenburg, Ray. *The Great Good Place: Cafes, Coffee Shops, Bookstores, Bars, Hair Salons, and Other Hangouts at the Heart of a Community.* New York: Marlowe, 1997.

Omi, Michael, and Howard Winant. *Racial Formation in the United States from 1960s to the 1980s.* New York: Routledge, 1986.

Pain, Rachel. "Gender, Race, Age, and Fear in the City." *Urban Studies* 38, nos. 5–6 (2001): 899–913.

Park, Robert E., and Ernest W. Burgess. *Introduction to the Science of Sociology.* Chicago: University of Chicago Press, 1924.

Park, Robert E., Ernest W. Burgess, and Roderick D. McKenzie. *The City.* Chicago: University of Chicago Press, 1925.

Pattillo, Mary E. *Black on the Block: The Politics of Race and Class in the City.* Chicago: University of Chicago Press, 2007.

Pattillo-McCoy, Mary E. *Black Picket Fences: Privilege and Peril among the Black Middle Class.* Chicago: University of Chicago Press, 1999.

Peterson, Richard A., and Roger M. Kern. "Changing Highbrow Taste: From Snob to Omnivore." *American Sociological Review* 61, no. 5 (1996): 900–907.

Phillips, Debby A. "Punking and Bullying: Strategies in Middle School, High School, and Beyond." *Journal of Interpersonal Violence* 22, no. 2 (2007): 158–178.

Picca, Leslie Houts, and Joe R. Feagin. *Two-Faced Racism: Whites in the Backstage and Frontstage.* New York: Routledge, 2007.

Plesner, Ursula. "Studying Sideways: Displacing the Problem of Power in Research Interviews with Sociologists and Journalists." *Qualitative Inquiry* 17 (2011): 471–482.

Pope, Mark. "Fathers and Sons: The Relationship between Violence and Masculinity." *Family Journal* 9, no. 4 (2001): 367–374.

Poran, Maya A. "Denying Diversity: Perceptions of Beauty and Social Comparison among Latina, Black, and White Women." *Sex Roles* 47 (2002): 65–82.

Powers, Rebecca S., Jill J. Suitor, Susana Guerra, Monisa Shackelford, Dorothy Mecom, and Kim Gusman. "Regional Differences in Gender-Role Attitudes: Variations by Gender and Race." *Gender Issues* 21, no. 2 (2003): 40–54.

Prewitt, Milford. "Ties No Longer Binding: '21' Club Eases Dress Code Permanently." *Nation's Restaurant News* 31, no. 6 (February 10, 1997): 6.

Reagans, Ray E. "Preferences, Identity, and Competition: Predicting Tie Strength from Demographic Data." *Management Science* 51 (2005): 1374–1383.

Rieder, Jonathan. *Canarsie: The Jews and Italians of Brooklyn against Liberalism.* Cambridge, MA: Harvard University Press, 1985.

Riley, Sarah C. E. "The Management of the Traditional Male Role: A Discourse Analysis of the Constructions and Functions of Provision." *Journal of Gender Studies* 12, no. 2 (2003): 99–113.

Rivera, Laura. "Status Distinctions in Interaction: Social Selection and Exclusion at an Elite Nightclub." *Qualitative Sociology* 33 (2010): 229–255.

Rome, Dennis. *Black Demons: Media's Depiction of the African American Male Criminal Stereotype.* Westport, CT: Praeger, 2004.

Rose, Tricia. *Black Noise: Rap Music and Black Culture in Contemporary America.* Hanover, NH: Wesleyan University Press, 1994.

Ross, Lawrence C. *The Divine Nine: The History of African American Fraternities and Sororities.* New York: Kensington, 2000.

Rotundo, E. Anthony. *American Manhood: Transformations in Masculinity from the Revolution to the Modern Era.* New York: Basic Books, 1993.

Rubinstein, Ruth P. *Dress Codes: Meanings and Messages in American Culture.* 2nd ed. Boulder, CO: Westview, 2001.

Rudman, Laurie A., and Kimberly Fairchild. "The *F* Word: Is Feminism Incompatible with Beauty and Romance?" *Psychology of Women Quarterly* 31 (2007): 125–136.

Salling, Stuart. *Louisianians in the Western Confederacy: The Adams-Gibson Brigade in the Civil War.* Jefferson, NC: McFarland, 2010.

Shipp, Bill. *Murder at Broad River Bridge: The Slaying of Lemuel Penn by Members of the Ku Klux Klan.* Atlanta: Peachtree, 1981.

Silver, Daniel, Terry Nicols Clark, and Clemente Jesus Navarro Yanez. "Scenes: Social Context in an Age of Contingency." *Social Forces* 88, no. 5 (2010): 2293–2324.

Simmel, Georg. "Fashion [1904]." *American Journal of Sociology* 62 (1957): 541–558.

———. "The Metropolis and Mental Life [1903]." In *On Individuality and Social Forms,* edited by Donald N. Levine, 324–331. Chicago: University of Chicago Press, 1971.

———. "Sociability [1910]." In *On Individuality and Social Forms,* edited by Donald N. Levine, 127–140. Chicago: University of Chicago Press, 1971.

——— "The Stranger [1903]." In *On Individuality and Social Forms,* edited by Donald N. Levine, 143–149. Chicago: University of Chicago Press, 1971.

Simmons, Tavia, and Jane Lawler Dye. "What Has Happened to Median Age at First Marriage Data?" Paper presented at the annual meeting of the American Sociological Association, San Francisco, August 14–17, 2004.

Smelser, Neil J., William Julius Wilson, and Faith Mitchell, eds. *America Becoming: Racial Trends and Their Consequences.* Vol. 1. Washington, DC: National Academies Press, 2001.

Smith, J. Douglas. *Managing White Supremacy: Race, Politics, and Citizenship in Jim Crow Virginia.* Chapel Hill: University of North Carolina Press, 2002.

Smith, Sandra Susan. *Lone Pursuit: Distrust and Defensive Individualism among the Black Poor.* New York: Russell Sage Foundation, 2007.

Spradley, James, and Brenda Mann. *The Cocktail Waitress: Woman's Work in a Man's World.* New York: John Wiley, 1975.

Steele, Shelby. "On Being Black and Middle Class." In *The Best American Essays,* edited by G. Wolff, 395–408. New York: Ticknor & Fields, 1989.

Suttles, Gerald. *The Social Order of the Slum: Ethnicity and Territory in the Inner City.* Chicago: University of Chicago Press, 1970.

Swidler, Ann. "Culture in Action: Symbols and Strategies." *American Sociological Review* 51, no. 2 (1986): 273–286.

Sypeck, Mia F., James J. Gray, and Anthony H. Ahrens. "No Longer Just a Pretty Face: Fashion Magazines' Depictions of Ideal Female Beauty from 1959 to 1999." *International Journal of Eating Disorders* 26, no. 3 (2004): 342–347.

Tajfel, Henri, and John C. Turner. "An Integrative Theory of Intergroup Conflict." In *The Social Psychology of Intergroup Relations,* edited by W. G. Austin and S. Worchel, 33–47. Monterey, CA: Brooks/Cole, 1979.

Tatum, Beverly. *Why Are All the Black Kids Sitting Together in the Cafeteria: And Other Conversations about Race.* 1997. Reprint, New York: Basic Books, 2003.

Thrasher, Frederic M. *The Gang: A Study of 1,313 Gangs in Chicago.* 2nd rev. ed. Chicago: University of Chicago Press, 1936.

Tiggemann, Marika, and Suzanna Hodgson. "The Hairlessness Norm Extended: Reasons for and Predictors of Women's Body Hair Removal at Different Body Sites." *Sex Roles* 59, nos. 11–12 (2008): 889–897.

Tolnay, Steward E., and E. M. Beck. *A Festival of Violence: An Analysis of Southern Lynchings, 1882–1930.* Urbana: University of Illinois Press, 1995.

Tucker, Linda. "Blackballed: Basketball and the Representation of the Black Male Athlete." *American Behavioral Scientist* 47, no. 3 (2003): 306–328.

Utsey, Shawn O., Joseph G. Ponterotto, Amy L. Reynolds, and Anthony A. Cancelli. "Racial Discrimination, Coping, Life Satisfaction, and Self-Esteem among African Americans." *Journal of Counseling & Development* 78, no. 1 (2000): 72–80.

Veblen, Thorstein. *The Theory of the Leisure Class: An Economic Study of Institutions.* 1899. Reprint, New York: Dover, 1994.

Venkatesh, Sudhir. *American Project: The Rise and Fall of a Modern Ghetto.* Cambridge, MA: Harvard University Press, 2000.

Wacquant, Loïc J. D. *Body and Soul: Notebooks of an Apprentice Boxer.* New York: Oxford University Press, 2004.

Walsh, Anthony. "African Americans and Serial Killing in the Media: The Myth and the Reality." *Homicides Studies* 9, no. 4 (2005): 271–291.

Warde, Alan. "Dimensions of a Social Theory of Taste." *Journal of Cultural Economy* 1, no. 3 (2008): 322–336.

Watson, Rod. "The Visibility Arrangements of Public Space: Conceptual Resources and Methodological Issues in Analysing Pedestrian Movements." *Communication & Cognition* 38, nos. 1–2 (2005): 201–227.

Weber, Max. "Basic Sociological Terms." In *Economy and Society*, edited by G. Roth and C. Wittich, 3–62. Berkeley: University of California Press, 1978.

———. *From Max Weber: Essays in Sociology.* Edited by H. H. Gerth and C. Wright Mills. New York: Oxford University Press, 1946.

———. *The Methodology of the Social Sciences.* Translated and edited by Edward A. Shils and Henry A. Finch. 1903–1917. Reprint, New York: Free Press, 1997.

Weitz, Rose, ed. *The Politics of Women's Bodies: Sexuality, Appearance, and Behavior.* Oxford: Oxford University Press, 2009.

Wesley, Charles H. *The History of Alpha Phi Alpha: A Development in College Life, 1906–1969.* 11th ed. Chicago: Foundation, 1969.

West, Candace, and Don Zimmerman. "Doing Gender." *Gender and Society* 1, no. 2 (1987): 125–151.

Whyte, William Foote. *Street Corner Society: The Social Structure of an Italian Slum.* Chicago: University of Chicago Press, 1943.

Willis, Paul. *Learning to Labor: How Working Class Kids Get Working Class Jobs.* New York: Columbia University Press, 1981.

Wilson, Butler B. "Results of the Investigation." In *Social and Physical Condition of Negroes in Cities*, edited by T. N. Chase. Atlanta University Publications No. 2. Atlanta: Atlanta University Press, 1897.

Wilson, William J. *More Than Just Race: Being Black and Poor in the Inner City.* New York: Norton, 2009.

———. "The New Black Sociology: Reflections on the 'Insiders' and the 'Outsiders' Controversy." In *Black Sociologists: Historical and Contemporary Perspectives*, edited by J. E. Blackwell and M. Janowitz, 322–338. Chicago: University of Chicago Press, 1974.

———. *The Truly Disadvantaged: The Inner City, the Underclass, and Public Policy*. Chicago: University of Chicago Press, 1987.

Wirth, Louis. "Urbanism as a Way of Life." *American Journal of Sociology* 44, no. 1 (1938): 1–24.

Wolfe, Naomi. *The Beauty Myth: How Images of Beauty Are Used Against Women*. New York: HarperCollins, 2002.

Yamaguchi, Kazuo. "Homophily and Social Distance in the Choice of Multiple Friends: An Analysis Based on Conditionally Symmetric Log-Bilinear Association Models." *Journal of the American Statistical Association* 85 (1990): 356–366.

Young, Alford Jr. *The Minds of Marginalized Black Men: Making Sense of Mobility, Opportunity, and Future Life Chances*. Princeton, NJ: Princeton University Press, 2004.

Zielinski, Dave, and Daniel Guidera. "Cracking the Dress Code." *Presentations* no. 2 (February 19, 2005): 26–27.

Index

About the Author

Reuben A. Buford May is the author of the award-winning book *Living Through the Hoop: High School Basketball, Race, and the American Dream* (2008) and *Talking at Trena's: Everyday Conversations at an African American Tavern* (2001). He has been a fellow at the W.E.B. Du Bois Institute for African and African American Research at Harvard University and a Dr. Martin Luther King Jr. visiting professor at MIT. May received his Ph.D. in sociology from the University of Chicago, and his research focuses on race and culture, urban ethnography, the sociology of sport, and the sociology of the everyday. In addition to his books and other scholarly publications, May has been featured on radio and television and in print media.

CPSIA information can be obtained at www.ICGtesting.com
Printed in the USA
BVOW07s0803180714

359186BV00001B/2/P